PRAISE FOR *STRESS WISELY*

"Dr. Robyne Hanley-Dafoe is a truly remarkable scholar and speaker whose expertise lies in resiliency and wellness. With twenty years of experience, she has a wealth of knowledge on how to navigate stress, challenge, change, and self-identity. Dr. Robyne's ability to help people incorporate these practices into their everyday lives is remarkable, and she has shared this world-class thinking in *Stress Wisely*. We are living through the most significant global health crisis in our time with no end in sight. Yet there is hope if we apply the new ideas that Dr. Robyne shares with us. She weaves together knowledge, ancient wisdom, and deep practice to elevate our mental, emotional, and spiritual lives with clear and powerful stories and strategies. Reading *Stress Wisely* is like having a conversation with Dr. Robyne where she shares practical wisdom and hope directly with you so that you can stop the negative stress cycle and return to joy, happiness, and thriving."

GREG WELLS, PhD, bestselling author of *The Ripple Effect* and *Rest, Refocus, Recharge*

"Dr. Robyne Hanley-Dafoe once again has brilliantly brought together her deep professional insights and experience with her own journey. Through COVID and beyond, she has helped and positively impacted the lives of countless individuals with her care, compassion, and practical tools. *Stress Wisely* takes her insights and impact to the next level in helping us all live with greater peace and fulfillment in today's world."

KATHERINE DUDTSCHAK, former executive vice president at RBC and corporate leader, director, and community builder

"Wellness is now a $4.2 trillion global industry. And yet somehow, levels of stress and burnout are at all-time highs across professions. Cutting across this paradox while synthesizing the vast and unruly world of resilience research down to practical insights, enlightened behaviourist Dr. Robyne Hanley-Dafoe has gifted the world with an original, refreshing, and empowering perspective on how to be well in an unwell world. *Stress Wisely* makes the science-backed case that stress is inevitable in pursuing the good life. But this situational awareness is hardly a cause for despair. Instead, it's optimistic permission to choose differently. Everyday choices that prioritize wellness are revolutionary acts. Rich with heartfelt stories and original research, Dr. Robyne's book is candid yet comforting, nuanced yet holistic, scholarly yet colloquial, and timely yet timeless. It's a sprawling journey that oscillates between micro and macro contexts, uplifting and challenging wellness seekers from every walk of life. With *Stress Wisely*, Dr. Robyne offers weary voyagers true calm in a time of chaos. For everyone experiencing stress and burnout, *Stress Wisely* is what you've been waiting for."

HAMZA KHAN, future of work expert and author of
Leadership, Reinvented

"Dr. Robyne Hanley-Dafoe combines lived experience and scientific expertise in perfect measure to provide a comprehensive approach to make stress less stressful. I can't imagine anyone more qualified to take us on this journey. *Stress Wisely* offers up both a novel mindset and a new skillset when it comes to reconciling and wrangling the stress in your life. These are ideas to last a lifetime."

LIANE DAVEY, PhD, organizational psychologist and
bestselling author of *The Good Fight*

"We all have stress in our lives. Some of it is good and helps us get things done. Some of it is bad and can impact our ability to live our lives to the fullest. Get ready to unlearn, learn, and integrate Dr. Robyne Hanley-Dafoe's stress-wisely principles. Through research, data, and amazing storytelling, you'll feel your stress release as you turn the pages. You'll name it, claim it, and tame it! Breathe and enjoy."

BILL G. WILLIAMS, speaker, executive coach, and author of *Electric Life*

"Dr. Robyne Hanley-Dafoe's fresh take on established science and thought leadership on wellness is a blueprint for how to live your life. This book is a wonderful gift, and it's laced with heartfelt moments and examples that we can all relate to. *Stress Wisely* is a tune-up for the soul."

GLENN VOLLEBREGT, president and CEO of St. Lawrence College

"Dr. Robyne Hanley-Dafoe's valuable perspective on prioritizing the power of connection and personal recovery will inspire you to become an unstoppable force for wellness in your community."

RIAZ MEGHJI, keynote speaker and author of *Every Conversation Counts*

"*Stress Wisely* was like having a coffee with Dr. Robyne Hanley-Dafoe. It provided me with a better understanding and useful tools to help me deal with the challenges of running a business, having a family, and trying to navigate my health. Dr. Robyne's book came at a time when I was feeling stretched like a bear skin, desperate for the tools to loosen the tension. Through her gift of storytelling and expertise, I am feeling better equipped to handle my life."

STU SAUNDERS, founder and head gardener of Peregrine ECE, YLCC, and the EPIC Community

"*Stress Wisely* is a deeply moving and insightful book that has the power to transform the way you live your life. Dr. Robyne Hanley-Dafoe's passion for helping people to navigate stress and cultivate wellness is evident in every page, and her warm and approachable writing will make you feel like you're having a heart-to-heart conversation with a trusted friend. She draws on her extensive research and experience in the fields of stress, resiliency, and wellness to provide practical guidance on how to navigate the complexities of modern life. What sets *Stress Wisely* apart is Dr. Robyne's ability to communicate complex concepts in a relatable and engaging way, using personal anecdotes and a conversational tone to create an emotional connection. As you read, you'll feel a sense of empowerment and inspiration to take control of your life and make positive changes. Her emphasis on self-awareness and self-care will leave you feeling motivated to cultivate a healthier and more balanced lifestyle. Above all, you'll feel a deep sense of gratitude for Dr. Robyne's wisdom and guidance, and a renewed hope for what's possible in your life."

NATALIE TYSDAL, journalist, media expert, and host of
The Natalie Tysdal Podcast

"Combining the power of courageous storytelling, scientific insights, and unapologetic authenticity, Dr. Robyne Hanley-Dafoe invites readers to be the engineer of their own wellness. She offers instantly implementable tools and relatable aha moments that spark understanding, wisdom, and commitment to growth toward a life of purpose and health. *Stress Wisely* is a gift for all who want to unlock their wellness potential and thrive personally and professionally."

SAMRA ZAFAR, author of the national bestseller *A Good Wife*

"Dr. Robyne Hanley-Dafoe is the kind and wise guide that we need for these times. In *Stress Wisely*, she shows us that resilience, healing, and thriving is for anyone and everyone. Full of insightful research and relatable personal stories, this guide is a gift for happiness and well-being."

"Dr. Robyne Hanley-Dafoe has created an absolute must-read for anyone feeling stress in today's ever-changing, fast-paced world. Her approach to stress and the effects it has on one's overall life is grounded—not just in research, but also in the realities of everyday life. No pretence. Just the reality of being real. That life is not easy, and you don't have to make it look so. She introduces her Eight Realms of Wellness framework and how stress in one area can affect all other areas of one's life and overall wellness. Using research, personal experiences, and her incredible ability to make science relatable and digestible, Dr. Robyne looks at the individual puzzle pieces of wellness and how they fit into the big picture of life. This book is not about being perfect. It is about becoming aware of the factors—the stressors—that may be preventing you from living your best life. *Your* best life—not the one that others think you should be living."

"People are becoming so stressed that they are stressing out about how stressed out they are. Finally, someone has documented something really honest, kind, and above all else, useful. Thank you for helping us make sense of it all."

HOW TO BE WELL
IN AN UNWELL WORLD

PAGE TWO

STRESS WISELY

DR. ROBYNE HANLEY-DAFOE

Cataloguing in publication information
is available from Library and Archives Canada.
ISBN 978-1-77458-262-6 (hardcover)
ISBN 978-1-77458-263-3 (ebook)

Page Two
pagetwo.com

Edited by Kendra Ward
Copyedited by Jenny Govier
Proofread by Alison Strobel
Jacket and interior design by Jennifer Lum
Interior illustrations by Jeff Winocur
Indexed by Stephen Ullstrom
Printed and bound in Canada by Friesens
Distributed in Canada by Raincoast Books
Distributed in the US and internationally by Macmillan

23 24 25 26 27   5 4 3 2 1

robynehd.ca

This book is dedicated to my first teachers,
Lesley and Michael,

to my greatest teachers, Ava Lesley, Jaxson, and Hunter,

and to "little" Robyne
My love for you all has no end.

I respectfully acknowledge that this work was written upon the treaty and traditional territory of the Michi Saagiig Anishinaabeg. I am a settler on these lands. I offer my gratitude and give thanks to the people who have walked before me.

CONTENTS

66

Nothing lasts forever—
not even your troubles.

ARNOLD H. GLASOW

66

And now that you
don't have to be perfect,
you can be good.

JOHN STEINBECK

GETTING TO OKAY

M ORE THAN HALF the events I have gone through in my life, I was not ready for. If I had seen the path that was before me in its entirety, I can only hope I would have had the strength to take the first step. We are taught that life is a journey with endless possibilities and promise. There will be moments that take our breath away. Experiences that define our true purpose. Insights that irrevocably change how we see the world. Love that will transform us. If we do right, put in the work, and follow those golden rules, we will be rewarded with the good life. What is not as explicit in this promise of a good life is that, while we are doing our best to achieve it, we will also experience stressors that will bring us to our knees.

How do we even begin working toward living the good life when the global landscape is ever changing? What even is the good life anymore? The ancient philosophers had theories about this. In overly simplified examples, Plato said it was finding your function or purpose in being here. Socrates believed it was fulfilling your inner life with an expanded mind. Spiritual texts like the Bhagavad Gita talk about dharma. Buddhism teaches the Eightfold Path. The Bible promises the good life in heaven, and to get there, we are encouraged to act righteously, forgive, and be humble while we are here. But as we try to sift through the philosophical and spiritual components of living a good life, where does a clean house, remembering teacher gifts at the holidays, working under a mediocre boss with unreasonable expectations, and our jean size fit in? Imagine this full continuum of a "good life," with every aspect of our health and wellness dialed in, with oneness with God at one end and ageless skin at the other.

But for real, life is not only hard as hell but also joy-filled, complicated, contradictory, and messy. Think about it: the same brain and body are supposed to be "all things" to everyone, all the time, while being selfless and self-centred. In the same twenty-four hours, we are challenged to find higher purpose, meditate, and be altruistic, while also signing permission forms and trying to match socks. And the reality for many people is far more grievous. Some are trying to do everything while also managing food scarcity, discrimination, or violence. To top it off, somewhere along the line we were taught that we are supposed to make all this look easy! My friend, let this be your first permission slip of this book. You do not have to make your life look easy.

Exhale.

If you feel as though you are trapped in a vortex of demands, wants, desires, dreams, obligations, evaluations, expectations, and commitments, you are not alone. If your life is fuelled by "shoulds," "have-tos," and "musts," you are not alone.

The pace of life has dramatically increased, and the bodies that carry us through it are desperately trying to catch up. The problem is that human evolution does not progress as quickly as our technology. Our whole self is underdeveloped for the tasks at hand, and the bar keeps rising. Many of us spend our waking hours trying and grasping. We keep chasing "enough" and coming up short. This repetitive state of striving, juggling while on wobbly footing, convinces many of us that we are the problem. The self-help industry confirms it. We are failing at our own lives. How have we let this happen?

Let's pause for awareness here: we are not the problem. When we look at everything society tells us about our priorities and what they should be, it appears we have essentially brought a Fruit Roll-Up to a knife fight. We are underprepared and did not understand the assignment.

Thankfully, awareness of our situation is a gift. Awareness puts us in a precious place where we can choose differently. Some may choose a different weapon—perhaps the keto diet will save us this time—and others will choose to walk away. When you choose to walk away, please know I am here to walk alongside you. Let's chart a new course together. All collectives—people changing *their* world and then *the* world— started with one person who dreamed it could be different.

THE CURRENT LAY OF THE LAND

Unparalleled stress, unrest, and uncertainty are becoming common. As a result, the blast radius is wide. Often in such challenging seasons, the collateral damage is our wellness, our sense of self, and our dreams. The average pace and complexity of most people's lives tends to be full, heavy, and wildly unsustainable. I have had times of "running" my life at such a pace that a sick child, a dog on the loose, forgotten gym shoes, or needing to stop for gas would send my day to hell in a hand basket. Every minute was scheduled and accounted for and required precision execution. When we constantly operate at 100 per cent, we have little to no room for errors, surprises, or do-overs, let alone learning, reflection, stillness, or healing. Our physical, emotional, and mental health are being tested and taxed every day. And at no other time in history have we had access to such vast information and resources to address our problems, yet many of us feel more lost and alone than ever before.

Then there are others who, it seems, have figured out another path. I want to learn about that path! The one where my worth as a mother is not contingent on my children's grades or the cleanliness of my baseboards, and my value as a woman is not contingent on my job, hobbies, level of fitness, or how well behaved my dogs are when a package is delivered.

Chances are that you too have noticed that your world is heavy. You carry it well, yet it comes at a cost. Many people I work with are feeling discouraged. Rightfully so. Feeling good and living a good life feels so elusive. Sustaining our wellness is like shovelling snow in a blizzard or cleaning the kitchen while the teenagers are awake. Everywhere we turn, we hear and see messages that are designed to make us feel as though we are failing. There is always more to do. People are watching, judging, and commenting on our every move. Social media is built on the psychology of social comparison under the guise of social connection. "Us versus them" is rampant. Deltas form between who we are, how we want to feel, and our realities.

These cuts run deep. Our egos are bruised. Our minds are full. Our hearts are longing. Our bodies are depleted. We are

a whole other level of tired. We ache in our bones. And gosh—
we could really use time at home to finally get organized and
get our lives on track. "I just need a week off to get my life
in order." I said something like this on March 5, 2020. I just
need a day at home. Maybe I should have been careful what
I wished for?

STRESSED OUT IN A STRESSED WORLD

In 2021, my research team and I conducted an informal survey, asking people all over Canada, coast to coast to coast, to
describe how they were feeling that day using just one word.
By this point, our world had entered its second year of a
global pandemic. A resounding amount of people responded
with the word "DONE." People have had enough. As a collective, we have all experienced varying degrees of micro
and macro traumas since March 2020. We are permanently
changed from living during COVID-19. And many people
were already in a precarious place emotionally, physically,
economically, and mentally before the world was engulfed
by this deadly virus.

We are living through the most significant global health
crisis in our time while also facing a needed racial reckoning. Meanwhile, travesties that have been and continue to
be committed against Indigenous communities are coming
to light, as are many other social injustices. We are seeing
educators, health practitioners, and families pitted against
one another. The divides among ideas, beliefs, values, and
actions have become expansive. We are weary, wobbly, and
discouraged. And meanwhile we are fully in it, facing seasons upon seasons of devasting environmental catastrophes
as our climate swings wildly out of balance. We are in a dire

situation with no end in sight, yet we persist because that is what we do. "I don't know how much more I can take," shared one person during a call. "I am scared that now after feeling everything, I can't feel anything. I am numb." This is a very normal response in abnormal times. Dr. Charles Figley calls this compassion fatigue, often described as the cost of caring.[1] This is a feeling of numbness and hopelessness resulting from direct and indirect exposure to pain, suffering, and uncertainty. It is hard to hold hope after such stressful events. And being told that personal resiliency and self-care will remedy the situation only exacerbates our collective weariness.

BANDAGES ON BULLET WOUNDS

Telling someone to be resilient or "self-care" themselves back to good when the world is on fire is like putting a bandage on a bullet hole. It might stop the bleed for a millisecond, but the injury needs a proper intervention. As a scholar of resiliency and wellness, I am deeply concerned with how resiliency and wellness are being weaponized. Amid systems of corruption and social injustices, telling people to just "be more resilient" or to "up their self-care" is cruel. The reality is that governments, organizations, systems, and companies also need to carry responsibility in addressing the demands on their people. The demands are rising, and our supply of self-care is not proportionate. Professional care is also needed. Self-care is what we bring. Professional care is what an organization or community can do to mediate and address the stressors.

Perhaps you have heard the old adage that calm seas don't make strong sailors. Well, my friend, that is very true! Yet being in the storm and letting it knock you around is not what makes the sailor strong; rather, a constellation of variables working concurrently does. Honouring the mighty force of nature while knowing how to trust your instincts and use key skills, techniques, and strategies is going to keep you alive. Navigating through storms also requires leaning into your prior knowledge and lived experiences while being open and nimble so you can apply, execute, evaluate, adjust, and persist, all while waves are crashing over the front of your boat. Navigating through storms involves knowing how, above all else, to meet the waves head on, bow forward, because when the waves hit us from the sides or from behind, we are likely going under.

The same is true for stress. Simply being in hard times or situations doesn't make us any better at managing stress. It is what we do before, during, and after the experience that fosters and strengthens our resolve and capacity. This is what my work on learning how to stress wisely is all about.

The practice of "stressing wisely" that I lay out in this book encompasses radically accepting that stress is a natural part of every single season of our lives in some form or another and choosing to engage with those stressors in a well way. In the chapters that follow, I will share with you key insights about stress from multiple perspectives and thought systems. I will unpack and present research-informed practices with the Eight Realms of Wellness framework that can positively impact your daily life in practical and sustainable ways. I will invite you to challenge yourself to build upon your prior knowledge, sometimes by unlearning long-standing beliefs about your wellness. I will also embolden you to face the excuses you may have been using to hold yourself back from being truly well. This book is not intended to fix you or your life, because neither is broken. I whole-heartedly believe that each and every person is doing the best they can in this moment with the histories, knowledge, and resources they have. This book is intended to show you that you are not alone. I vow to share things that can help you navigate every aspect of your life. Because you are worthy of being well. I know this because you are still alive, which means better ways and days are ahead. Together we will become stronger sailors for the seas of our lives.

BRAIDING TOGETHER KNOWLEDGE, PRACTICES, AND WISDOM

As a behaviourist, I deeply appreciate the use of tools and strategies to help people adapt, cope, learn, and grow. I can also read the room, and I know the last thing people want to be told is that they need to do more or do it differently. A popular meme captures this so well: Someone asks an exhausted person, "What are you doing?" The person replies in an exasperated voice, "I am doing my best, that is what I am doing. I am doing my best."

You are doing your best. For sure.

I also believe that many of us are so inundated with misinformation that we might not even know what we are doing anymore, or why. I see this when people finally slow down and then the tsunami of emotions hits. We stay busy so we don't have to experience all the feelings that many of us are running from. The feeling factory is relentless, though. Eventually it catches up with us, despite our best efforts. We cannot think our way out of this.

In this book, I aim to help you find your way back to good feelings again, even when you are in a storm. I want you to find ease, spaciousness, and a sustainable pace in your life so you can respond rather than react to the world around you. I want you to find unconditional safety within yourself, knowing you can work with stress. I want you to see your skills, talents, and gifts. I want you to recognize and know your worth. I want your soul to smile at the wonder and mysteries of your life. I want you to know that you can do hard things and you can do great things. Each chapter contains stories, theories, applications, and refreshing perspectives that build your capacity for charting new ways of showing up in your life. By challenging and unpacking long-standing misconceptions and barriers within each realm of wellness, we can finally break free from the chokehold of misinformation.

My promise is to braid together knowledge, practices, and wisdom through storytelling. I share with you the insights that I and my team have come upon in our research and pass along what we have learned from other researchers and scholars, too. This is the knowledge. I offer ideas about how to build lasting systems and habits for sustained wellness. These are the practices. And I share what I have learned from people all over the world who have discovered what it takes to be well, even when the world is not. This is the wisdom.

As we explore an alternative path for working with stress in a well way, I encourage you to take kind and compassionate steps and walk gently with yourself. To achieve a more sustainable and human-centric way of co-creating your good life, there may be some "unlearning" required. Be patient. Be brave. Be present.

Consider this your personal invitation to walk alongside me. Come as you are. You are welcome here. You pick the pace. You pick the next steps. Let's discover, together, the art, science, and craft of stressing wisely.

PS The tools presented here are specifically designed for people who are tired of tools.

PPS I am so glad you are here.

PART I

HOW "FINE" GOT US INTO THIS SITUATION

"How are you?"
"I'm tired, overwhelmed,
scared, angry, frustrated,
hopeful, excited, nervous,
hungry, bored, inspired …"
"I'm fine."

CHAPTER 1

IT'S THE END OF THE WORLD AS WE KNOW IT

"How are you?"

It must be one of the most common questions asked in the English language. And our responses are equally as common—"good," "okay," "not bad," and, perhaps more recently, "busy" or "tired." But the word "fine" is by far the most common and complex response of them all.

I recall a teacher asking me, "How are you?" in my early high school days. I was barely holding on. I had just moved to a new school. I had just gotten out of a toxic relationship. I was experiencing violent bullying. My mental health was spiralling out of control. My risk-taking behaviour was frequent and escalating. I was hurting, in one of the darkest seasons of my life. When the teacher asked me, "How are you?" I answered, "I'm scared I'm losing it. I don't think I can survive another day. This school is worse than hell. I don't want to be here anymore. I hate feeling this way. I don't know what to do." Tears slowly ran down my cheeks. In a moment of absolute truth and vulnerability, I bared my weary heart to this teacher, who stopped in their tracks, shook their head, and said, "God, Robyne, why do you need to be so dramatic? A simple 'fine' would do."

In my first book, *Calm Within the Storm: A Pathway to Everyday Resiliency*, I shared with radical candor my struggles with mental health, learning disabilities, addiction, loss, grief, and pain. I also shared parts of my story that involved healing, recovering, and making the next right decision. Professionally, I have studied and taught human resiliency and wellness worldwide for over two decades. My work braids personal and professional insights with research and application. I want to be of service to those navigating the hard parts of life. I can sum up my work with two truths and one big idea:

- People can do hard things.

- People can do great things.

- When we believe.

The reality is that often we are not believed. Or perhaps we have lost hope that things can be different. Many suffer in silence. Others try to seek help, only to be condemned or gaslighted. Somewhere in our lives we have picked up the idea that we are supposed to make our lives look easy. Or that there is one right way things should be. Just think about how many times a day you "should" on yourself. I should have prepared my meals on Sunday. I should not have said that to my colleague. I should be better at this. I should have said no. I should not have dated him. I should know better by now. The "shoulding" is relentless—we do it as naturally as breathing.

Our lives and the world we live in are not easy. We are doing a disservice to one another every time we claim they are. The weight of our personal worlds cannot be carried by our own two hands. Perhaps it was never meant to be. We are drowning in the worlds we created. We are lost in our own lives. And all most of us have the energy to say when asked if we are okay is that we are fine. "Fine" is the real four-letter f-word.

Saying we are fine when we are not has led us down a path we do not want to travel.

TWO PERSPECTIVES, ONE LIFE

My adolescent years were riddled with challenges. Despite growing up in a solid, loving, faith-filled home with devoted parents, I lost my way. I spent my early years experiencing mental health and emotional challenges in parallel with a beautiful childhood filled with wonderful experiences. I believed that I was somehow different from my family and peers. Something inside my head and heart made me see and feel the world differently. My internal struggles finally broke through, and I developed complex maladaptive behaviours in a desperate attempt to cope. With my adult eyes reflecting on little Robyne, I can see that she was fighting for her life in all the wrong ways. But, God knows, she was trying.

My tumultuous adolescence was riddled with maladaptive behaviours. I was just so desperate to feel anything other than the constant bombardment of thoughts that were telling me I wasn't enough, that I was unlovable, and, ultimately, I was the problem—the villain in every story. My risk-taking behaviours had me spiralling from poor impulse control, to blatantly ignoring rules and appropriate social norms, into addictions, self-harm, and suicidal ideations in a heartbeat. It is hard to explain to someone who has never experienced an inner war, you against yourself, how frantically and fiercely you grasp on to anything that can bring you a moment of peace and relief.

That is one side of the coin. But I have recently come upon a truth about the twenty-five years that followed my teenagerhood: my coping strategies remained maladaptive and destructive, but they had become socially accepted, celebrated, and even praised.

The pendulum of my life swung so rapidly. With that same fierce and frantic drive, I went from addict to counsellor. High school dropout to university professor. Larger-bodied to marathon runner. Single to married, more than once. I went from living well below my own human potential to exceeding everyone's expectations. I ran so hard and fast into my "recovery" that I refused to look back. I never slowed down long enough to notice that I was replacing old addictions with new ones.

I held amazing jobs and achieved a bunch of degrees. I had status. I had experiences, opportunities, and adventures often found on bucket lists. I was afforded so much privilege. Please don't get me wrong: I appreciate dearly the life I created. Every single moment of it. *And* I also know now that this season of my life, which brought so many external wins and a few losses, was fuelled by the same insecurities, fears, and trauma of my adolescence. Underneath it all, I was still hurting. I felt broken, lost, unworthy, and scared. I repaired my social self, the part of me that was out there for the world to see and judge. But the more I achieved, the worse I was suffering internally. Parts of my life were still filled with the constant themes of strife, conflict, and stress. I felt like my own worst enemy, again.

From the outside looking in, I was fine. Yet these years presented a new fear: I now had a life I could lose if I didn't get it right. And, most importantly, I had three babies depending on me.

I had done the "head work" in therapy and the "checking-off-life-achievement-boxes work" in my everyday life. I had learned so many lessons that allowed me to flourish, yet there was more work to be done. A different kind of work. It was time to do the heart work. I needed a union between the extremes. I needed a path to real wellness, not just surface physical health and social acceptance. I wanted wellness that would permeate my soul. Oneness and unity with all parts of my life. I sought that mysterious and majestic wellness that means when we are told, "All will be well," we believe it in our bones. "Fine" was not going to cut it anymore.

So, my dear friend, when did you first learn to be "fine"?

FOLLOW THE PLAN AND YOU'LL BE FINE

Take a moment to reflect on how you thought life was supposed to go. What was the master plan you believed in when you were young? What was the norm? Go back as far as you can remember. We are groomed to have a "right path." Social norms are created and presented to us as "the way." What was the story you were told, and what were you promised?

I grew up thinking that there was one right path and an order to everything. Like a master-life checklist. Be good. Do good. Go to school. Fit in. Finish high school. Go to university. Study a subject that gets you a job. Don't rock the boat. Get married. Buy a house. Get a dog. Maybe a cat. Have two kids. Keep your job for life. Take two weeks of holiday a year. Visit your parents. Grow old. If you do everything just so, you will be fine. Even the creation story I was taught was about one man named Adam and one woman named Eve. And watch out, that woman did her own thing and ended up unleashing hell on the world.

For many of us, our difficulty with sticking to that plan is often where our patterns of maladaptive behaviour start. Our stress and threat systems are activated. We need to fit in. We try everything to ensure we feel accepted and are safe. That struggle grows. Eventually we might start rebelling against the path we "should" be on. We may even scorch the earth so that no one can even try to put us on that path again.

Our greatest human drive is to survive. We need nurturing when we are babies. Then we need our caregiver's acceptance so that we can stay in the community. Our survival depends on our ability to belong within our group. When we realize that the norms established by the group may not align with who we are, it is scary. We might be rejected. Our threat system is on high alert. And through it all, we fight to appear fine. The reality is, though, we are not fine. None of this is fine.

STRESS, WICKED PROBLEMS, AND WELLNESS

Stress research is quite similar to resiliency research. It is vast and unruly and depends on who you ask! I came upon this quickly in my own scholarship on resiliency: there is a multitude of theories, and it really depends on who you choose to listen to. Through empirical research combined with real-world applications and my own lived experiences, I formulate working theories of how we show up or practice resiliency in our lives. It is a dance of learning, testing, reflecting, circling back, and—mostly importantly—then sharing with others wherever and whenever I can. I want to make this knowledge accessible and share it with those who need it most. I am proud and deeply honoured to see my work circle the globe, offering sound theories and techniques to individuals and to the largest organizations in the world! I never saw it coming—how widely my resiliency work would be welcomed.

I attempted to use a similar avenue in my stress studies as I took to my work on resiliency—an explorer's approach. More formally, this is called action research, or "an approach in which the action researcher [me] and a client [people, groups, and organizations I support] collaborate in the diagnosis of the problem and in the development of a solution based on the diagnosis."[1] Essentially, I generate knowledge and insights for practical settings or situations while working collaboratively with the stakeholders to plan, act, observe, and reflect on the effectiveness of the proposed solution. This approach to research and scholarship has served me well.

I wanted to learn all about stress and stress management. I was curious if stress mastery was even a possibility in this day and age. I did not have an idea in mind that I was trying to substantiate or prove. I entered this realm of research with both an open mind and a wounded heart, looking for direction. What questions do I ask? Where do I look? Who is a trusted source? And does any of this align with my lived experience? Does it fit with the truths I have discovered in my own life and in the lives of people I support? I looked for threads I could weave together, to deepen my understanding of stress from both a personal and a professional perspective.

What I found was a wicked problem.

In education we use the theory of wicked problems to describe a situation where the solution to a problem is complex and may seem unsolvable. The theory of a wicked problem was introduced in 1973 by Horst Rittel and Melvin Webber. They were design theorists who explained that many problems in planning and social policy did not have one solution. Wicked problems are difficult to resolve because of the interconnected nature of the problem and solution itself. There are no risk-free attempts at solving the problem because of the real impact on people's lives. Rittel and Webber proposed ten markers that make a problem wicked:[2]

1 It lacks a definitive formulation. You cannot sum it up as one thing since it has so many parts, nor can you write it in a typical problem–solution formula.

2 It has no stopping rule that determines when a solution has been found.

3 It has good or bad solutions rather than true or false solutions or absolutes.

4 It lacks immediate and ultimate tests of proposed solutions.

5 It has proposed solutions that are "one-shot" operations versus experiments.

6 It lacks criteria that indicate all solutions have been identified.

7 It is unique.

8 It could be viewed as a symptom of another problem.

9 It has discrepancies that can be explained in multiple ways.

10 It requires that the people attempting to solve it be held accountable because it has real-world impacts.

Global warming, poverty, educational inequity, religious conflict, war, discrimination, and health care inequities are a few major wicked problems we face today. There are many.

On a much smaller and individual scale, our stress-filled lives have become a personalized wicked problem. When I dove into the research on stress, I was stunned by the contradictory information. Even defining stress was contentious. Stress can be viewed from nearly every lens: biological, psychological, physiological, social, philosophical, and even spiritual. Where do we begin? And how do we even talk about solutions? Heck, stress was relatively easy to identify and understand compared to the *solutions* to stress.

Stress is our wicked problem, and the even more wicked solution is wellness.

There is so much information and knowledge about what it takes to be well, yet there is no one solution for everyone. Even the concept of measuring your "wellness" is abstract. If you are completely overwhelmed and confused about your next right decision regarding your stress and wellness, you are definitely not alone. This is where I come in. Let me bring some clarity to this maze of information, because our lives and the quality of our lives depend on it. And it is never a good idea to tackle a wicked problem alone.

UNLEARNING A POINT OF VIEW

There is a Chinese parable that talks about the power of "We'll see."

A farmer and his son had a beloved stallion who helped the family earn a living. One day, the horse ran away, and their neighbours exclaimed, "Your horse ran away! What terrible luck!"

The farmer replied, "Maybe so, maybe not. We'll see."

A few days later, the horse returned home, leading a few wild mares back to the farm as well. The neighbours shouted out, "Your horse has returned and brought several horses home with him. What great luck!"

The farmer replied, "Maybe so, maybe not. We'll see."

Later that week, the farmer's son was trying to tame one of the mares, and she threw him to the ground, breaking his leg. The villagers cried, "Your son broke his leg. What terrible luck!"

The farmer replied, "Maybe so, maybe not. We'll see."

A few weeks later, soldiers from the national army marched through town, recruiting all the able-bodied boys for the army. They did not take the farmer's son, who was still recovering from his injury. Friends shouted, "Your boy is spared. What tremendous luck!"

To which the farmer replied, "Maybe so, maybe not. We'll see."

The "we'll see" perspective holds a huge amount of power and opportunity. As someone who personally has a paradoxical love of everything control and order *and* uncertainty and freedom, I am tipping my toe cautiously in the "we'll see" world, walking gently, thoughtfully, cautiously, and perhaps even slowly in any area of my life that feels like I am test-driving a new way of being. It feels foreign. I feel like a beginner. Yet, it also feels oddly familiar. Like this is how we were made to be. Like it is in our nature to be present.

When I tapped into this way of being, as in setting the intention to show up steady, grounded, and open, I noticed the natural pull and push of moments. Minutes, hours, days, weeks, months, and even years started to take on a natural season, filled with ebbs and flows. There is an ever-present current of energy to harness oneself to. Like how the wind guides a sail or how water dances around rocks. There is a natural rhythm to all things, including our lives. "We'll see" is more than a mindset; it is wisdom. My invitation for you is to be curious and gentle with how your stress-wisely practices form and unfold in your life. I believe observing life from a higher vantage point is a crucial first step. Awareness is a powerful teacher. So, where do you go from here? "We'll see." Trust that you know your next right move. Trust your wise self.

PERSONAL WISDOM

When I started my educational recovery, as in actually trying to learn and not viewing school as a version of purgatory, I quickly discovered I had virtually no learning-to-learn skills. I read appreciably below grade level. My spelling and writing were atrocious. I didn't know how to study or take tests. I had big ideas yet struggled to communicate them in a way that fit with the expectations of teachers and the whole schooling system. I stumbled my way through and did my best to fill in some major gaps. By this point, I had learned to work with parts of my attention deficit hyperactivity disorder (ADHD) and learning disabilities, yet I had not been formally diagnosed or medicated. Over time, I cobbled together the skills needed to do well in the last few semesters of high school. Using correspondence I made up the courses I missed after having dropped out. Much later in life, I told Jaxson, our youngest son, about how I did my grade eleven year through correspondence, and he asked me, "Was the Pony Express involved too?"

Through it all, I never felt particularly smart, but I did have this emerging feeling of being wise, for some reason. I felt that I knew about things most people my own age didn't know

"What is the topic of
your next book?" they asked.
"How to stress wisely,"
I replied.

Laughing in a
doubtful tone, they asked,
"Can that be done?"
"We'll see,"
I said, smiling back.

about, and maybe even some adults. My definition of being wise meant I had a deeper understanding of how parts of the world worked: the good, the bad, and definitely the ugly.

I knew firsthand about things like grief, abuse, loss, addiction, and recovery. I was starting to recognize worldly concepts like social justice, injustices, and privilege. I also knew the darkness of mental health episodes. I learned painfully that there were adults out there who didn't follow the rules. And that some adults used their positions of power over teenagers in harmful ways. I recall reading the anonymous quote, "For with much wisdom comes much sorrow; the more knowledge, the more grief." This felt pretty right. I knew sorrow, and the more I knew of it, the more grief I carried. So, yeah, I did feel wise in that realm, yet not particularly smart academically.

Having a deeper understanding of the world around you is crucial to recognizing your own wisdom. You are your own expert. No one knows you better than you do. We may have knowledge holders in our lives, those people who have been our witness to the stages of growth and development. For me, it is my father; he is the only person left who has the full understanding of what my journey has been. This is a precious gift. I hope that you have someone who has witnessed your valleys and your summits, too. Yet, those people only know part of our whole experience. We are the only person who knows what it is like to live our own lives. To know what it is like to be us. How we feel. How we think. How we experience all of it. I implore you to tap into this personal wisdom. It is your data. It is valid. It is absolutely yours to know.

BRIDGING WISE WITH SMART

Despite not feeling all that smart, I could navigate to post-secondary education. One institution, St. Lawrence College, was instrumental in my educational journey. This is where I finally let go of the label of "not smart." I discovered "smart" is quite relative! The skillset I learned that snapped the ties that bound me was critical thinking. I raise this because critical thinking is a tremendous support for people learning how to stress wisely.

Now, you might be wondering, what the heck is critical thinking anyway? I know when I started to think critically about knowledge and tried to apply critical thinking skills to the real world, I struggled. Most of us have been taught that there is one right answer to every problem. The idea of thinking critically seemed to me to be so enmeshed in some philosophical tango of rhetorical questions with no real answers that I wasn't very interested in learning about it, let alone practising it. Yet, eventually through the support of educators, I came to see how thinking about our thinking, which is called metacognition, allows a person to take what they know and dive deeper. It allows you to "know what you know" in the context of the much bigger picture. Being able to critically think about something allows information to shift to knowledge, and that knowledge can create a bridge to becoming wise. I share this because I want you to apply critical thinking to everything you learn, hear, and read about on the topic of your wellness. Here are some questions you can apply to any area of your life:

- What do I think about this?

- How do I feel about this?

- Why do I think/feel that?

- Where did this idea/feeling come from?

- How do I know this?

- What is missing for me?

- What questions do I still have?

- What do I need to learn more about?

This practice of critical thinking became part of how I began to see the world. My natural curiosity and wonderment were set ablaze. I felt a force growing inside me. I came upon a truth. I didn't want to learn anything in particular just for learning's sake. I needed to understand and apply what I was learning. This is important for you, too, and I am confident you can do this. Start asking the questions and let your truth rise to your awareness.

When it comes to stressing wisely, we can read all the things. We can buy every book. We can set lofty goals and have all the best intentions, yet if we are not critically thinking about our wellness, it is like the iconic lines from Coleridge's poem "The Rime of the Ancient Mariner": "Water, water, every where / Nor any drop to drink." Information is everywhere, yet what do we really know?

Rather than drowning in all the things you should be doing, ought to be doing, and could be doing, I invite you to stop and take a personal inventory. We are so conditioned to get to the doing parts, we don't allow ourselves the time to think, process, reflect, and imagine. Yet this is where the magic happens. True insights are discovered. Old wounds surface. New learnings take root. New ways of being in the world seem possible.

Hold space for this moment in time. Before rushing your way forward, pause long enough to have one big and meaningful reckoning with yourself. What brought you to this moment? Why this book? Why now? What are you hoping to come upon? When we have an intention or at least an inkling of what we are hoping to discover, it is more likely we will find it!

Past behaviour may be the best predictor of future behaviour, but you can hit the brakes and choose a different path. If you are like me, you have likely plowed through so many books on personal development looking for answers. We need to interrupt that cycle. As the popular sentiment goes, if you always do what you've always done, you'll always get what you've always gotten. So let us use our critical thinking skills for good here—for our own good. Pause. Stop what "else" you are doing in this moment. Unclench your jaw. Release your shoulders. Feel back into your body. Elongate your spine. Wiggle your toes. Now push your feet firmly into the ground. Breathe in for four counts. Hold it for four counts. Release the breath for four counts. Hold the empty space for four counts. Breathe in again.

Now, ask yourself this: Where is my emotional home?

EMOTIONAL HOME

The concept of an emotional home means that each of us has a learned emotional state of being. It is where we seek out and stay most of the time. Here is an example: Let's say someone's emotional home is "anger." On any given day, they find their way home to anger. That person could be looking out at the most beautiful vista in the world and would still find something to be angry about. Another person's emotional home may be "worry." They spend all their time trying to manage what could go wrong or predicting the worst possible outcomes in every situation, and they worry their life away.

Your emotional home is the place you feel the most comfortable and familiar with. You retreat there even if it is not necessarily good for you. Yet, going there has become a habit. You have been conditioned by life to seek refuge there. You feel safe there, even if the feelings are unsafe, because it is a place you know.

Your emotional home is the pinnacle example of your adaptability to survive, practise resiliency, and be well. For those who have had a lighter load to carry in life, it may be more familiar to have emotional homes of ease, gentleness, and friendliness. For others, emotional homes are more complex. If someone's emotional home is fear and rejection, they might have people-pleasing behaviour because that it is what has kept them safe. People whose emotional home is chaos and dysfunction find themselves in workplaces that are chaotic and dysfunctional because on some deep level this feels "normal." If someone was raised by an absent caregiver, they seek out relationships with people who are not emotionally available because that is all they know about love. One woman shared with me that her emotional home was "should." She reflected that she could take any pleasurable thing and turn it into a heavy obligation.

Before we jump into stressing wisely, please take note of your emotional home. This is the starting place from which to move into truly transformational change. When you know your emotional home and take inventory, you can use that deep and personal insight to chart your course. Now, you may have several rooms in your emotional homes, so my invitation is to pick the one room that you know needs some tender nurturing and radical support. I really like the practice of referring to my mood or my feelings as "parts": "Part of me is feeling lonely" or "Part of me is feeling frustrated." This simple word shift allows for more space and nimbleness within my emotional home. It is not all or nothing. Just think of how much stuff you have in a home. There are lots of layers and pieces to our emotions.

WHEN-THEN

I have occupied many different emotional homes during the seasons of my life. While some were more maladaptive, others were adaptive. Nevertheless, they *all* served a purpose. Meet the evolution of your emotional home with compassion. It is very much "you," after all. As I write this book, I have come upon another room in my emotional home that I didn't know was still there. This room is the "when-then" room, and it has served me very well over the years. But for me to really embrace stressing wisely, I needed to shine a light on this habitual practice. *When* I get X or do Y, *then* I will be . . . Z. When I lose these ten pounds, then I will feel good in my clothes. When I finish my doctorate degree, then I will feel smart enough. When I fix that one family relationship, then I will feel as though I belong. When I have the right house or at least a clean house, then I can relax. When I find the right meditation practice, then I will feel peaceful.

I am very confident that many of you can relate to this mindset. Our society has deeply conditioned this way of being in the world. What are your when–thens? Notice how many when–thens you have had in your lifetime. Perhaps you had "thens" but in the moment didn't realize it. For example, it is quite irking to look back at photographs and see yourself clearly, or to remember when an extra $500 in the bank felt like winning the lottery. In the "when–then" cycle, we will never truly be well.

According to Dr. Ann-Louise Lockhart of the Gottman Institute, if you can learn unhealthy patterns, like "when–then," then you can unlearn them too.[3] This is logic I can get behind. The system is simple, but I have seen just how radical this approach can be for changing any behaviour.

1 Write it down. You can't change what you are not measuring. Use a journal, a note pad, or even just your notes app on your phone. Identify one behaviour. Name it. Now track it.
   Example: *When-then thinking*

2 Determine the trigger. What starts or activates this behaviour?
   Example: *The emotional trap that says I have to earn my worth. When I graduate with a doctoral degree, then I can let go of the label of being a high school dropout.*

3 Determine your response. How do you respond to the trigger?
   Example: *Automatic thoughts of "just one more time." I will really feel better when I achieve this one last thing.*

4   Develop a hypothesis. Why is this behaviour part of your emotional home? (This may be big, heavy work here— finding support to do this work may be necessary.)
Example: *Work with my therapist to uncover root emotional injury causing me to not feel good enough.*

5   Is this belief or behaviour serving you? Remember, every single thing we do serves a purpose. Often the behaviour you are trying to change is being reinforced somehow or somewhere. Be honest with yourself here.
Example: *This "when–then" behaviour has been extremely motivating, and I have achieved wild success, yet I am choosing to unlearn this pattern so I can be more present and at ease. My worth does not have to be externally measured.*

The real recovery needed for adopting a stress-wisely way of being in the world starts with radical personal honesty. All wellness behaviours (adaptive and maladaptive) are symptoms of our relationship with ourselves. As spiritual teacher Vernon Howard said, "Just be honest with yourself. That opens the door."[4] And Thomas Jefferson said, "Honesty is the first chapter in the book of wisdom."[5] Start there. It is hard, especially if we have been lying to ourselves for such a long time, but it is worth it.

THE RECKONING

I love the idea of a reckoning. Even the word "reckoning" sparks a sense of boldness. Courageously and unapologetically, you show up and say, "No more." I remember reading Colleen Hoover's novel *It Ends with Us* and throwing the book across the room! I have different categories for books' transforming effects. The highest rating is saved for books I throw. It is a visceral reaction to having my mind blown or just being stopped in my tracks. Hoover's main character has a reckoning, and it was *exactly* what the character needed. And gosh, that reckoning hurt like hell to read. Reckonings are not for the faint of heart. They are hard. Thankfully, we can do hard things. We can also do great things! I might have written a book about that already.

To be able to do the hard things, we need to be sure we are okay in the moment. At the beginning of this chapter, I shared that "fine" got us into this mess of stress, burnout, and disconnection, and, my friends, "okay" is going to get us out of it.

So, you may be asking, now what? I am being honest with myself, but what do I do now? I am thinking critically about my wellness, but how do I fix it? How do I be okay in all this discomfort of not being where I want to be? Is okay even possible when I need to make changes, stat?

My research on resiliency was built upon this idea of "okay," and being okay is fundamentally what life is all about. When a first responder arrives at an accident, the first thing she tells you is that you are okay. You beg to the heavens for your child to be okay on their first day of university. You pray that you will be okay when you lose your job. Being okay is absolutely everything. A person once told me that my model of resiliency, which holds the idea that okay is enough, was not ambitious enough. This critical scholar commented, "She is making resiliency so practical that almost everyone could achieve it." I took that as a compliment, although I am certain that was not how it was intended! To me that is exactly the goal: debunk the idea that resiliency is only for a chosen few.

We all have the capacity to show up even in the hard parts of our lives.

Just as my work on resiliency is built on an accessible path, so is the idea of your reckoning and your recovery. Once you have had your personal reckoning, whatever that looks like for you, you are invited to a path of recovery—recovery is what you need to be okay in the moment. You don't have to change all the big stuff in this very moment. I invite you to allow yourself the time, spaciousness, and ease in your life right now. I want you to start feeling well today. When you give yourself permission to let "good feeling thoughts" into your day, you can hold space for self-compassion, acceptance, perspective, and even humour. Once you hold those good feelings again, you can see more clearly what matters most, and the "work" of wellness naturally unfolds.

SET AN INTENTION

In all my beginnings, before each day, and before every event, I set an intention. I am going to invite you to set one, too, for yourself. It takes courage to learn and unlearn. The topic of how you live your life is a hard one to explore! It is okay to be nervous about making this personal, but I do invite you to try. Borrowed courage and real courage produce the same result: you keep going. Please take a moment to set your intention as you read this book. What are you searching for? Are you looking for quick fixes? Are you looking for real insights into your life? Are you hoping to support others with their stressors? Are you searching for ideas about embracing the change you desire? Are you hoping to connect with and awaken that part of you that once felt whole?

Regardless of why you are here, you are here. That matters. Just calling to mind what you are looking for raises your awareness and helps you recognize your need when you read it. This is how I see it. If you know what you are looking for, great—I hope you find it. If you do not know why you are here, that is perfectly okay, too. I hope you will come upon something you needed to learn. My goal as an educator is to share that piece of knowledge you need, exactly when you need it most. Our paths have now crossed. And with all the paths in the world, that in itself is a wonderful mystery! Aren't mysteries grand? Our imaginations are free to explore and entertain the idea anything can happen. Everything is possible. Maybe even solving a wicked problem like learning how to stress wisely and to be well in an unwell world.

Now let's adventure this wicked problem together, shall we?

66

Don't let your mind bully your
body into believing it must carry
the burden of its worries.

@ASTRIDALAUDA

CHAPTER 2

STRESS AS WE KNOW IT

'M BEYOND THE normal running late, with a cold coffee in hand, hoping I posted today's lecture notes for my students, thinking of all the other things I will not get done today. I am scrambling to get forgotten basketball shoes to a panicked child before practice begins. The very same practice I had already driven to, while asking said child to double check they had their shoes! "Check your shoes" had become a family joke ever since Hunter travelled to a soccer match with a 7 a.m. start time, in flip-flops, only to discover his cleats were still "airing out" back at home, two hours away. Hunter, who wears men's size 14 shoes, played a full soccer match in his coach's size 10 cleats. I should have bought that coach new cleats since by halftime Hunter's big toe had popped through the front of the shoe.

As I'm texting said child that I am in the parking lot with his shoes, I'm reading the red glowing letters on the school sign. A series of reminders scrolls by: *Don't forget pizza orders due Friday. Donate to the school band's trip. Sign up for parent-teacher interviews by Tuesday. Have you thanked your bus driver today? Remember—refuse to let yourself stress over things you cannot control. If you cannot handle your stress, you won't be able to handle success.*

Six reminders in six seconds. Hunter comes running out the main school doors and, with a sheepish smile, collects his shoes through the passenger window. "Thanks, Mama. You always come in a clutch." He blows me a kiss and dashes back into the school. I call out to him, "Did you thank your bus driver today?" Hunter glances over his shoulder and nods, winks, and disappears into the building. Well, I am 1 for 6, according to the sign. No, wait, Hunter is at least 1 for 6. He thanked the bus driver. Mom, 0 for 6. Because I sure as heck have already stressed over things I cannot change, and I am pretty confident that my track record of handling stress means success is out of the question!

Today is also the day my dad goes in for major surgery. Because of COVID protocols, he went in alone. My only living parent's life is in the hands of the medical community. My mom didn't make it out alive. A memory awakens. "Yes, you're right, Robyne," the doctor said, looking up from my mother's autopsy report. "People don't die in 2012 from this, especially someone as young as your mother. We definitely have more questions than answers here."

That always-present grief grabs my attention as I am sitting in the parking lot, remembering what is at stake today: my father's life. All of our lives are at stake every single day, but some days that is more obvious. Knowing that, on any given day, a life can change in an instant ignites the grief I hold for my mom. Before, that grief would have overcome me. The waves of pain, loss, anger, and sadness pulverized me for years. It was visceral. Now my grief is familiar enough that I know to tuck my chin, clench my jaw, and push my ribs against my spine as far as I can, to make space for my splintered breaths and bruised heart to coexist in the chamber of my chest. *This too shall pass*, I whisper in my mind. Will it? I wonder. Will life ever let up?

A string of rapid-fire email notifications wakes me to the present moment. "Dr. Hanley-Dafoe, the lecture notes aren't posted." Another thirty emails confirm this. Deep breath in. Strong exhale out. Game face on. It's time to work. As if managing life isn't work, but the day job calls! I throw the car into drive. As I do, I knock my cold coffee from the cup holder. Coffee covers the dash and the passenger seat and is halfway up the windshield. I freeze. I am curious to see how I am going to react. Tears or swear words? I'm waiting for it. Surprisingly, I notice the radio; a classic song fills my awareness. A magical guitar riff sends memories ricocheting between the past and the present. I hear the Indigo Girls wondering how long it will be until their souls get life right. They go on to sing something about looking at what you have to overcome from your last life. My mom bought me that album when I was sixteen years old. The Indigo Girls, *1200 Curfews*, released in 1995. I was the same age as Hunter, the one who now has basketball shoes on his feet. Those same Indigo Girls taught me an important lesson on that album. You have to just laugh in some moments or you will cry your eyes out. I can't muster a laugh, but I am able to snicker and smile at the mysteries of my life. All before 8 a.m. Out loud I share a truth. Maybe it's a prayer. It is the only comfort I can find. "Today, Dad, it will be either Mom or me there when you wake up. Either way, we've got you covered."

The easiest thing in the
world is to be what you are, what
you feel. The hardest thing
to be is what other people want
you to be. Don't let them put
you in that position.

LEO BUSCAGLIA

THE INESCAPABLE TRUTH

Stress permeates every part of our lives, yet we get little training or teaching on how to navigate it effectively. More often people share with us how to ignore, avoid, or ward off stress. People and society offer an infinite number of maladaptive ways of running for cover from that enemy known as stress! Just like telling an upset person to calm down, which has never in the history of the world worked, telling people not to stress about something is equally ineffective. I promise, if I could avoid stressing about whatever is gripping every part of my consciousness, I would. But I can't. Stress is inescapable because it originates inside us.

Despite how familiar we are with the idea of stress, and given that it is entwined in our nature, it is shockingly difficult to define stress clearly. In my previous book, I devoted an entire chapter to stress. I had identified that stress was a barrier to practising resiliency. I will revisit some of those key ideas because the foundations and science of stress are relatively consistent. I will also offer new insights that are shifting our understanding of stress.

Some researchers define stress as a normal biological reaction to potential danger. When you encounter a stressful situation, your brain floods your body with chemicals. This definition introduces the variables of adrenaline and cortisol. The Canadian Mental Health Association defines stress more broadly, explaining that stress can be cognitive, emotional, physical, or behavioural.[1] The traditional medical model defines stress as physical, mental, and emotional factors that cause bodily or mental tension.

For our purposes, I like to think of stress as similar to gasoline. Stress hormones can be inert. But when they contact certain triggers or mix with other elements, they can run a car, start a fire, or send a rocket into space. The body and mind work in tandem. The mind activates our internal fire alarm, which signals a batch of hormones and chemicals to call us into action. Our body will respond or react, depending on our state of consciousness. We may fight, flee, and freeze our way out of the danger zone. We don't get to choose what reaction we have. It happens to us.

Most of us are familiar with the fight-or-flight idea, and the idea of freezing has been talked about more over the past few decades. Freezing is that stunned response. You are paralyzed in that moment when your body registers danger. You can't run. You can't fight. You just stand there, lost in that million-miles-away stare, oblivious to the world around you. Or, in a more common example, you watch Netflix for so long that the "Are you still watching?" prompt pops up. Those are freezing responses.

The newest addition to this list of stress reactions is the fawning response. Although the fawning response has likely always been part of our stress response system, it is gathering more attention recently. The fawning response occurs when someone is triggered and, instead of fighting, fleeing, or freezing, they acquiesce. Like a helpless fawn, the person becomes soft, gentle, nice, or accommodating in a threatening situation. They exhibit any behaviour needed to show the enemy that they are not a worthy opponent.

THE FAWNING RESPONSE UNPACKED

Psychotherapist and trauma expert Pete Walker, who introduced the term "fawning," explains that it is when people
seek safety by appeasing the needs and wishes of others
in a self-sacrificing way.[2] It is often referred to as a trauma
response. And it is an automatic response. All stress reactions
happen to us; we don't get to choose which one to experience.
It would be helpful if we could, but our physiology, biology,
and the oldest parts of our brain take over in reaction to threat,
stress, and danger. Our body and mind, without giving our
higher-order thinking time to process, are making decisions
on our behalf. With fawning, the evolutionary part of our
brain, the one that knows how to survive, reads the situation
and reacts by placating. We placate because that is our best
option for survival in that moment.

When we fawn, we erase ourselves. We push aside our
own needs, feelings, and even thoughts. The reptilian part of
our brain cannot even consider speaking up, setting boundaries, or being honest in that moment. It doesn't have that
capacity. But even if the more advanced parts of our brain
engaged, we wouldn't say anything anyway. That would be
self-damaging. On some level we might be aware of our
needs and feelings, but it is extremely scary to express them,
so we become monotropic. We focus only on the other person.

If fawning is a new concept and it is really resonating with
you, take some time to explore. Remember that fawning is
an automatic response. You are not flawed or broken. There
is no place for judgement or shame here. I remember doing
my own work to unpack fawning and felt weakened somehow.
"How come other people fight their way out of dangerous situations, which sounds brave and courageous, yet for me, when

I want to fight back, instead I roll over and show my belly like a puppy?" Far enough away from the threatening situation, I am all talk. I visualize myself speaking my truth. Standing tall and proud in the face of mistreatment. I'm not taking any guff. Then, when I am actually in a situation, the first words out of my mouth are, "Sure thing, I can do that."

We cannot control the stress reaction we are going to experience, but we can make decisions about how to respond to the reaction. Learning to work with your stress reactions takes insight, effort, and a heck of a lot of practice. And still, sometimes nature wins.

MEETINGS UNDER THE INFLUENCE... OF STRESS

Not that long ago, I recall being belittled, mocked, and shamed in a one-to-one professional meeting. Every part of my being knew that what was transpiring was not okay. If that person had talked to anyone else like this in front of me, you would have probably mistaken me for a Spartan princess warrior. I would have kicked him into the death pit while cursing him to hell. Yet this passive-aggressive attack was happening to me, and I took it. It was also on Zoom, for goodness' sake! All I had to do was hit the "end meeting" button.

The feelings of humiliation started to grow when I could hear my husband and children in the kitchen. On one side of the door, my family was preparing dinner. I was on the other side of the door with a grown person mocking me. "Do you even know how to write a sentence? Can you tell the difference between a noun and a verb? Show me. Share your screen and type me a sentence that shows me you know how to write a letter with proper grammar." I placated. I shared my screen and started typing sentence after sentence. My inner Spartan was screaming so loud that I thought my ears would bleed. Yet, my fingers still found their way to the keyboard, and I complied. He watched. When I finished the corrections to a letter, he told me to open the other six letters and make those corrections, too, with my screen shared, just to make sure I got it right. At one point, he stopped to remind me this was "collaborating," with a smile that made me uncomfortable.

Classic gaslighting. Gaslighting is a form of psychological manipulation. The person makes you question the validity of your own feelings and thoughts. You question your perspective and the reality of what is happening. The person who is gaslighted is often left thinking they are the problem. As this call carried on, I recall wondering if maybe I was just being sensitive. I do have ADHD and learning disabilities. Maybe I was not following properly. He was just trying to help. A boss wouldn't act that way. I was confused. Was this a joke? I stayed on that call for way too long.

When the call finally did end, only after I finished those letters, I felt ashamed of myself. I was angry, but not at him as much as at myself. I felt embarrassed and furious that I had fawned. I was also confused about that reaction when the threat was not even in the same city as me. It was over a screen. Well, my friends, we are working with a very underdeveloped nervous system. My brain didn't compute that the other person was not physically present with me. The size of his face on my computer screen suggested to my brain that we were nose to nose, the classic fighting stance between two boxers. I was toe to toe with a threat. As I cried that night, talking with Jeff, my husband, who has the superpower of remaining calm and grounded, I said with a weary smile, "Jeff, I think my trauma is showing." My therapist confirmed it in our next session.

If the fawning reaction is something you want to explore, here are some questions to help guide your thinking:

- How have I used fawning in the past to keep me safe?

- How has fawning helped me?

- What are the patterns when I react with fawning? For example, am I triggered by certain situations or a type of person?

- What's at risk if I don't fawn here?

- How can I hold space and appreciation for this part of me?

- What is needed to make alliances with this part of my nervous system?

- How would I like to coexist with this part of me, moving forward?

Remember, there is no need for shame or guilt. All behaviours serve a purpose. Fawning is not a choice, and it has served you well.

WHAT WE THINK STRESS WILL DO TO US

All stress is stress—and I prefer not to think about it as a moral issue, as good stress versus bad stress. Even with what we perceive as "positive stress"—like a new job, the birth of a child, starting a relationship, or even holidays—the hormones that inundate our bodies, the cortisol and adrenaline, are the exact same as when we experience "negative" stressors. Our cells don't look at the cortisol and say, "Oh, that's a *good* cortisol molecule—that's triggered because I have a hot date tonight!" Or, "Ah, that's a *bad* cortisol molecule because I have a flat tire." As Dr. Henry Emmons says, "Your body can't differentiate between a sabre-toothed tiger attack and a bad job review," and the same applies to a sabre-toothed tiger versus a new kitten.[3] Chemicals are chemicals; hormones are hormones. Good stress, bad stress, neutral stress—it is all the same stuff. The judgement provides little benefit. However, our perception does. *Our perception is the key.*

Now, before I jump into this idea about our perceptions of stress and its impact, I want to assure you that I'm not oversimplifying or minimizing the effects of trauma. For anyone who wants to learn more about complex trauma, *The Body Keeps the Score* by Dr. Bessel van der Kolk is a brilliant resource. The studies I reference below did not control for complex trauma to the best of my knowledge.

We are bombarded with messages that suggest a stress-free life is available or that being stress-free and happy all the time is the ultimate goal. We are presented with the notion of good and bad stress. Thankfully, we also have thought leaders like Kelly McGonigal, whose work breaks through those narratives and provides critical insight into what is really going on with our stress. Dr. McGonigal's key insight is that getting rid of stress shouldn't be the goal. Getting better at it is the secret.

McGonigal's book *The Upside of Stress* is an excellent read for revisiting our understanding of biological stress. McGonigal does not suggest how to minimize stress but rather how to get better at it. In chapter 1, McGonigal shares results from a groundbreaking 2012 study, conducted by Whitney Witt from the University of Wisconsin–Madison, that also changed how McGonigal thought about stress.[4] With more than 29,000 people in their study, the researchers examined how a person's perception of their stress affected their physical health. Participants rated whether their stress levels influenced their health "a little," "a moderate amount," or "a lot." Eight years later, the researchers used public death records to compare to their original sample. In a shocking discovery, people who had reported that their stress affected their physical health "a lot" had an increased prevalence of death by 43 per cent! Participants who reported that their stress levels affected their health "a little" were less likely to have died compared to everyone else in the study. What we can learn from this is that if we believe that our stress is going to kill us, we're probably right. If we believe our stress is not affecting our health, we're also probably right. Telling ourselves that stress is killing us is not helpful—it is damn well harmful.

Another group of researchers, Alia Crum, Peter Salovey, and Shawn Achor, categorized stress as either debilitating or enhancing, and found similar results.[5] I would invite you to think of these two categories not as good or bad but as adaptive and maladaptive, or as helpful for moving us forward or holding us back. Their findings support the idea that the story we tell ourselves about our stress matters. The researchers developed a tool to measure a person's perception of stress. I have adapted their Stress Mindset Measure tool to provide an example of how you would measure your perception of the impacts of stress.

STRESS MINDSET MEASURE

This eight-item measure was developed by Crum, Salovey, and Achor to address the extent to which an individual adopts a mindset that considers the effects of stress as enhancing or debilitating. Consider whether you agree or disagree with the following statements:

1 The effects of stress are negative and should be avoided.

2 Experiencing stress depletes my health and vitality.

3 Experiencing stress inhibits my learning and growth.

4 Experiencing stress debilitates my performance and pro-ductivity.

5 Experiencing stress facilitates my learning and growth.

6 Experiencing stress enhances my performance and pro-ductivity.

7 Experiencing stress improves my health and vitality.

8 The effects of stress are positive and should be utilized.

This measure can help you explore your ideas about the impact of stress on your health. Take a moment to reflect on your answers. Do you believe that stress is bad for you? Do you think stress should be avoided? And most importantly, do you believe that your stress is going to kill you?

Once you have explored what you hold as truth, then investigate where those beliefs came from. By understanding your beliefs and their origins, you can develop new perspectives and plan a course of corrections when unhelpful beliefs come up.

Here are some questions to stimulate your investigation:

• Who first taught me about stress (directly or indirectly)? What was the message?

• When have my stress perceptions served me well? When have they led me off course?

- What is one step I could take to reframe one stress belief that no longer serves me?

- What is one new stress belief that I want to strengthen?

- How can I reinforce this new stress belief?

Thankfully, McGonigal shares more strategies. In her work, which interconnects with that of Crum, Salovey, and Achor, she frames three additional productive beliefs about stress that are helpful for minimizing its harmful effects:[6]

- View your body's stress response as helpful, not debilitating or harmful; view stress as energy.

- View yourself as able to handle, and even learn and grow from, the stress in your life.

- View stress as something everyone deals with and as a natural part of our humanity.

Each one of us will have a different way of internalizing these beliefs. Some may read them once, a switch will go off, and they will just know differently from then on. Others may have to write the beliefs down, reread them, or even make notes or screen-capture images to constantly remind themselves of their new outlook; for example, "This situation isn't going to kill me." Whatever your case may be, I hope this helps you reframe stress and minimize the needless harm and worry. But don't be too hard on yourself: learning to reframe and revisit stress may take some time. But with intention and commitment, we can start to adopt a new way of thinking and being. We need to be intentional with our thoughts about

If there is a meaning in life at all, then there must be a meaning in suffering.

DR. VIKTOR FRANKL

stress and the doses of stress we experience every day. You may also have to keep reminding yourself and the people around you that stress is not the enemy.

START BY KNOWING WHERE YOU ARE STARTING FROM

To start this work, we need to know where we are starting from. What is the lay of your land? Take note. You can ask yourself this: "Has the way I have worked with my stress worked for me in the past?" I am confident that most of us respond with "sometimes." We all have adaptive and mal-adaptive stress behaviours. We all have seasons and cycles. For example, people often tell me that their number one stressor is their weight. This is very common in our cruel, fat-phobic culture. People share with me that when they lose the weight, then they will finally feel better. They share success stories about their fad-diet past. "This program worked for me, and I lost forty pounds two years ago." Yet they have regained the weight, because most of us do. Did that really work? Or is that evidence of diet cycling? The lower weight just happened to be a part of the diet cycle they liked. Or maybe they hated every minute of restricting their body yet loved the social acceptance and praise they gained.

All behaviours, both adaptive and maladaptive, serve a purpose. They keep us safe. No judgement. We have been conditioned to think there is only one right answer to the problem.

The problem of stress is a wicked problem with no one solution. And as we start to take a stand against the parts of our Western culture that promote stress-living and hustle as a sign of accomplishment, we are going to need thoughtful and careful steps. We will need a plan. We will need a map. And probably snacks.

There will always be stress in our daily lives. Our very nature is designed on a living stress system that cannot be turned off. There is no switch, although some of us try to make one. We numb out in various ways. Some work themselves into exhaustion. Others use substances. Others use people. Numbing behaviour is widely accepted if it fits within certain social norms. But alas, there is no switch, my friends. So, let's stop looking for one. Let's shift our energy and focus into learning sustainable ways of coexisting with our stressors. Our greatest ally in this emerging way of living with our stressors will be our relationship with our wellness. Now, that is a wicked solution! Is wickedly well a thing? It can be when we learn how to stress wisely.

What happens when you are stuck in
the stress-storm-cycling lifestyle?

SHORT TERM:
You win a lot of daily battles.

LONG TERM:
You eventually lose the war.

CHAPTER 3

BUCKETS FULL OF STRESS

HAVE YOU EVER been in such a stress state that you could barely hold it together, and someone suggested, "Oh, you should try drinking chamomile tea!" I have come to appreciate that part of me that feels instant rage yet has learned not to share it. I remind myself that they are just trying to help.

Recently, I was on a flight, and the man next to me refused to wear his mask. Flight regulations still required passengers to wear masks on planes. This grown man made such a fuss but eventually put on the mask so we could take off. Within seconds of the flight being air bound, he slid the mask to his chin. Several flight attendants, and even a pilot who was just catching a ride, asked him to keep his mask over his nose. The situation was escalating quickly. I am not a fan of conflict anywhere, let alone at 38,000 feet in the air!

The difficult passenger was mocking the flight crew. "What are you going to do about it, huh?" he sneered. The flight crew was doing their absolute best to remain calm but assertive. The man, now yelling, said, "I can't keep it up! It just slides down."

Without hesitation, in my loudest teacher voice, I proclaimed, "It is really a common problem that some men can't keep it up. You shouldn't feel embarrassed. Seriously, keeping it up is a real issue." Everyone was stunned, even me. But a few snickers from the elderly women sitting in front me and the smiling eyes of the flight attendants, who remained absolutely professional, were assuring. I was among friends! The man snapped that mask on his face so fast, put on his headphones, and ignored everyone for the remainder of the flight. At the end of the flight, as I exited the plane, the pilot who was catching a ride home tapped me on the shoulder and let me know that he would be sure to tell all his colleagues about what had happened. My intention is never to make someone uncomfortable, even that guy who was behaving poorly, but I will not be a bystander ever again.

Learning how to work with our stressors and being able to recognize our stress thresholds and states takes work. We need to be aware in the moment. This requires mindfulness: the act of focusing awareness on the present moment. And please, if even reading the word "mindfulness" prompted an eye roll, stick with me.

The data does not lie. Well, data can be manipulated, but the overall consensus that mindfulness is a superpower for self-management and self-regulation is true. In full disclosure, this idea of staying present used to seem like a bunch of woo-woo nonsense to me. I grew up needing the focus and ferociousness of a tiger to take down this big world, not the serenity of an eyes-closed, grass-eating gazelle. Mindfulness felt like the gazelle. I wanted to be the predator, not the prey. Mindfulness felt soft. The world taught me I had to be hard. Of course, yet again, clearly I had some unlearning to do!

Despite my resistance, the data is remarkable. Individuals who develop consistent mindfulness practices see improvements in overall physical health, including a reduction in symptoms of chronic diseases, improved immune function, reduction in physical pain, and improved sleep.

Mindfulness has also been associated with improved performance in learning, motivation, self-regulation, problem solving, and decision-making. It is attributed to enhanced personal and professional relationships, lower stress, and increased life satisfaction. And as if that were not enough, mindfulness also improves emotional well-being by increasing tolerance of difficult situations and by reducing reactivity and repetitive negative thinking. It also fosters self-compassion, which can decrease self-criticism and promote more positive emotional responses. It increases our sense of belonging and connection with others by reducing feelings of loneliness and isolation.[1] "Okay, fine. I will try it," I said to a friend.

I approach most things in my life with a "full-on, all-in, sign me way up" kind of energy. This is the ADHD symptom that works for good, most of the time. When I want to learn something, I plan to be a card-carrying expert by the end of it.

But when I hit the mat at my first meditation retreat, I wasn't even remotely knowledgeable about any of it. At least I couldn't have impostor syndrome since I was so obviously out of my element. A few years earlier, I would not have been okay in such a foreign situation. But the Robyne at her first retreat had learned to lean into the unknown with more ease. Shedding my ego, or at least putting her in the back seat of my mind with an iPad and ear buds, helped me explore new situations.

The retreat location and energy were magical—abundant nature, gentle and kind humans, ancient smells, glowing warmth radiating from every square inch, and nourishing sounds that my ears and mind softened around. The guide, with the most divine voice, welcomed us to circle up. We each had our own mat and pillow. We were about to explore a fifteen-minute guided meditation. This felt like a warm-up for the main event, a two-hour session later in the day. "I've got this," I told myself. We were guided into a collective experience; her words welcomed us into a still and quiet place in our own minds. The meditation began. We would be in peaceful stillness for fifteen minutes. "I can quiet my thoughts for fifteen minutes, right?"

My mind took full advantage of the lack of motion and stimuli. It started as a whisper, then my inner voice grew louder, grabbing at my attention.

"Wait, her voice reminds me of someone. Oh, it's that Australian actress from the *Lord of the Rings* movies. I loved that trilogy! Cate Blanchett was the Elf Queen, or was it Kate Winslet? Gosh, I love Kate Winslet. Wasn't Orlando Bloom in *Lord of the Rings* too? Those movies were long. Was Orlando in that movie before or after *Avengers*? Wait, Orlando Bloom wasn't in the *Avengers* movie; that was Jeremy Renner playing Hawkeye, but they made a Legolas joke in the battle scene in New York, and Legolas was Orlando's character in *Lord of the Rings*. Right. That's it. Wow. I forgot the author of *Lord of the Rings*, J. R. R. Tolkien, was friends at Oxford University with C. S. Lewis, the author of *The Lion, the Witch, and the Wardrobe* series. I wonder what the J. R. R. and the C. S. stand for. Oh, and C. S. Lewis also wrote my favourite book on grief. Oh, for goodness' sake, grief, grief, grief. I miss my mom. I don't want to do this anymore..." When there is stillness and a lack of stimuli, all thoughts lead here, eventually. When I stop, the grief is never far behind.

Pushing through the waves of grief, my mind sought out the teacher's voice. She let us know we were one minute into our meditation. One minute! *This may not be my scene. These may not be my people.*

For the next ten minutes, I panicked, bounced back from panic, and then planned a birthday party for my daughter and decided to paint the accent wall in the family room a new colour since it hadn't been painted in at least a year. With only a few minutes remaining, our guide invited us to imagine sitting on a beach, alone. She offered prompts about complete ease, freedom, spaciousness, and peacefulness, and she reiterated that we were safe, content, and fulfilled. She described the sound of the waves, a bird in the distance, and a tropical forest behind us that caught the breeze rolling in from the ocean. My mind was desperately trying to be on that beach with her. It sounded amazing. I was using all my mental energy to stay there. And then I heard it. My mental attention spun around to see the image being held in my mind's eye. I saw the tree line of the forest, and it was absolutely full of baby monkeys smiling at me. Within a moment, the pristine beach in my mind was taken over by loud, playful monkeys. I settled onto my mat, the corners of my mouth rose, and I let the circus show begin. This is my mind. This is also my circus. These are my monkeys!

Thankfully, with all things, including mindfulness, practice makes better. Mindfulness practices need practice, and they are always just one breath away. The present moment is really the only moment we ever have.

The little things?
The little moments?
They aren't little.

JON KABAT-ZINN

So, yes, in later chapters we will explore practical ways to build awareness, and mindfulness is one of them. But to understand why so many of us struggle to do things like mindfulness, which we know help with our wellness, we need to discuss stress theory a wee bit more. When you understand the why, the how to make it work for you becomes clearer.

In the previous chapter we examined the biological reactions to stress: we interpret a threat, and our biology takes over. It seems like quite a finite relationship. Cause and effect. There is so much more than just our lizard brains commanding the ship. Thank goodness! Let's talk about the diathesis-stress model.

DIATHESIS-STRESS MODEL

The diathesis-stress model is a psychological theory that explains how behaviours can be attributed to both biological and genetic predispositions as well as to external variables in a person's environment. This means that some people have a susceptibility or predisposition to certain diseases, illnesses, or disorders. When stressors are present, these underlying conditions or tendencies emerge. This theory has widely been used to appease the nature-versus-nurture debate, or at least has added some useful considerations.

Most textbooks trace the origins of the diathesis-stress model to the 1950s. However, researcher Dr. Kenneth Kendler discovered multiple descriptions of similar theories in psychiatric texts written well before then, suggesting it was recognized much earlier. With very outdated language, the idea is that "insanity could be usefully divided into those that predispose to illness and those that excite onset."[2] This theory is used extensively in both physical and mental health work today, with an emphasis for onsets of depression and anxiety. It is used with other mental health diagnoses, as well. In the classic study by Irving Gottesman and James Shields in 1966, identical twins were used to understand the heredity of certain mental conditions.[3] The researchers discovered that even though the identical twins who all had the gene for schizophrenia had the same DNA, sometimes only one twin developed schizophrenia. They concluded that certain genes may predispose someone to a particular condition, but an environmental stress or trigger activates that gene. Nurture and nature were both at play.

Although this work is from the medical perspective, it is useful to understand that underlying factors influence how our bodies experience stress, especially anxiety. There will always be things outside our control, and there are also things within our control. I think of this theory as a "dual risk model." We have certain vulnerabilities, and how we work with our stress, or do not work with our stress, can also be a risk factor. Another remarkable finding from the research on the diathesis-stress model is what is known as the stress-vulnerability and protective factors.

STRESS-VULNERABILITY AND PROTECTIVE FACTORS

Researchers Joseph Zubin and Bonnie Spring expanded the work on the diathesis-stress model to introduce the components of psychological and social protection factors. This work explains that while some components are outside our control, we can influence some parts of our biology.[4] The big idea is that our biology and being predisposed to certain conditions, combined with our lived experiences, make us vulnerable to certain types of challenges as we grow older. In psychology this is known as adverse childhood experience.[5] Certain experiences can be detrimental to our development, especially if we have underlying biological vulnerabilities. Interestingly, there are also protective factors that can minimize the impact of stress vulnerabilities. For example, for a child who may be susceptible to anxiety, having one solid, consistent, caring adult in their life can make a difference. To support this idea, take a look at Josh Shipp, an award-winning author and speaker who candidly shares about his life "from foster care to Harvard." Shipp has devoted himself to spreading the message that "every kid is *one* caring adult away from being a success story."[6] His work highlights on a global scale how people can overcome both biology and environment. (I like to think that it is not so much about overcoming as it is learning and growing through our circumstances.) When the right protections are in place, people can thrive.

In other situations, this could take a community. When I'm asked about how a community can rally around youth who are at risk, I often share the stories of NBA legends like DeMar DeRozan or Kawhi Leonard. Both athletes forged their way out of one of the most dangerous neighbourhoods in the US, Compton. In interviews, DeRozan talks about how, growing up in that city in LA County, he had "a circle to teach me the right way to go about things," even though "it was so easy to get caught up ... in a lot of temptation to go the wrong way."[7] Some of the strongest people I have ever met speak with deep reverence about the people who stood by them during hard times. It reminds me of the saying, "Take notice of who stood by you in hard times, who helped you out of hard times, and never forget who put you in those hard times."

Internal factors serve as protectors, too. We will explore those factors shortly, but first, let's look at our stress and capacity in action.

THE YERKES-DODSON HUMAN PERFORMANCE AND STRESS CURVE

When working with others to help unpack stress and capacity, I love introducing to them to the Yerkes-Dodson Human Performance and Stress Curve.[8] This is my go-to framework for learning to see stress on a continuum.

The Yerkes-Dodson Human Performance and Stress Curve

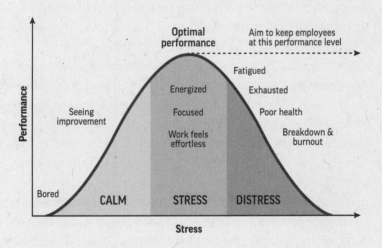

Researchers Robert Yerkes and John Dillingham Dodson discovered that there is an empirical relationship between stress (what they called arousal) and performance: performance increases with physiological or mental arousal, but only up to a point. What this means is that stress will actually improve our performance. When there is no stress, performance is lacking. When stress builds, we start seeing improvements, and when we are in our peak zone, we experience optimal performance. The work feels energizing and effortless. Once the stress level gets too high, however, our performance will decrease.

When coaching people with this framework, I use the notion that the peak zone is our "A-game." We feel great. We are getting things done. We are proud of ourselves. This can be referred to as eustress, or good stress. What is important to remember here is that the stress itself is not good or bad. It is how the body experiences the stress that is either positive and productive or excessive and destructive. In the peak zone, the body responds to the stress in a productive way. I also think it helps to think about the "doses" of stress we experience each day. Think about how many times it is not just "one thing," but a combination or accumulation of things that pushes us into a zone of distress or overwhelm. Most things on their own wouldn't be an issue. It is the unrelenting doses of stress that does a number on us.

In an adaptive stress experience, the body responds to a challenging task as it should. The brain's alarm has gone off briefly to let us know this work is important, and we experience the chemicals and hormones that help produce fluidity to our work. But once we cross the threshold of too much stress, too many tasks, or competing demands, we feel fatigued and our performance starts to decrease. This is when we have shifted from adaptive to maladaptive stress experiences. Once we are in the zone of distress, we start making mistakes and everything feels urgent. You know you have crossed into the zone of distress when you can't string a sentence together, find your keys, or remember basic information. In my case, I start dropping things—physical things like phones and coffee mugs, but also mental things, like who needs to be picked up from where or why I walked upstairs. If we spend too much time in the distress zone, we get sick, feel constantly overwhelmed, and risk burnout.

Imagine how strange that would sound in a conversation if I told you that I was desperately trying to stay in a constant state of stress! But that really is the goal when we think about the correlation between stress and performance.

I used to think of stress as a full-body reaction to anything in life that I didn't see coming, I didn't understand, I couldn't control, or I couldn't protect myself or my loved ones from. Stress was an external event that manifested as a physical reaction. It was an intruder. It was only after I started learning about mindfulness that I first came upon the idea that my stress was attacking me not only externally but internally as well. Our minds can conjure up stress too: how and what we think about events or tasks create the reaction or initiate the series of biological events. This idea led me to think about stress beyond isolated events that fit on a bell curve and about how it compounds and grows exponentially over our lifespan.

STRESS BUCKET MODEL

What's in your stress bucket? Here is another tool I use often in my work, with everyone from toddlers to top CEOs.

The stress bucket model was introduced by Alison Brabban and Douglas Turkington in 2002.[9] The tool was designed for use in the mental health field. It provides a visual representation of our stress and our capacity, and introduces the idea of release. The bucket represents what we carry. The size of our bucket, the materials, and how it was built relate to our vulnerabilities. These things could also relate to our privilege and lived experiences. (I added that last part to this work.)

The size of our bucket is relative. If you have ample resources, supports, and opportunities, your bucket may be larger. Conversely, some people start with smaller buckets simply because of the situations they were born into. At the bottom of our bucket, we have what we always carry. These contents are relatively permanent. They are our personality and temperament as well as predispositions or biophysical conditions. For me, diabetes runs in my family. For other people it may be mental health conditions like depression or anxiety. This is also where generational trauma takes up space. Cycles of trauma change a person's DNA—trauma gets passed on and impacts future descendants. Whatever your biological and genetic underpinnings, they are in your bucket. They take up space. Then, everyday life stressors are added to the bucket. If we have a lot at the bottom already, new stressors don't have much room before they overflow.

With each of our buckets, we also have a buffer zone. This is the space in our lives between our stress levels and our overflow point. Our buffer zone is our greatest ally. This is where the work of learning how to stress wisely will show rich benefits. In our buffer zone, we are invited to live our well life.

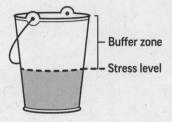

Our buckets also have a release valve in the form of coping strategies. We make room in the bucket by letting go of stress. Some coping strategies are adaptive and helpful, such as the Five Forces of Recovery—solitude, connection, music, nature, and gratitude—which we will talk about in much more detail later. Other behaviours may be maladaptive, such as bingeing on Netflix when you have a deadline or online shopping without the funds. They may release stress in the moment, but these behaviours often either don't work long term or they become problematic.

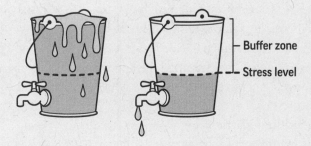

Even with the best adaptive strategies in place, if our bucket is 95 per cent full (which it is, for most of us, most days) and the stressors are coming in faster than we can process or release them, we will experience overflow or what we feel as "overwhelm." There is not enough emotional, physical, or mental buffer to manage the unexpected. In such cases, maladaptive behaviours (the release strategies) work like a circuit.

Instead of releasing the built-up stress, we recirculate it. This could look like substance use, overspending, isolation, procrastination, or any form of self-sabotage. Self-sabotaging behaviours may work in the moment to provide relief but ultimately interfere with big-picture goals.

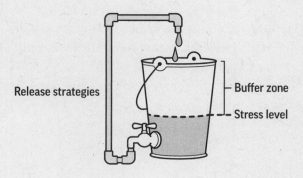

This final image of the bucket model portrays an optimal bucket experience. An optimal bucket experience includes a manageable stress level, adaptive release strategies, and a generous buffer zone. Yes, there are stressors, but there are also actions that provide us with relief from those stressors.

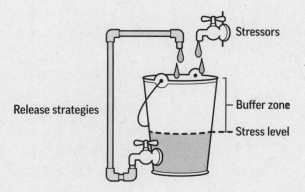

BURNOUT IN OUR BUCKETS

Stress and burnout are often confused, and it is easy to understand why that is. After all, the physical manifestations are often quite similar. However, unlike stress, which is a *response*, burnout is a very real *condition*. Dr. Jeremy Sutton explains that burnout is the accumulation of stressors over time, resulting in unmanageable stress levels.[10] In other words, burnout is the natural evolution of chronic stress that has gone unchecked or unrelieved.

From a clinical perspective, burnout is characterized by three marked symptoms:

- Emotional exhaustion
- Cynicism
- Personal inefficacy

Sutton explains that burnout is an extended period of stress that feels as though it cannot be ameliorated. If stress is short-lived or tied to a specific goal, it is most likely not harmful. If the stress feels never-ending and comes with feelings of emptiness, apathy, and hopelessness, it may be indicative of burnout. Coined by psychologist Herbert Freudenberger in the 1970s to describe the effects of extreme stress placed on "helping professionals," the term "burnout" has evolved to include the loss of our ability to cope.

When we think of burnout, we often consider workplaces to be the culprit. The World Health Organization defines burnout as "a syndrome... resulting from chronic workplace stress that has not been successfully managed."[11] Not only do people suffer emotionally, but work productivity suffers as well. Researchers from Stanford explained that working fifty hours a week decreases productivity, but working beyond fifty-five hours is like letting our work fall off a cliff![12] Our work at that point becomes riddled with errors, and so we spend additional time revising and correcting.

Although workplace burnout is very real, its scope and impact on our health reaches beyond the work environment. What became evident for my research team and me is that "non-work burnout" is also a factor. Yet it is definitely lesser known, and I believe that's because there is so much shame and stigma attached to the reality that sometimes personal roles also cause burnout. Complain about a ruthless boss—that's acceptable. Share your frustrations about your teenager going through troubling times—that is unbecoming of a parent. It is socially acceptable to say that you are sick and tired of a difficult colleague, but say that about your family and people judge.

Our cultural norms play into this awkwardness and double standard. A parent who has an adult daughter with a disability shared with me that every time she takes her daughter out into the community, it is an ordeal. "People either look away or tell me I am the strongest, bravest, and most resilient woman they have ever seen. But," this parent said, "I am a mom. Doing what moms do. I don't need to be congratulated for having a child with a disability. We need better supports." Having worked with other caregivers, I see this too often. Many families lack the supports, resources, and respite care to leave their homes. They suffer under the weight of their responsibility to their child. They're exhausted beyond measure. Of course, they love their child, but often at the cost of their own health.

BURNOUT REFRAMED

The volume and time in work is leading to burnout, and so is the time we spend outside our values and in invisible labour. Here are some examples that you might be familiar with over these past few years: You value family above all else, yet you send your children away because you are in online meetings, or you put them in front of screens for hours, and you feel like a terrible parent. You value being a present parent, but in fact you are a distracted parent, and that takes its toll. Or you value collaboration and community, but you are working in a silo. Without your mates next to you, your work becomes heavy and unfulfilling. I have spoken with frontline nurses who pride themselves on excellent patient care, yet during the peaks of COVID, they were forced to fill medical gloves with warm water to leave on patients so they would have a sense of someone being with them as they died. When we spend time living and working outside our values, it erodes our soul.

RESET AND RECOVERY TO ADDRESS BURNOUT

According to Steven Kotler, burnout is not just extreme stress; it is peak performance gone off the rails.[13] He says that burnout costs you motivation and momentum. My dear colleague Dr. Greg Wells explained burnout to me this way: "Your brain and the frequency at which it is functioning means your brain is actually sizzling. You need to change the frequency." That resonated with me. We use the expression "my brain is fried." It literally might be! By the end of some days, stringing a sentence together takes effort and my inbox looms as large as Mount Kilimanjaro. Don't even try to ask me, "What's for dinner?" As the hilarious Canadian social-influencer duo Cat and Nat say, "Asking what's for dinner should be a swear word."

For people who are experiencing burnout or feel as though they are at the threshold, about to cross over, researchers recommend starting with deep rest to promote active brain recovery. The goal is to shift brainwaves into the alpha range. This can only be achieved through a complete interruption of our routines. So the first recommendation and the first line of defence in a state of burnout is to stop. Stop everything. For some, recovering from burnout is body work. You need to address the body for real rest and recovery. For others, it will be mind work. You need a literal break from thinking, being productive, and holding your life together. You may also need to stop being the one steering the ship. I call this the need for full "suspension of responsibility" when overwhelm hits.

Each person's recovery will look different. For some it takes a week; for others it could be years. It all depends on how far you have depleted your resources. I can, however, assure you: it is not just a weeknight or a weekend off. That is not enough time to repair the damage we have done to ourselves.

But there is hope. People can and do recover. Often, people return to their lives with a renewed passion and purpose. A terrific example of this is Arianna Huffington. Huffington was conquering the world as the chief editor of the *Huffington Post*. On April 6, 2007, while at the top of her game, Huffington woke up on the floor of her office in a pool of her own blood. She had collapsed and broken her cheekbone. The doctors diagnosed Huffington with extreme burnout. This experience prompted new thinking. Huffington questioned if this was what success should really look like. Thrive, a global platform that specializes in beating stress and burnout, was born.[14]

There are several different approaches to addressing and recovering from burnout. Dr. Wells's work is a brilliant resource for all things recovery. Check out his book *Rest, Refocus, Recharge*—it is the best in the field.

The bottom line is this: You cannot out-think burnout. You cannot self-care your way out of it either. If the demands in your life outweigh your available resources, real change is needed. When you recognize that you are experiencing burnout, to minimize the blast radius and prioritize active recovery immediately, you must stop. There is no shame in asking for and getting help. This road to recovery is not meant to be walked alone. Here is a thought to help shift your thinking: you are not only over-worked, but under-rested, too.

DISTRESS AND BURNOUT'S NEXT FRONTIER

An issue related to burnout is compassion fatigue. This is a unique type of distress. Unlike burnout, it is not depletion from everyday stressors; it is depletion from feeling another person's pain. Compassion fatigue is a condition in which someone becomes numb to the suffering of others, feels less able to display empathy toward them, or loses hope in their own ability to help. Coined by nurse Carla Joinson to describe the unique form of burnout experienced by caregivers, compassion fatigue is often associated with health care professionals, soldiers, and anyone regularly exposed to human suffering.[15] The concept was further developed by Dr. Charles Figley, who likened compassion fatigue to secondary traumatic stress and summed it up as the "cost of caring."[16]

Compassion fatigue dramatically affects our ability to practise empathy for others and for ourselves. Therefore, well-being and recovery practices collapse. People lose hope that they can feel any differently. In my practice I see a correlation between compassion fatigue and self-neglect. People are waiting for something or someone to fix it. They are desperate to feel better again. Unfortunately, a decrease in self-efficacy goes along with compassion fatigue. Self-efficacy is our belief in our ability to do something, and in this case, our belief that we can change our behaviour has disintegrated.

Dr. Sherrie Bourg Carter, a registered psychologist and author, notes that the Compassion Fatigue Awareness Project identifies denial as "one of the most detrimental symptoms" of compassion fatigue because it prevents those experiencing it from effectively assessing how fatigued they are, which prevents them from addressing it or seeking out help.[17]

Dr. Robin Stern of the Yale Center for Emotional Intelligence refers to emotional labour as the effort needed to manage a discrepancy that often emerges with compassion fatigue: the "happy face" those experiencing it put on for the rest of the world regardless of how they are feeling on the inside.[18] Further, Dr. Stern identifies the "overwhelming emotional residue" of other people's trauma, such that those with compassion fatigue no longer know how to "nurture their inner life." They cannot make themselves care anymore; they cannot care for others nor for themselves. This is where the "I'm done" feeling comes in. You have given everything you have, and it feels as though it didn't make a difference at all.

BURNOUT IS THE CURSE OF THE STRONG

As global citizens we have cared so deeply, for so long, about so many things. Many people are feeling numb, disconnected, and uninterested in or incapable of caring anymore. We just have no more empathy to give. What is amazing about the human condition is that we can heal and reframe our perspective. Many people I work with share that they believe they are not allowed to feel bad or have a bad day because they are living in an abundance of privilege. I hear, "People have it so much harder than I do, Robyne. Who am I to feel bad?" Even when you live with privilege, you can still have a bad day! The reality is that when you stop practising empathy for yourself, you stop showing empathy to others. The more you show empathy for your own situation, the more you have to offer the world. If you are overwhelmed right now, allow yourself to be overwhelmed and tend to your needs. Whether you are drowning in two feet of water or ten, you are still drowning. Take the side of the boat. Reach for the hand. Every human has the right to receive care, compassion, and recovery.

If we are going to stress wisely, we need to have an honest look at our stress ecosystems. I appreciate that they are complex. I would argue that no two are alike. I trust that honouring what makes up our buckets and acknowledging burnout are critical for our next steps. I invite you to let go of any shame, guilt, or judgements about your bucket. Judging and shaming does not change behaviour. I also invite you to reframe the idea of burnout. Burnout is not a skill deficit. It is not just about the work or our lack of boundaries. Burnout is very much the curse of the strong. It strikes the hardest workers in every room. Those people who are diligent. Those who care deeply. Those who live to serve. People who experience burnout are trying to carry the weight of the world with their two hands and rarely ask for help. The people who don't care, or those who cut corners, or those who are okay with others carrying the load—they are not burning out.

We need to rally around those who are burned out. They are the best of us. I appreciate that this all can seem like a lot. It is a lot. It is a wicked problem for this very reason. Yet when we start to understand all that is involved and we realize what is at stake, we are well positioned to explore solutions. This is how I can best prepare you for what's next. The brilliant Dr. Maya Angelou shared with her dear friend Oprah that when we know better, we can do better.[19] And thankfully, practice makes better. Better days are ahead. Buckets full of better days are ahead. Let me show you.

I'm at the stage in my life
where I don't want crazy in love
anymore. I wanna be calm in love,
patient in love, happy in love, and
understood in love.

UNKNOWN

CHAPTER 4

STRESS MEETS HER ALLY

RE WE THERE YET? This is what I would be asking right now, reading this book. *Okay, I get it, stress is a big deal. When are we going to get to the part about what I can do about it? I have a full bucket of stress—it over-flow-eth; let's move on.* We are. Right now. Just as a gentle reminder, though, that sense of urgency or even frantic energy to get to the point is also a stress experience. And this energy fuels many of our days and we may not even be aware of it because it is just so familiar. Our stress is not only the big stuff. Building awareness of this is important. Stress has the propensity to creep into every part of our day. Noticing it, in a non-judgemental way, can help in unexpected ways.

Our greatest ally in managing stress is our relationship with wellness. I use the word "relationship" on purpose. Our wellness is a relationship with our whole self. It is a series of give-and-takes. When we nurture different aspects of our lives, we build patterns, connections, and trust.

The idea of stressing wisely came from this simple truth. When I started taking care of *all of me* and accepted that my wellness was a relationship with myself, I found an abundance of energy, purpose, and productivity. I also found a deep sense of sufficiency and confidence. Most importantly, though, I found a richness of peace that I never knew was possible. As someone with a lot of water already in my bucket, I didn't know I could ever feel or be this way.

THE ORIGINS OF WELLNESS

When I first started studying stress and burnout, I was looking for some quick fixes. I wanted a clear and concise list of actionable items that could help people think and organize their way out of stress. As a behaviourist, I wanted to know what behaviours needed to be reinforced or punished so people could feel better while juggling the watermelons of their life. I needed that list for me, too! Within a year, I observed that a strictly behavioural approach would work for a short time, yet almost inevitably, people would regress.

The problem was that a behavioural approach was missing the undercurrents of life. Yes, we could make short-term changes, but as soon as stressful seasons returned, people would regress into old patterns. Like an explorer who finds a dead end, I retraced my steps and sought a new path. Soon, I discovered that my definition of wellness was the issue. I was using the word "wellness," but I was only capturing physical health. No eating program, sleep schedule, time-management system, boundary-setting activity, fitness app, yoga class, or scorecard was going to make lasting changes to stress.

The Western approach to wellness is often dominated by physical health. Our medical system is built on the disease model. It is "sick care," not always health care. Treatment is the major focus, with fewer resources for prevention. Dr. Ajai Singh writes, "Modern medicine is mostly palliative, and rather proud of it. By palliation, I am not talking of cancers. I mean reducing or easing the severity of a pain or a disease without removing the cause, or effecting a cure (from Latin *palliare*, to cloak)."[1] Here is an example: You can go to a medical appointment and have no symptoms of a particular illness or condition. The doctor can give you a clean bill of health, but are you well?

My broken heart was inaudible to the stethoscope. My trauma couldn't be detected in a blood test. My skin cloaked an eating disorder. My addictions never came up in those visits. We might be without disease or illness, but we are not truly well. This is the system of "wellness" I grew up in. As long as you were not bleeding, you were fine. And if you were bleeding, you were probably fine, too.

The term wellness, when properly used, implies a more holistic and comprehensive view of health. Scholars, practitioners, and even philosophers have been talking about various components of wellness for what seems like forever. Yet Halbert L. Dunn, who is recognized as the "father of the wellness movement," first termed "wellness" in 1959 in the *Canadian Journal of Public Health*. He explained that "wellness . . . signifies something quite different from good health."[2]

High-level wellness for the individual is defined as an integrated method of functioning which is orientated toward maximizing the potential of which the individual is capable, within the environment where he is functioning. This definition does not imply that there is an *optimum level* of wellness but rather that wellness is *a direction* in progress toward an ever-higher potential of functioning.

Wellness is a direction, not an outcome. There are no finish lines to wellness. It does not fit within a check box. Dr. Dunn's conception of wellness included

- "direction in progress forward and upward towards a higher potential level of functioning,

- an open-ended and ever-expanding tomorrow with its challenge to live at a fuller potential, and

- the integration of the whole being of the total individual— [their] body, mind, and spirit—in the functioning process."

Imagine for a moment a medical doctor, in 1959, presenting this idea to the medical community. He actually used the word "spirit," and it was published in medical journals!

Dunn believed in the totality of a person, which included their uniqueness, their available energy, their inner and outer worlds, and the interrelation of self within it all. Furthermore, Dunn expressed that people have twelve basic needs. At the time, Maslow's hierarchy of needs, first introduced in 1943, talked about the five basic needs of humans: physiological, safety, love and belonging, esteem, and self-actualization.[3]

This was the predominant view at the time. Abraham Maslow's theory argues that once a need is met, we move up the hierarchy. But Dunn believed there were other basic needs required at the minimum. Dunn's work was radical at the time. Even to this day, some are reluctant to embrace such a progressive, holistic view as represented by these twelve basic needs:

- Survival
- Communication
- Fellowship
- Growth
- Imagination
- Love
- Balance
- Environment
- Spirituality
- A way of life
- Dignity
- Freedom and space

When challenged by others on his views, Dunn responded,

> To integrate self in a changing world calls for a continuum of reintegration of the self with full realization of the nature of [a person and their] basic human needs... The challenge must be met both by individuals and by society within its various groups, ideologies, races, religions, and cultural patterns. Self-assurance will be needed to meet this challenge. We must have the courage to change ourselves when this is called for and to trust ourselves and our fellow [humans].[4]

I know many influential leaders who have President Theodore Roosevelt's "Man in the Arena" speech framed in their office. I have both Roosevelt's speech and Dunn's response on my wall! Dunn's passage is so powerful because it unpacks so many truths. Wellness is within a person's own capabilities. To function in an ever-changing world, we need to grow and adapt. Our needs will change over time, as they should. When we adopt an inclusive and comprehensive view of wellness, it will serve as a buffer to protect our emotional and mental health, and those areas are basic human needs, not secondary to physical health. Wellness practices serve to not only prevent breakdowns and burnout but also to cultivate our highest and most authentic potential. And the responsibility for our wellness is shared between us and the systems of our world. Society needs to be held accountable, too. And lastly, Dunn believed we need the courage and self-assurance to trust ourselves and others. We need this courage to find what works best for us. And to trust that we can navigate our lives to unlock our truest potential.

So, this is where the next step of our journey begins.

THE EIGHT REALMS OF WELLNESS

For transformational wellness and change, we start with theory, but theory alone does not equal change. We need to bring theory into application. The Eight Realms of Wellness framework is based on the theories of wellness, most notably Dunn's work and that of other thought leaders. It is the foundation of how we stress wisely.

Each realm holds an important role in a person's overall wellness. And sustainable wellness practices are unlocked where these realms intersect. In Part II of this book, each realm will be explored in greater detail with tools, strategies, and loads of real-world examples to bring this work into your life. In the meantime, here is a snapshot of the Eight Realms and their key factors:

1 **Physical Realm (The Body):** The biological basics, including sleep, nutrition, movement, touch, physical safety, and absence of disease

2 **Emotional Realm (The Heart):** The inner world of feelings, thoughts, and attachments

3 **Intellectual Realm (The Mind):** Our learnings, knowledge, memories, and creativity

4 **Social Realm (Community):** Relationships, identities, and social and cultural norms

5 **Environmental Realm (Our World):** Outside parts and systems and the natural world around us

6 **Occupational Realm (Our Roles):** Responsibilities, duties, and contributions

7 **Financial Realm (Resources):** Tools, money, and exchanges within our system of currencies

8 **Spiritual Realm (The Soul):** Purpose, meaning, and values— the greatest good

The Eight Realms of Wellness

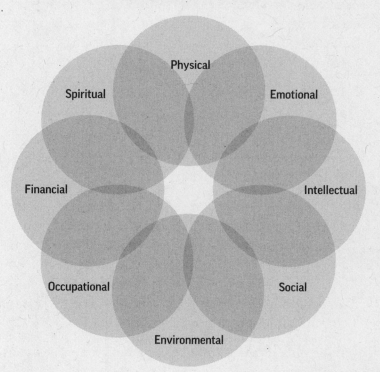

When we slow down long enough to pay attention, most of us know on some level that something isn't working the way we had hoped. It may be a persistent whisper or a sudden wail, but regardless of how it presents, we sense it. If you look into the shadows of your mind and tap gently into your heart's longings, what do you find? What do you feel? What truth wants light? As you check in with yourself, I have one important reminder: Your true inner voice is kind. It is gentle and wants the best for you. An exhausted, weary colleague once asked me, "How do I know what voice in my head is the real one I should listen to?" I knew the answer to this one. "The voice that is the most loving. Listen to that one. Make room for that one."

RUMBLES AND RESETS

I'm sitting in a chair worth more than my car. My eyes are transfixed on a desk that looks like it should be in a museum. The floor-to-ceiling windows from the highest-floor corner office offer a stunning view of the downtown core and harbour. This office screams, "I made it!" A friendly smile meets me. Retirement looms for this business powerhouse, so he asked me here to talk about resiliency. The conversation starts with common questions about how to make his senior team more resilient. He is concerned that the next generation of leaders doesn't have the same level of grit he has to make it in this business. He wants to best prepare them but is concerned it's a losing game. This leader made enormous sacrifices. His success came at the cost of relationships and his physical and emotional health. He also knows his business negatively impacts the environment. "Robyne, I am not leaving this business and how we do this work in a better place than when it was given to me." He knows what this type of work lifestyle costs, and he is deeply concerned about the next person repeating the cycle. "I wouldn't wish this life on anyone, not even my enemy." He has clearly succeeded in certain domains of wellness, but he is not well. There is a rumbling that something is missing.

Later the same day, at a local coffee shop, I am awe-inspired by an artist's work. Her talent is better described as a gift. What she creates in her medium is breathtaking. She paints spectacular portraits that should be celebrated and sought after as real treasures of the modern world. There she is, painting this art, sitting in the corner of a coffee shop. She doesn't have time to talk now about my purchasing her work. She is late for her shift as a server at the local pizza shop. "A girl still has to make a living." She looks at me, eyes full of discouragement and frustration. This woman is so talented as an artist, yet the reality of needing a steady income keeps her in a paycheque chase. How can we be truly well if we are not using our gifts?

And speaking of gifts, as I drive home, I listen to an interview with an Olympic gold medallist. The host asks guests on his show to describe the moment when they "beat the world." With radical candor, they share that they don't remember much about what it felt like. Anxiety and depression robbed them of the memories of that year. One athlete says, "I see myself in pictures, but I don't remember it. I only remember a hollowness in my chest when they placed the medal around my neck. I was scared it would fall right through me. I thought the medal would make me feel again. Nothingness, still." This athlete had hit the pinnacle of their career. They used their gifts and achieved their goal, yet the toll on their mental health was costly. Despite the physical realm being mastered, they were not well either.

At this point in my day, I am feeling waves of concern and a heaviness. Physical tiredness is one thing, but when my heart hurts and my soul whimpers, I have learned I need time. Holding hope and choosing to live hope-filled requires tender care and patience. I make a cup of tea and absolutely do not look at my phone! Just as I am settling into a quiet moment of reflection, Hunter comes in. "You free tonight? I got a movie for us!" That sounds about right. I can handle that. "I'm in,"

I say to Hunter, grateful that my teenager still wants to watch movies with his mom.

The movie is based on the story of Kurt Warner, the American Underdog of the NFL, who went from stocking grocery shelves to winning the Super Bowl. Whoa, this guy knows a thing or two about resiliency and wellness! The St. Louis Rams' football seasons with Warner were described as The Greatest Show on "Turf." However, before Warner made his miraculous journey into the NFL, he knew that success in his sport wouldn't mean anything unless his wife, Brenda, was there with him. The movie captures how Warner knew what mattered most and built a life around that.

As the credits rolled and tears streamed down my cheeks, my heart smiled. I'd needed that. It was a reminder that we can figure all this stuff out. Two hours later, inspired by an amazing story, still holding the same cup of cold tea and cuddled up next to Hunter, my heart and soul were realigned and reignited. Tomorrow is a new day. Anything is possible.

THREE-LEGGED STOOL

Every person has a story. We know intuitively when our lives are in alignment. Things just seem to unfold on a frequency that feels real, authentic, and true. The stress is present, because let's face it, stress is omnipresent, yet we feel steady. We also intuitively know when our lives are out of balance. We have a "knowing" when something is off. We may try to block it out, avoid it, or ignore it, but in the quiet moments, especially at night, it resurfaces. The collateral damage of poor health, lost relationships, and good things missing in our lives is another sign.

As we dive deeper into the realms of wellness, I must reiterate that this is personal development. It is meant to be personal. There is no one right sequence, balance, or degree of wellness that benefits two people the same way. Your uniqueness and your situation are all parts of the equation. Wellness is an orientation toward maximizing the potential of your capability, within the environment you are living in. People ask me, "What is the most important area of wellness? If I only have time for one area, which one should I focus on?" My answer is not very helpful, I'm afraid. Asking what area of wellness is most important is like asking which leg is the most important on a three-legged stool.

As we move into Part II, keep an eye out for what speaks to you. Cast aside the old stories that no longer serve you about your relationship with wellness. Bring your experiences with you as data, not determinants. This is a new adventure. Be led by your curiosities. Be open to what calls to you. You are already on your way to stressing wisely, my friend. Let the self-stewardship begin!

I'm glad you are here.

Stress has met her ally: wellness. You have also met an ally: me. And I'm ever so excited our paths have crossed.

PART II

HOW WELLNESS CAN HELP US OUT

"

If you don't pick a day to recover,
your body will pick one for you.

DR. JESSI GOLD

CHAPTER 5

THE BODY

NOTHING LIKE JUMPING IN with both feet! The first realm to explore is the body, which is code for "complicated." Our bodies and our relationships with our bodies are so personal and complex. I am mindful of my own resistance in writing this chapter. This topic makes me feel vulnerable yet also empowered. I have come upon some major insights into how our relationship with our body can be nurtured and tended to in meaningful ways that align with wellness. I am also assured by knowing that you, too, may feel like this topic is a war zone. So, I will go first.

My first recollection of me not fitting in with the master plan was sitting in circle time in junior kindergarten at four years old. Apparently, already by then, I thought that to live the master plan you also needed to have blond hair and be fair-skinned and small. I still recall noticing that my red hair stuck out, my freckles were odd, and my body took up more space than those of my peers. The teacher was reading a book and talking about letter patterns. I didn't understand or know what a letter pattern was. She was asking children to repeat the letter patterns. Each child responded as if on cue, and the teacher rewarded them with a friendly smile and classmates cheered. "Do you see how the letters E and A go for a walk, and the A does the talking?" the teacher asked. My classmates nodded and smiled in chorus. My little brain was scrambling. I had absolutely no idea why letters were going for a walk or why the letter A was talking. We were being read a story about bears! *What the hell is this?* I thought, looking around stunned. Everyone was in on this conspiracy! I felt the stress growing in my body. I was the next child to be called. I was wearing jeans, indoor running shoes, and a white Jem T-shirt, and my hair was half in my eyes from my falling-out ponytail. I remember it with such clarity even thirty-nine years later. Because stress does that. You see it all. You feel it all. You are paying attention; stress makes sure you are.

Of course, I didn't know I was having a stress reaction or my first panic attack in that moment. At first it started in my cheeks. They went red. Redder than my hair. Then my hands became hot, sticky, and sweaty. My heart started beating wildly in my chest, and then the deafening sound of my heartbeat travelled to my ears. I closed my eyes. I was scared of the dark. I opened them again. My little limbs started to tremble. Then the worst wave hit. Burning hot tears were building up behind my eyes. I did not think my wee body could hold in this volcanic eruption of feelings much longer. This energy was about to level me. In a scrambly moment, I tried to stand. To find my escape. I was prepared to run the five kilometres home. That was my plan: run, find the main door by the office, break out of the school, and run. Don't stop until you see your front door.

As I took one frantic yet brave step toward the door, the teacher told me to sit down. I froze. My kindergarten teacher was *that* kindergarten teacher—the one with the softest, kindest, almost whimsical voice. She wore sweaters that matched the holidays and styled her hair like Princess Diana. I locked eyes with her. I couldn't move; I was standing in the middle of the circle, frozen. Other children started to laugh and snicker. My teacher, while still reading from the book and showing the pictures, stood up from the rocking chair, reached for my hand, and with the gentlest of gestures pulled me toward her and guided me to sit on the carpet next to her chair. She still held my hand in hers as she turned the page with one hand and her thumb. She never skipped a beat. As the flood of chemicals that had just ravaged my body started to dissipate, I stared at one loose carpet thread. The tears retreated. My limbs went numb. My chest still hurt from the thumping and my ears still rang with the faint drumming of fear. The teacher held my hand for the rest of circle time, and I clung to her like a lifeline. She made me feel safe. Safety was outside of my body. This was the moment I met one of my greatest enemies: fear. I also learned that I don't like what stress feels like.

OUR BODY'S STORY

My relationship with my body is still a work in progress. This is hard work for so many of us. I notice that some of the women I respect most on this planet, who do brilliant and thoughtful work, still talk on their platforms about needing to lose weight. I wish this weren't such a conversation point in our society. But it will continue to be because it affects so many of us.

I share with you, with candor, that I abused and neglected my body for most of my life. My body was also abused by others. No nutrition or exercise plan can address this. Support is needed in this case. Our physical pursuits of health are often attempts to heal emotional parts of our lives. Our bodies are our protectors, not the enemy.

In my adolescent years, my self-harm took many forms, including cutting myself. Although after my teenage years I vowed never to physically hurt my body externally, other forms of harm persisted. To stop cutting, I used a "tell, don't show" strategy with therapeutic support. I learned how to talk about my pain versus show my pain. But I replaced the physical behaviours with disordered eating. At my lowest weight, and at the height of my eating disorder, as my hair was falling out and teeth enamel dwindling way, the outside world praised me. Society treats you differently when you are a size 0. This season of my life was riddled with pain, suffering, and toxic relationships. Yet in pictures, I finally met what I thought was the standard of beauty. I got there, and it was fu*&ing awful. I sought treatment and made gains, but the impulses to control my world by controlling my food were always just under the surface. The turning point for me for releasing these maladaptive eating behaviours happened in the most unexpected way.

My parents, my children, and I were participating in a community walk fundraiser. Mom and Dad had Jax in the stroller, and Ava was toddling beside me. Hunter, who was seven years old at the time, wanted to run ahead to the finish line. The trail was well marked, and several volunteers lined the course that wound through a provincial park. I let Hunter go on ahead and prompted him to keep an eye on the course. It was less than a thousand feet to the finish line.

When my parents, Ava, Jax, and I finished our walk, I looked for Hunter, and he wasn't there. I spoke to the officials, and they said they had never seen him cross the finish line. We started asking people in the area if they had seen a boy with a neon yellow goalie shirt come this way. No one had. The officials announced it over the loudspeakers, and everyone started looking for our lost boy. Over the walkie-talkies, people along the course reported back that there was no boy to be seen. The officials said they would start looking in the woods. I met my mother's eyes, and she was afraid. My mom was my rock. She was the only one who could keep me calm. But now, all I saw was fear.

"Find him, Robyne," is all my mother said, and I took off running into the woods. By this point in my life, I had run several races and knew how to run. I knew what my body could do. Driven by a fear I had never felt before, I ran. I ran back to the last turn in the course Hunter had needed to take and went straight. My body carried me as my heart prayed. I focused on the rhythm of my breath and pushed beyond the piercing pain in my heart. My heart ached with the thought of how scared Hunter must be.

It was well over an hour since I had taken off into the woods, and more time than that since I had last seen Hunter. I knew he was still missing without even checking my phone. I felt my son was somewhere, but not here. He was not safe yet. With easily ten kilometres between me and the racecourse now, I started to think this solo mission into the woods had not been the right call. I was running full stride, screaming in my own mind that I didn't know what to do. The size of the world grows exponentially when your child is lost in it. I refused to let my mind imagine the unthinkable, yet my thoughts darted around memories. Memories of Hunter as a baby. Memories of my work with parents who had lost children. Memories of my time working in a prison and learning about crimes of opportunity. My mind, my heart, and my faith started failing me in that moment. Every part of my being knew what was at stake, and I started to panic. It was the muscle memory of running that kept me going. My feet, lungs, muscles, blood, and bones kept me in the fight. And then, I saw him, in the distance, my boy, in his neon yellow goalie shirt, running toward me. We closed the distance between us quickly, and Hunter threw himself into my arms. "You found me, Mama, I knew you would find me." Through tears I assured Hunter that we had found each other.

Despite every horrible thing I have ever done to my body, my body has never failed me. It has come through for me every time I needed it to. Whether surviving a catastrophic car accident at sixteen years old, bringing three precious souls into the world as a mother, finding a missing child in the woods, or withstanding the pain and grief of losing my mother tragically, exactly when I needed her most in my life, my body has shown up for me.

My body has carried me through the worst moments of my life, and it still took in air when I couldn't breathe. It fought for me when I lost the will to live. My body has also held so much joy and happiness and the purest love. My body holds a fierce sense of devotion, faith, and loyalty. My body allows my soul to walk this earth in the most miraculous ways.

That day on the racecourse, I committed to changing the way I talked to myself about my body. It was about time I showed her the respect she deserves, don't you think?

OUR FOREVER HOME

What is your relationship with your physical body like? How have you traditionally cared for the body you have been entrusted with? Imagine your physical self was to give a report or even a grade on how well you have cared for it. Now, I want you to give your physical body a grade for how well it has worked for you.

In a workshop, I led this type of reflection. People scored themselves on how well they cared for their body. They reflected on how the care for their body changed over the years. Participants then listed everything that their body had seen them through. Years' worth of examples of growth, healing, movement, and pleasure were listed alongside examples of pain, betrayal, suffering, and damage. One woman shared that when she received her diagnosis of late-stage breast cancer, she felt as though her body had betrayed her. "How could something that could kill me have grown from inside of me? I hate my body for doing this to me," she confessed. Another person shared that losing her mother to Alzheimer's disease created a mistrusting view of her own mind. "It is inevitable. My mind is going to turn on me too one day. I am just waiting for it. Every time I misplace my keys, forget why I walked upstairs, it's the first place my mind goes. I live in fear."

But people also spoke about healing, recovery, and life. "This body created life. I marvel that my body brought my children into this world." "I was able to walk again even after the doctors said that was impossible." "My brain injury changed me, but I grew into a new version of me that I love." It is an extraordinary experience to witness people holding space and reverence for the miracle that is our physical form. Yet, despite the true miraculous nature of our bodies, our relationships with them are often fraught with negativity. "Yes, I beat cancer, but I still can't lose this last ten pounds," said one person. The group burst into laughter! As soon as weight was mentioned, it was as though a vacuum sucked out all the appreciation, gratitude, and reverence. Now, it was about jean sizes. I felt the energy and tone in the room shift to this odd "knowing," like finally we were really talking about the real "physical" stuff. Weight loss, diets, and exercise. I also noticed people sitting up straighter in their chairs, tugging at their shirts and pulling up their pants. People were readjusting their physical bodies now that everyone was looking at one another through a different lens. The lens of comparison. Before it was all about the internal, embodied experiences of our physicality, but now it was about external physical appearances.

In Western culture, there is an astonishing focus on physical appearance that has very little to do with actual health. For decades, psychologists have studied the so-called attractive-person benefits or attractiveness biases. Higher levels of perceived attractiveness have been correlated with everything from moral character (beauty equals goodness) to intelligence, trustworthiness, political favour, occupational success, relationship status, life satisfaction, overall health, self-esteem, and confidence.[1] Even babies favour faces they perceive as attractive.[2] There is an abundance of privilege associated with being perceived as attractive in our society.

Interestingly, perceptions of attractiveness vary greatly by culture and geographical region. In a study conducted by Superdrug Online Doctor, a UK virtual medical practice group, they commissioned a digital marketing firm to investigate perceptions of female beauty around the world.[3] The marketers took one photograph of a woman and shared it with fashion design teams from eighteen different countries. Each country edited the photograph to best reflect the cultural standards. The project was named "Perceptions of Perfection Across Borders," and the results were wild. Depending on the geographical region, perceptions of what is attractive vary. Yet consistent across all eighteen countries was that none of the standards was realistic or healthy. Most countries produced an image of a woman remarkably underweight or otherwise consistent with an adult with disordered eating. And in countries where the woman was depicted as being in a larger body, the hip-to-waist ratio was so exaggerated that she would be unlikely to have lower ribs!

DIET CULTURE IS THE LIFE THIEF

I love sharing with people books that changed my life. The book *Anti-Diet* by the extraordinary dietitian and journalist Christy Harrison is in this category. By page 29, I had bought ten copies to share with friends. *Anti-Diet* first introduced me to the roots of diet culture, and they are downright horrific—riddled with racism, prejudice, coercion, cruelty, abuse, oppression, and control. So, my dear friend, if you have ever rebelled against a diet, said "screw it," and ate that cupcake, I salute you. I believe something deep within our souls recognizes how absurd and irrational dieting is.

Our current view of thinness as the desired physical size is another ugly legacy of colonialism. Whiteness and thinness were associated with civility and godliness. Colonizers placed a sense of morality on food and body shape as a means of differentiating themselves from other groups of people. Rarely in our human history has the notion of restricting food ever made sense. The goal was always about getting enough food to survive, and larger bodies signified prosperity and well-being. Thinness represented poverty, illness, and even death.[4] The view of the body and food as it related to status and significance shifted dramatically over the centuries following the age of exploration. The predominantly privileged white male view, often attributed as "science" or the "civilized" way of being, upheld the prejudicial status quo. To maintain the colonizer supremacy, larger bodies were deemed semi-civilized at best but mostly barbaric and even savage.

THE INFAMOUS LETTER ON CORPULENCE

Diet culture as we know it today was born in the nineteenth century in the US. And during the late nineteenth century, the narrative started to change from "civility and nobleness" to "health and safety."

Meet our first weight-loss guru. In 1863, British funeral director William Banting wrote his "Letter on Corpulence, Addressed to the Public." I consider this the first "If I can do it, so can you":

> Of all the parasites that affect humanity I do not know of, nor can I imagine, any more distressing than that of Obesity, and, having just emerged from a very long probation in this affliction, I am desirous of circulating my humble knowledge and experience for the benefit of my fellow man, with an earnest hope it may lead to the same comfort and happiness I now feel under the extraordinary change, which might almost be termed miraculous had it not been accomplished by the most simple common-sense means.[5]

The letter included, with remarkable detail, a diet that most would recognize as an Atkins diet or keto approach, minus the daily requirement of brandy! The diet is still practised today. The term "banting," a method of dieting by avoiding sweets and carbohydrates, is even in the *Merriam-Webster* dictionary.[6] The letter also introduced a new element to the diet culture: the use of a scale.

Banting recorded his weight on a scale, which was not a commonly used instrument for human weight measurement at the time. But when Banting showed the world how he had lost forty-six pounds and twelve inches off his waist, penny scales became popular and the people who owned these penny scales made an extraordinary amount of money.

Another legacy of Banting's letter was a chart. Adolphe Quetelet, a mathematician in the early nineteenth century, was interested in statistical probability and ratios of large groups within a population, so he developed the Quetelet Index, a formula that determined the "ideal" height and weight for people, or at least for the average (read "white European") man. He created this formula for general predictions, not individual use, but insurance companies began applying it to people.[7] That's right, insurance companies! They wanted to sort people and their policies, and they normalized categorizing people with a chart based on their height and weight.

Shockingly, the formula behind what later became known as the BMI—the body mass index—stayed consistent for 183 years. In 1998, the US government changed the criteria, but the change was not positive. Over 35 million Americans waking up the next morning were now classified as overweight.[8] Researchers at Michigan State University explain that the tone of the major flaws in the BMI is an overall lack of diversity—age differential, muscle versus fat ratios, and over-all fitness.[9] Why does the medical community still use this outdated and inaccurate tool? Short answer: it is cheap and easy to use, and insurance companies have built an empire with it.

THE CALORIE ADDS INSULT TO INJURY

As dieting, restrictive eating, shaming, and body dissatisfaction grew around the turn of the nineteenth century, another ugly side of the physical health shit-show emerged: the calorie. Most of us associate the word "calorie" with food, not steam engines, right? One calorie is the energy required to heat one kilogram of water by one degree Celsius. It is an equation for steam engines from the eighteenth century! In the 1860s, with the new focus on losing weight, the calorie as a unit of measurement found its way into the food world. Our under-standing of a calorie is actually a kilocalorie. Most food manufacturers now use what is known as the 4-4-9 method. Each gram of protein and carbohydrates contains four cal-ories, and a gram of fat contains nine calories. This was determined by how long it took food to turn to ashes when they lit it on fire. An avocado has so many pesky calories because it takes so long to burn into ashes, hence raising the water temperature, in a lab. This measuring process uses what is called a bomb calorimeter.

Based on this practice, the idea of daily calorie require-ments was first introduced, to the detriment of women.

CALORIE RESTRICTION AS A POLITICAL TOOL

In the late nineteenth century, many women started to collectively campaign for women's rights, with the focus on a woman's right to vote. Momentum for the suffrage movement had started. Then, in response to a lack of male workers, since they were fighting during World War I, women took on predominantly male work outside the home both in North America and overseas. After the war, in 1918, the suffrage movement won some women the legal right to vote in Canada, mostly those of European descent. But it was not until 1929 that a woman was declared a "person" in Canada. It is important to note that, for other groups, the battle for rights took decades. Asian Canadians, including women, won the right to vote in Canada in 1948; Inuit in 1950; and First Nations people in 1960.

Feminist writer Naomi Wolf argues that as women were making their greatest gains politically and socially, transforming the place of women in our society, new standards of beauty were being introduced. A new push for thinness, meekness, and submissiveness was an attempt to distract and weaken the women fighting against the patriarchy because, as Christy Harrison writes, "if women are busy trying to shrink themselves, they won't have the time or energy to shake things up. It's hard to smash the patriarchy on an empty stomach or with a head full of food and body concerns, and that's exactly the point of diet culture."[10] Harrison goes on to quote Wolf: "Dieting is the most potent political sedative in women's history; a quietly mad population is a tractable one."

It is also fascinating that as the women's suffrage movement was gaining steam, the "1,200 calorie rule" was introduced by Dr. Lulu Hunt Peters in 1918. Dr. Peters's book became the first bestselling diet book.[11] Peters claimed her method was developed from personal experience. She had lost more than seventy pounds and proclaimed a person could eat whatever they wanted as long as they didn't eat more than twelve hundred calories in a day. She also argued that since many countries were still rationing food after World War I, eating only twelve hundred calories made rationing more pleasant. "For every pang of hunger we feel we can have a double joy, that of knowing we are saving worse pangs in ... little children, and that of knowing that for every pang we feel we lose a pound."[12] Peters offered calorie counting as a patriotic and moral duty that women should undertake to support the troops, and perhaps the patriarchy? The twelve-hundred-calorie limit is still used to this day in the medical community and by so-called health experts. There is nothing even remotely healthy about eating only twelve hundred calories a day, unless you are a toddler!

Our bodies need nutrients throughout the day. Most people I know partake in crescendo eating patterns. Whether you call it intermittent fasting or being "not a breakfast person," most people consume their calories later in the day. This triggers the brain into scarcity mode, and our bodies are so deprived that we struggle to feel full, and so we eat beyond comfort. You are allowed to eat food. All the foods. Free yourself from being a prisoner to diet culture. For more information on this topic, please check out Evelyn Tribole and Elyse Resch's work on intuitive eating.[13] It is possible to unlearn and relearn the principles of nourishing a healthy relationship with food.

NOW WHAT?

That was a lot to "digest"! I get it. Why did I invite you on this nightmarish history tour of nutrition and diets? Well, to stress wisely, we need to build our wellness practices on sound theory. The reality is that many of our physical health beliefs and subsequent behaviours are not built on solid foundations. As just demonstrated, what has been taught and practised when it comes to our nutrition is questionable, damaging, and even unethical. This misinformation has created a $71 billion a year diet industry built upon the sad truth that 95 per cent of diets fail.[14] That means that when a medical doctor recommends dieting as a treatment, it is technically unethical under the criterion of evidence-informed treatment options.[15] No other treatment with a 5 per cent effectiveness rating could be prescribed. But although it is the diets that are failing us, we are the ones who feel like failures. And doctors keep telling us to just eat less and move more. Thank goodness, certain wellness practices can free us from the "diet-culture bush league hullabaloo" that leaves many of us miserable. Case in point: if you don't know if you can eat a full banana, then we have some unlearning to do! But first, let's explore two other dimensions of physical wellness that support a wise approach to stress: movement and sleep.

VITAMIN E: EXERCISE

As my favourite physiologist Dr. Greg Wells writes in his book *The Ripple Effect*, a new drug has been discovered, and it essentially can heal every ailment.[16] It reduces the risk of cancers, heart disease, and viral infections. It can reverse type 2 diabetes, prevent osteoporosis, alleviate depression and anxiety, and improve mental and cognitive function and your mood. It can also make you happier, more energetic, and even a better parent, partner, friend, and leader. The only catch is that you need to take it daily, for the rest of your life. And if you do take it every day, you are guaranteed these benefits. Will you take it? Dr. Greg is not talking about a new drug, obviously. He is talking about the benefits of exercise. Vitamin E!

Many of us are already familiar with the benefits of physical activity, but then why is it that we don't do it? Common knowledge does not equal common practice. But why not? As the saying goes, exercise is the most underused drug in our society and stress eating is the most overused one.

Research reports that people don't exercise for reasons focused on lack—a lack of motivation, of time, of affordability, of interest, of energy, and of conviction that exercise even works. We are playing a losing game here. Starting with a lack of anything perpetuates a scarcity mindset, which sends our nervous system into a state of panic. For example, the idea that "I don't have time to exercise" cues our nervous system that we are lacking something, and since lack is terrifying, we panic. This reaction of panic prompts avoidance, so we end up scrolling on our phone for an hour and watching television, because our body is just trying to avoid that feeling of not enough. We may have the time, but we don't feel as though we do. This may sound simple, but it is one reason why we avoid exercise.

I also see people struggle with exercise because of their personal narratives. Someone doesn't think they are an active person; or they think they are not athletic enough; or they are too old, too tired, too genetically predisposed to being an inactive person; or they are not interested in becoming obsessed with fitness, so they avoid it. I also hear people report external causes, like they don't have the right tools or memberships. But the primary reason we don't exercise is that exercise as we know it has become *way* too complicated!

Exercise is another billion-dollar industry built on you feeling like you are not enough as you are, and you need it (the industry) to fix you. My friend, the health benefits Dr. Wells and countless other physiologists claim are based on movement practices that you can realistically do anywhere. You just need to start somewhere. The benefits of movement are not only reserved for professional athletes or those with an extra two hours a day to spend in the gym or people who have a Peloton! The misinformation about what constitutes exercise has created a barrier for many of us. With all the conflicting and misleading information, we have experienced a decrease in our personal knowledge that we feel better when we move. Many of us think we are not moving correctly or enough, so what's the point? Then we don't move at all. Or we rely heavily on devices like fitness trackers. I remember a colleague asking me to come to their office across campus instead of meeting me in my office as we had originally planned. They'd forgotten their Apple Watch at home, so there wasn't any value in walking!

Another component worth discussing is the intention behind exercise or a movement practice. We cannot hate ourselves healthy or punish our bodies into submission. If you think having a six pack will solve your problems, you will likely have a six pack with your problems intact, despite the brutal punishment of restrictive eating and hours in the gym. The intention behind your activity is more important than the activity itself. Your physical self cannot change your inner world without the emotional work. You need the right mindset, aligned intentions, and self-awareness to make the physical changes most people are seeking.

Lastly, most exercise material suggests pain. No pain, no gain! As a species, we prefer pleasure, or not pain, over pain. Most exercise regimes guarantee pain, so it only makes sense that watching Netflix feels like the kinder activity. This choice is not about willpower or motivation. It is about self-preservation, which is not a weakness. Why would I want to hurt myself?

Exercise does not have to be complicated, painful, or all-consuming to provide the benefits of movement. But it does need to be consistent.

SLEEP

Sleep deprivation has been used as a form of torture for a reason. A lack of sleep wreaks havoc on the human condition. Johns Hopkins Medicine researcher Patrick Finan explains that not getting enough sleep negatively affects a person's mood, memory, and health more than any other form of deprivation. Dr. Finan shares that sleep deprivation can age a brain by three to five years because it is not getting the time needed to refresh and restore itself. Forty-eight per cent of people developed an increase in heart disease when they consistently did not get at least seven hours a night of sleep. Those same folks were three times more likely to catch a virus or develop an infection and three times more likely to develop type 2 diabetes.[17] Healthline reported that sleep deprivation, since it impacts concentration, balance, and reaction time, increases a person's risk of accidents.[18] Sleep deprivation also exacerbates mental health conditions and negatively impacts relationships and overall life satisfaction.

Professor Matt Walker from the University of California explains it this way: "We found that the emotional centre of the brain... was about 60 percent more active in people who had been sleep deprived, which was quite a frightening amount... As the frontal lobe puts the brakes on the brain's emotional centre, it shows that when you're sleep deprived you're all accelerator and no brakes. You don't have control over your emotions."[19] The effect of poor sleep is even considered a public safety issue by Harvard Medical School and other researchers, citing catastrophic events like the Chernobyl disaster, the Three Mile Island nuclear plant reactor meltdown, and the *Challenger* space shuttle explosion as influenced by sleep deprivation.[20]

If sleep is so important, why do so many of us struggle to get enough? Short answer: We are not very good sleepers anymore. Since 1985, the average number of people getting less than six hours of sleep a night has increased by 31 per cent. The average amount of sleep is reported to be 6.8 hours now, compared to nine to ten hours fifty years ago. It is estimated that 45 per cent of the world's population has issues with sleep![21] And people between the ages of forty-five and fifty-four are getting the least amount of sleep.

Why is all this so? Here are some quick insights. People are not getting enough daylight or time outdoors anymore. There are more distractions and activities to do at nighttime. Our sleep habits have changed. Many of our bedrooms are also home offices, gyms, or spaces shared with other people and animals. Our stress levels are elevated, which makes it harder for the body to produce melatonin. We are always on high alert. Anxiety and other mental health conditions are more prevalent. We are not moving as much as we used to. And we have also made sleeping more complex, especially with ideas

Even if you are on the right track, you'll get run over if you just sit there.

ATTRIBUTED TO WILL ROGERS

like the 5 a.m. club (where you wake up an hour earlier than everyone else in your household to get your uninterrupted "me time") paired with the busyness of our lives, requiring a solid stream of caffeine to function.

STRESS WISELY FOR PHYSICAL WELLNESS

We are more than what we weigh or how we look. We are more than the lack of sleep that hustle culture preaches. Our physical form is really a marvel of science, and we need, desperately, to get back to this truth.

Let me introduce you to the marvel of *you*!

You have 206 bones in your body, with 54 bones in your hand and wrist alone. Your largest bone, your femur, can support 30 times your body weight. You weren't born with kneecaps, but you grew them by two months old. As a baby you could also breathe and swallow at the same time. You have over 600 named muscles in your body, but scientists think you might have as many as 800. It takes 17 facial muscles to smile and 43 to frown. The muscles of your heart pump almost 1,000 litres of blood every day. Every 28 days you get a complete new set of human skin. Brand new skin every month! Your skin can also repair itself, although it can't regrow hair on a scar. You also have somewhere between 95,000 and 160,000 miles of blood vessels! If those vessels were outside your body, they could wrap around the earth— three times. Your teeth are as strong as a shark's. Your brain emits electricity. Your heart can imitate the music you are listening to. Your thoughts travel at 400 kilometres per hour! On an average day, you will take 20,000 breaths. Your eyes can distinguish 10 million different colours. You even have stardust in your bones! Your body is the most sophisticated organism on earth. It is a scientific marvel, and so much about our bodies still remains a mystery. Why am I telling you basic facts about your body? Well, this is the first step in body appreciation. Focus on the parts and how well they work, not on what you think needs to be fixed, shrank, or built to be happy.

Taking care of your body is a lot of work. Of course it is—it should be. You are working with the most sophisticated organism on earth!

BODY APPRECIATION

You may have heard about how important it is to have a positive body image. But striving for a positive body image holds us captive to the negative body image, as well. Our body is not a moral issue. Body appreciation is what makes real and lasting change. Researchers Bettina Piko, Annabella Obál, and David Mellor found that "body appreciation was most strongly related to self-esteem, as well as being positively associated with life satisfaction, self-perceived health, being in control of diet, and engagement in sport."[22] This is a significant finding. Increasing your appreciation for your body as it is brings about the positive changes that diets and unhealthy exercising behaviours promise to but never deliver. Imagine healing your relationship with your body through body appreciation and reaping the benefits of feeling better from the inside out!

Researchers Tracy Tylka and Nichole Wood-Barcalow developed a tool that measures a person's level of body appreciation.[23] It includes statements such as "I respect my body," "I feel that my body has at least some good qualities,"

"I appreciate the different and unique characteristics of my body," and "My behaviour reveals my positive attitude toward my body; for example, I hold my head high and smile." Shifting to a body appreciation focus shows remarkable effects in healing our relationship with our body.

I have developed this series of questions based on the work of brilliant experts in the field who have shared critical questions for us to explore.

Nutrition

- Every cell in your body needs water. Are you getting enough water every day?

- How can you ensure you are having three meals and snacks each day? Notice how you feel when you eat regularly.

- What are your food and nutrition fantasies? What are your beliefs about weight? Who can you talk with to sort through some of these beliefs?

- What formed your ideas about nutrition and eating? Where did they come from? What rules do you need to unlearn?

- What do you need right now to accept your "here and now" body?

Body

- What has your body carried you through? What have you healed from? How has your body served you?

- What steps can you take to forgive yourself for how you have treated and judged your body?

- Our clothes are meant to fit our bodies, yet we live like our bodies are meant to fit our clothes. What work do you need to do here? A closet cleanse? How can you let go of the socially created labels, sizes, and measurement rules? What would it feel like to wear clothes that fit your body comfortably and respectfully?

- Before any activity, are you willing to ask yourself for your own consent? Consent to work out today. Consent to be touched. Check in with yourself. Trust is how we build relationships, and that needs to be with ourselves as well.

Movement

- You cannot hate yourself healthy or punish your body into wellness. What could a healthy and respectful relationship with movement look like for you?

- How can you incorporate movement that supports flexibility, nimbleness, stamina, and heart and muscle health into your daily routines?

- How can you spend more time in nature? Anything outdoors allows our bodies to regulate faster and more efficiently.

- How can you slow down your pace?

- What is your optimal movement rate and frequency? What activities do you enjoy that involve movement? How can you work toward resetting your baseline for more steadiness and groundedness while you are moving about your day?

Sleep

- What is a realistic sleep schedule that you can hold most of the time?

- What does a supportive bedtime routine look like for you?

- How do you know if you are well slept?

- What does fatigue look like for you? What does exhaustion look like for you? What is your sleep recovery plan?

- What is healthy sleep hygiene for you? How can you protect your best sleep habits and practices?

FINAL THOUGHTS ON THE BODY

Your relationship with your physical wellness is vital for stressing wisely. Your body will carry you through every moment of your life. Find patterns, systems, habits, and practices that cultivate a respectful, kind, intentional, and practical way of meeting your physical needs. You deserve to feel physically well. You can be physically well. Remember, your body is the most significant organism on the planet. And it is all yours. You have been entrusted with its care, so care for it wisely.

66

And sometimes I have
kept my feelings to myself,
because I could find no language
to describe them in.

JANE AUSTEN

CHAPTER 6

THE HEART

MY DEEPEST MORAL INJURIES were born from how I *felt* about myself in the world. My earliest childhood memories are of feelings so complex and all-consuming that, even as an adult, I struggle to understand them. When I was happy, I felt like I had stumbled upon a second sunrise in a day. And when I was sad, I thought the sun would never shine again.

Emotions have a profound capacity to shape our lived experience. After all, people may forget what you said or did, but they won't forget how you made them feel. This is true for how we feel about ourselves and our situations, too. Feelings and emotions are so powerful, unruly, and magnificent. They spark everything from world wars to life-altering love stories. Emotions are complex enough on the best of days, even when they are positive or high-vibrational feelings like love, joy, and gratitude. And on the worst of days, almost out of nowhere, emotions can trigger deep hurts, old sadness, and even traumatic recall.

Often, especially after physical injuries heal, emotional scars linger. Although you cannot see emotional fractures by looking at someone, these are the wounds that require deep care. There is such a dichotomy when it comes to emotional healing; we are so bloody strong and vulnerable, concurrently. I recall talking with a surgeon who said that despite how invasive and violent surgery is to the human body, it is nothing compared to the mental and emotional work required to truly heal from trauma. Comforting, right? Physical wounds heal at a relatively known rate. We cannot heal faster than time can go, despite our efforts to rush the physical healing process. Yet emotional wounds have no timeline. Healing time and recoveries from emotional traumas are what I call "unknowables." There is often a disconnect between how long it takes for our emotions bruises to "heal" and when we actually feel as though we have recovered from the experience.

Recently, my gifted and skilled attachment therapist Ayla, who has been a lifeline for me these last few years, guided me through a treatment approach related to EMDR (eye movement desensitization and reprocessing) to support my residual trauma. Since my teenage years, I have successfully learned to manage maladaptive behaviours through cognitive-behavioural interventions. But that never really addressed the root causes. I reached a point in my adult life where I was finally ready for the heart work. I was finally ready for real healing. (Quick side note: I am often asked how to find the right therapist. Or I hear stories from people who tried therapy "once" and it wasn't for them. Finding the right therapist, at the right time in your life, can fundamentally change your life for the better. Although I had worked with several therapists, Ayla helped me heal from my old trauma in a way that I didn't even believe was possible. My work with Ayla changed my life and freed me from chains I believed were permanent and irrevocable. So, my gentle invitation: find the right fit for you and your needs. Be ruthless in your search to find your Ayla! Don't settle. Your paths will cross.)

EMDR is a technique used to rewire traumatic memories. My first encounter with EMDR treatment was a year after I had a catastrophic car accident such as nightmares are made of. As the first anniversary of the accident approached, I experienced post-traumatic stress disorder from the accident for the first time. Up to that point, I was okay talking about my accident and surrounding events with people who asked curious questions. I felt rather indifferent to the whole thing, although I knew it was a substantive and life-altering experience. Intellectually, I understood the significance on every front and the risk a random person, just driving home from work, took in saving my life. Joseph Todd was awarded the Governor General's Medal for Bravery for his actions. I was just sixteen years old, a troubled teenager without much hope for my future, and a brand-new driver.

On a lonely stretch of road, on a cold winter's night, a blizzard rolled in quickly, and I lost control of my car. It veered off the road and plummeted into the frozen Otonabee River, smashing through the ice. The car, with me in it, was viciously swept away. Imagine, one minute you are driving, listening to a song on the radio, working your way home in a snowstorm cautiously but confidently, and then the next minute you are sinking, trapped, as numbingly cold water rushes into the car. The metal, plastic, and glass of the car were no match for the fury of nature. There was no escape. The noise of cascading water pierced my ears as the song on the radio started to fade.

Lights flickered. Then darkness. Water filled every square inch of space. My body rose, but the seat belt firmly pinned me down. Now it was silent. Dead quiet. I was entombed in a watery grave.

I was drowning. Frigid water tore at my lungs. My chest heaved uncontrollably. I felt completely helpless and hopeless. My thoughts ricocheted until they landed on my mom, Lesley. This brought on a deep sorrow, not for me but for her. I didn't want my dying, and her losing a child in a car accident like this, to be part of her story. She had told me that no parent should outlive their child. I held on to my mom with every part of me, and my sorrow shifted to a sorry. *I am so sorry, Mom; I cannot protect you from me.* Then I felt it. A deep, familiar knowing. The bravest part of me dared to say, *Yes, you can.*

I recall the tender but mighty words of my mom. "Robyne can do hard things." Clinging to my mom's steadfast confidence that I was able to problem-solve myself out of any situation, I wiggled out of the locked seat belt, pulled the window off its track within the door, and escaped by swimming out through the window. I tried to fight my way through endless water. With a winter coat, boots, and jeans restricting my ability to move, I willed myself to swim to the surface. The water fought back and aggressively tried to pull me deeper. Ridiculously outmatched against the current, I lost my bearings. I couldn't differentiate up from down. My body was tossed around like a ragdoll in the forceful current. While I was attempting to steady myself, a new idea sparked. I exhaled all the lingering air in my lungs. And I saw air bubbles in front of me. I followed them as they whimsically guided me to the surface. Then, bang. Something smashed my face so hard that my teeth shook. A searing pain cut my frozen skin. Ice. A thick slab of ice over the river pinned me underwater.

Scrambling, completely out of air, I moved toward the deeper, faster moving water in the middle of the channel. I fought to get my torso onto the edge of the ice. The river relentlessly tried to swallow me. The pull of my boots tugged me down. I clawed my frozen fingers into the ice the best I could, but they kept slipping, the flesh on the palms of my hand torn open. I was clinging for my life, alone, in the middle of the night. In a blizzard. Desperately trying to just hold on.

My fierce sense of determination made way for a new feeling: resignation. Every time I tried to pull myself onto the ice, it cracked and I went underwater. I was losing strength in my arms; despite being frozen, they burned. I had done absolutely everything in my power to survive, but this was as far as I could go. I accepted it. As this acceptance flooded my weary heart, I was not afraid. My emotions were steady. My mind was clear. I was comforted knowing that my mom would at least know I had fought. *I fought for us. I tried, Mom. I'm sorry.*

Then I heard it. A faint voice in the distance calling out into the darkness. Someone was out there. A stranger frantically looking for me. I screamed with every ounce of energy I had left, as a wave of fatigue pulled me toward a sensation of warmth and release. My body was surrendering to the harsh conditions of hypothermia and exhaustion. They felt like a longed-for embrace. Then resignation turned to urgency. My mind fiercely kicked in and I screamed again, but nothing came out. Not a sound. I begged my voice to help me one last time. As though I had swallowed razorblades, cracked sounds emerged. I didn't recognize my own voice. But somehow, in this winter storm, Joseph heard me.

Taking wood and a chain from his pickup truck, he crawled out onto the precarious ice to rescue me. Using the wood to support his body weight, Joseph manoeuvred onto the ice as far as he could, then slid the chain out to me. On the third try my ravaged hands grabbed hold. Although there were only two of us in this moment, I felt an army of people spiritually around us. We were not alone. Even in my darkest hour, clinging to the edge, fighting for my life with the help of this stranger, I came to this knowing. We are never truly alone.

I survived a near-death experience in the most miraculous way. I knew it was my personal miracle, and it was already in motion before my car accident. This was a comforting thought and realization—knowing that miracles are at the ready! I had renewed evidence that even in the most dire and urgent situations, I can do hard things. I can do great things, too. My faith was restored that night. I believed that I could have a future and that there was more life to be lived. I could hold hope again. After years of darkness, the light started to edge into view. I used this event to propel me into a big, bright future.

As the first anniversary approached, I continued to intellectualize my accident in every way, but I didn't really *feel* anything when I talked or thought about that night. I had survived it. It had happened. But it was as if my mind wouldn't let my body hold any feelings about my accident, until one day, it did.

NIGHTMARES WHILE YOU ARE AWAKE

At seventeen years old, after dropping out in grade eleven, I was re-enrolled for my final semester of high school. With the help of correspondence courses, I was graduating on time. Then, on a normal, nothing-out-of-the-ordinary kind of day, I slipped into the driver's seat of my car and nonchalantly unloaded my backpack on the passenger seat. I pulled my keys from my coat pocket. As I slid the key into the ignition, I looked up and out the front windshield.

Like a scene from a movie, the accident played out in front of my eyes. I was there again. Bone-chilling terror pierced my body. The headlights illuminated a scene of eerie green glowing water peppered with sediment and bubbles. I heard the water crashing through the floorboards. I felt it rushing up my legs. My skin recoiled at the pain. My head whipped back. As I screamed, arctic-cold water choked me. I gurgled as the water overtook my airways.

I frantically scrambled with the door handle, and this time, the car door opened, and I fell onto the driveway, smashing my face against the asphalt. I tasted blood. My ears were ringing, my head was throbbing, and my body shook uncontrollably. I could not catch my breath—I tried to breathe in, but there was no air to be found. I was gasping and my lungs were heaving against my ribcage, trying to make room for even one drop of relief. Tears finally broke free from behind my eyes. I clung to the first sip of air. I ground my teeth and tried to stand, but my legs couldn't hold my body weight. I fell again.

I reached for the steering wheel, and I pulled myself up and slid back into the driver's seat without closing the door. I was scared to close my eyes because I knew what I would see. I slowly took in the world around me. I saw the large evergreen tree in front of our house. I saw the house. Then I saw a face looking out the front window. It was our family dog, staring at me. Apparently, the only witness to my first "flashback trauma episode" was my dog. Dogs can keep secrets. Not wanting to burden anyone, I too tried to keep the secret of the flashbacks and nightmares. I was given a second chance, and here I was not even emotionally able to accept this miracle.

And like secrets do, these tore me apart until they eventually made their way into the light.

EMOTIONAL REPAIR

A year after my accident, under the supervision of an extraordinary medical psychotherapist, Dr. Bob, trained in EMDR, I started rewiring the traumatic memories. This intervention does not remove your memories or the feelings that go with them. It is a sophisticated process of pairing new connections with traumatic memories, which then minimizes the physiological arousal those memories produce. Dr. Francine Shapiro, the psychologist who developed this treatment, explains, "EMDR therapy facilitates the accessing of the traumatic memory network, so that information processing is enhanced, with new associations forged between the traumatic memory and more adaptive memories or information. These new associations are thought to result in complete information processing, new learning, elimination of emotional distress, and development of cognitive insights."[1]

Here lie important truths. Emotions are real. Feelings can hurt as much as physical pain. Emotions are a multiplex mosaic that shape the lens through which we see the world. You cannot *out-think* trauma. Trained support is needed; we are not meant to do this work alone. No amount of yoga, thought-stopping exercises, journaling, essential oils, healthy eating, love from friends and family, professional success, or accolades can address trauma or emotional wounds. We cannot see or touch those scars, but they are real. Our brains and our nervous system are markedly different now. We are not broken people, but we do have an injury.

EMOTIONS AS WE KNOW THEM

There are so many theories of emotions, ranging from the evolutionary theory proposed by Charles Darwin (we feel so we can mate and survive), to the James-Lange theory (we see a bear, we tremble, and we feel afraid, not because we see a bear, but because we feel ourselves trembling), to facial-feedback theory (which claims that when someone smiles, they have a better time, even if they don't feel like being at the party!). There is also the Schachter-Singer theory, which claims that we have a physiological reaction and then we try to make meaning of that reaction by giving it a name and a classification, usually good or bad. These theories are classified as physiological, neurological, or cognitive. From another perspective, Saint Thomas Aquinas proposed that emotions are something the soul undergoes.[2] Regardless of the theory, there is one commonality that Oscar Wilde reminds us of: our emotions are stirred more quickly than our intelligence.[3]

The inner world of feelings, emotions, and thoughts is complex for even the most educated adults. Thankfully, the animation studio Pixar shed some much-needed clarity with its 2015 blockbuster movie *Inside Out*. In a wonderful telling of the biological underpinnings of emotions, the five core emotions are brought to life in the characters of Sadness, Disgust, Anger, Fear, and Joy. Researchers in psychology, anthropology, and sociology hold a consistent view that the idea of five core emotions is valid, although sometimes minus one (usually disgust).

This is how I keep emotions and feelings straight. Emotions are the biological reactions that are activated through our neurotransmitters and hormones released by the brain. Feelings are our conscious expression or experience of that emotional reaction. I experience the emotion of sadness, then I feel lonely, lost, abandoned.

With such a small allotment of basic emotions, it should be relatively easy to manage them, right? Unfortunately, no. This is because emotions can vary in intensity. We may feel anger at a ten, but sadness may be there, too, perhaps at a two. We can combine two or more core emotions, and sometimes the combination is mismatched. In a new relationship we may feel nervous and excited, but fear may make us behave counter to what we want. We may push people away when we want to get close.

Challenging, as well, is that four of the core emotions are socially hard to feel and express compared to the more socially acceptable feeling, joy. This idea ties back to our nervous system being underdeveloped for today's world. The nervous system is hardwired to keep us safe and alive using four profoundly strong emotions (fear, disgust, anger, sadness), yet society holds joy or being happy as the holy grail. We are not designed for max joy all the time. We feel many things, including difficult emotions. Being told to be happy all the time is just another way that society pathologizes normal fluctuations in emotions, making us feel like we are not doing "it" (as in our lives) right.

WE ARE FEELING FACTORIES

Another important consideration is that each core emotion has dozens of secondary expressions. I like to think of our emotions like key ingredients, and with those key ingredients, in your personal "feeling factory," you can make hundreds of different feelings. Dr. Tiffany Watt Smith, author of *The*

Book of Human Emotions: An Encyclopedia of Feeling from Anger to Wanderlust, argued that she has catalogued more than 150 feelings that can be created from the five core emotions.[4]

Depending on your culture, your lived experience, your geography, and even your values, your emotional tapestry will look very different. But there is a consistent practice of sorting emotions as being good or bad, moral or immoral, productive or unproductive, welcomed or feared. This rigidity—that emotions need to be black or white or in the extremes—is toxic to a weary heart.

We don't get to pick our emotions, just like we cannot pick our thoughts. Our control lies in how we work with our emotions, responding to them versus reacting. And this is effortful and requires us to be in the present moment, which, as we know, we are not particularly good at since we are so busy multi-tasking our lives away!

I appreciate that we are not always comfortable feeling certain emotions, or perhaps not skilled yet at experiencing them. Many times, I have wanted to stop being a nervous flier or didn't want to miss people anymore or didn't want to feel intimidated by a brutal boss. I have felt tired of fighting hard against the urges of addictions. I have tried to wish, or self-help, away feelings of being unworthy, jealous, ashamed, angered, afraid, or envious. I have begged therapists to take away the barrage of feelings. I have even prayed that all the feelings would stop. I was willing to give up the good ones, too, just so the hurting would stop.

Thankfully, around the same time, when I didn't think I could keep carrying the weight of my heart in this hurtful world, my perspective shifted thanks to my work with a trusted social worker, John. He was the therapist who I needed for this particular season of my life. As my thirtieth birthday approached, I didn't celebrate with a party or trip like many do. I gifted myself therapy! I wasn't going to spend another decade white-knuckling my life.

"You want to stop feeling it all, Robyne? Is that what you want?" I nodded. I was embarrassed for feeling so weak. Emotions were my kryptonite. I recalled how many times I had been told to "take the emotion out of it," "pull yourself together," "just be more logical," "just get over it." Being so emotional was my downfall. John smiled knowingly back at me. He saw my struggle. "If the goal is to stop feeling everything, then we just have to change the goal."

In my head, I swore in every language. I did *not* have the energy for a goal-setting exercise, and I made that very clear on my face. John looked past my anger, then said, "You are setting dead-man goals, Robyne. Only the dead stop feeling."

Feelings, all of them, are the price of admission to this life. Tough emotions are part of the contract. Feelings make life memorable, remarkable, if we are brave enough to feel them all. Maybe you too have dead-man goals. Let's see what we can do about that, together.

STRESS WISELY FOR EMOTIONAL WELLNESS

Despite our best efforts, we cannot hustle our way out of discomfort. We cannot out-think the heart. To stress wisely emotionally, we need to honour, respect, and appreciate our emotional energy. We must feel our way through this life. I am not suggesting that we turn ourselves over to every impulse that crosses our mind. We need to live in community, so a completely unbridled approach to our feelings is not the remedy.

Life shrinks or
expands in proportion
to one's courage.

ANAÏS NIN

Instead, we feel all the things, and we learn how to work with them as information, guidance, and value alignment. Our feelings hold sacred knowledge of our internal world. When we tune into this insight, when we meet all the feelings with curiosity and compassion, we can find an inner strength and resolve that will serve us well. As the great fictional philosopher Coach Ted Lasso said, be like a goldfish (they have very short memories), and get curious rather than judgemental when it comes to your feelings. Be curious, less judgemental!

SOCIAL EMOTIONAL LEARNING

Thank you, Dr. Marc Brackett, for introducing us to the wonderful world of social emotional learning. For over two decades, Dr. Brackett has been on a mission to educate the world about the value of human emotions and the skills needed to navigate them successfully. He wants us all, grown-ups and children, to become emotional scientists rather than emotional judges. "We need to be curious explorers of our own and others' emotions so they can help us achieve our goals and improve our lives," he notes.[5]

When we learn to value our emotions, our lives improve. In his book *Permission to Feel*, Dr. Brackett gives us a tool to do just that known as RULER, an acronym for the five skills of emotional intelligence:[6]

- **Recognizing** emotions in ourselves and others

- **Understanding** the causes and consequences of emotions

- **Labelling** emotions with a nuanced vocabulary

- **Expressing** emotions in accordance with cultural norms and social context

- **Regulating** emotions with helpful strategies

In my work, I use a simplified version:

- See it.
- Name it.
- Place it.
- Action it.

Here is how this can work for you.

First, notice you are feeling something. This is why being mindful, or at least having a practice of self-check-ins throughout the day, is so important. How am I feeling right now? It is hard to notice feelings when you are on autopilot.

Second, name the feeling the best you can, and as specifically as you can. Try to use words other than "fine," "busy," or "tired." So, let's say you notice you have low energy. Instead of saying you are just tired (let's face it, we have been tired for years), perhaps could you name it "depleted" instead? "Depleted" tells the brain that you need to restore something, that there is a lack or emptiness.

Third, place where this feeling is most likely coming from. Perhaps you are feeling depleted because you have not had a proper day off in several weeks (or years). You may be sleeping, but you don't feel rested. This is why we need to stop calling it "tired." The cause is more likely that you are depleted. Your soul and your spirit need uplifting!

Step four is to action it. For example, say to yourself, *I recognize I am depleted, and I am going to spend time with my dear friend this weekend to recharge my emotional batteries.*

As soon as we see it, name it, place it, and action it, our minds let it go. Our emotions are meant to trigger actions; when we plan, we can move on. This small practice makes radical improvements to your emotional health in record time.

EMOTIONAL MYTH-BUSTING

Another brilliant thought leader in this area of emotion is Dr. Susan David. In her book *Emotional Agility*, Dr. David writes about the importance of meeting our emotions with curiosity, compassion, and courage. One of my favourite activities to lead with groups is emotional myth-busting. This is when we explore the origin stories and rules of our emotions. Before we jump into this exercise, please know there is plenty of unlearning many of us need to do here. No judgement, just be curious.

Let's take a look at some myths about emotions:

- There is a right way to feel in every situation.

- Letting others know that I am feeling bad is a weakness.

- Negative or unpleasant emotions are bad and destructive.

- Being emotional means being out of control.

- It is better to be rational or logical than emotional.

- If others don't approve of my feelings, I obviously shouldn't feel the way I do.

- Emotions should not be displayed in the workplace.

- It's wrong or inauthentic to change my emotions.

- I need to be very emotional to be creative.

- If I let myself feel or cry, I will never be able to stop.

- I am my emotions.

What are some other myths about emotions you hold? As a gentle reminder, instead of being an emotional judge, be an observer. Get curious. Where are these feelings coming from? Be compassionate with yourself for feeling them. And have the courage to express them in a way that honours you and those around you. There is really no room here for judgement, blame, and certainly not shame! Self-awareness is a powerful tool in learning how to stress wisely, especially with our emotions.

EMOTIONAL WELLNESS

Our relationship with emotions is a vital component of our wellness. To be well, we have to feel well. To help explore your inner emotional topography, here are some prompts for reflection. My hope is they will cultivate self-discovery and awareness building. Be kind with yourself here. Your emotions have served you well in their own way.

- When I was growing up, I was encouraged to express the following emotions:

  _____

- When I was growing up, the following emotions were discouraged:

  _____

- It is easy to express these emotions:

  _____

- It is difficult to express these emotions:

  _____

- I most commonly feel these emotions:

  _____

- I want to feel more of these emotions:

  _____

- I try to avoid feeling these emotions:

  _____

- It is easy to deal with someone who is expressing the following emotions:

  _____

- It is difficult to deal with someone who is expressing the following emotions:

  _____

- I consider these to be negative emotions:

  _____

- When I am angry, it is helpful if the person I am speaking with does the following:

  _____

- When I am sad, it is helpful if the person I am speaking with does the following:

  _____

FINAL THOUGHTS ON THE HEART

Emotions are truly a miraculous part of the lived experience. At times, sure, they may feel like more of a curse than a blessing, but they are ours! Our emotions are extraordinary marvels intertwined in both the physical and spiritual realms. When we are moved by kindness, we put our hands over our hearts. When scared, we tremble. When held by the right person, we feel safe and free. I have learned that to hold the brightest, lightest, and most pure emotions in the world, I needed a frame of reference. Those enchanting emotions only felt that way because I knew pain.

One of the most beautiful moments you can experience in your emotional growth is realizing that you are handling situations better than you used to. Even when I have not handled a situation as well as I would have liked, personally or professionally, but I can see that I am handling the emotions of the situation better than I would have before, this is a major win. Emotions are the soundtrack to our lives. What songs are on your mixtape?

66

An unhealthy mind,
even in a healthy body, will
ultimately destroy health.

MANLY P. HALL

CHAPTER 7

THE MIND

"MY BRAIN HURTS!" Ava declared when I picked her up from gymnastics.

"Did you bang your head?" Given that she spends hours a week tumbling, this is very possible.

"No, I think I just was upside down too long, and we are learning a new unit in math, and I have a sleepover with Emy tomorrow, and I lost my lunch box today, and I miss my cat." Ava paused, looking contemplatively out her window. "Maybe it's just full of life." Ava was turning eight years old the following week.

"I hear you, sister! My head gets pretty full of life too sometimes."

BRAIN ON THE MIND (OR, MIND THE BRAIN)

There is a remarkable interconnectedness between the physiology and psychology of our brains and our minds and how they impact our wellness.

Our brain is a powerful, complex, and magnificent organ. In physical form, it is home to over 100 billion neurons—about as many as stars in the Milky Way galaxy! It is made up of blood vessels and nerve cells. It uses approximately 20 per cent of all our energy to run, and it never stops running in our lifetime. Our brain has a definite shape and structure; you can touch it, and it feels no pain. It is the main control centre for the entire body. The brain allows us to think, feel, remember, and communicate, while also coordinating all our actions and reactions and states of consciousness. This three-pound hunk of matter, made up of 60 per cent fat and 40 per cent of a combination of water, protein, carbohydrates, and salt, makes our lives as we know them possible.

Our mind, however, is truly a mystery! Our mind is not made up of biological matter. It is technically hypothetical, yet we ascribe it to being the very essence of who we are. We know it exists, but we cannot touch it. The brain is tangible. The mind is intangible. We can dissect a brain, but to study the mind, we must rely on self-reports. Another person cannot observe the human mind. They can assume, but there will always remain a degree of subjectivity, since one subjective mind is trying its best to interpret another subjective mind.

The brain and mind exist in a symbiotic relationship. They both affect one another and cannot be separated, yet the true nature of this relationship remains a scientific and spiritual phenomenon. We truly are a complex and intriguing marvel of science, mystery, and possibility. In this enmeshed discussion between the mind and brain, psychology versus physiology, the connecting thread that binds these two systems irrevocably together is the vital role of a healthy brain and mind in our overall wellness.

THE SOCIAL CONSTRUCT KNOWN AS INTELLIGENCE

Intelligence is a socially constructed idea. It is the same for something like money. Money is technically just paper, metal, or numbers, yet we ascribe meaning to it. Intelligence is a concept that people created and then built systems around, often with little validity, yet interest in studying the mind has a remarkably long history.

Ancient Greeks like Aristotle called intelligence "reason." Homer believed reason was claimed by personal experience or hearsay. In the seventeenth century, during the birth of the Scientific Revolution, brilliant scientists and "dangerous" thought leaders like Johannes Kepler, Galileo Galilei, and Isaac Newton each had a take on the value and nature of intelligence. Kepler wrote, "I much prefer the sharpest criticism of a single intelligent man to the thoughtless approval of the masses."

Galileo believed intelligence was a gift: "When I reflect on so many profoundly marvelous things that persons have grasped, sought, and done, I recognize even more clearly that human intelligence is a work of God, and one of the most excellent." Galileo also believed that these gifts were to be used. "I do not think it is necessary to believe that the same God who has given us our senses, reason, and intelligence wished us to abandon their use, giving us by some other means the information that we could gain through them." And Newton believed it was how you work with your intelligence that mattered: "If I have ever made any valuable discoveries, it has been due more to patient attention, than to any other talent."

Later, Charles Darwin called intelligence "mental powers." Darwin's half-cousin, Sir Francis Galton, is attributed as one of the first to formally study intelligence as a field.[1] In 1905, the psychologists Alfred Binet and Théodore Simon built the first intelligence quotient (IQ) test at the request of the French government. As a result, IQ is how most of us think about intelligence today—as a relatively fixed score of how smart someone is. Our entire educational system is built on this controversial foundation of analytical skills.

The Simon-Binet IQ test comprised a series of standard questions to identify which children would likely succeed in educational pursuits. It systematically sorted and classified people, with a heavy advantage to the upper class. The areas of focus were attention, memory, and problem solving. A score was factored by a person's age and compared to a set of standardized group scores. The comparative sample consisted of upper-class people, with little representation or diversity, yet everyone who was tested, regardless of background and educational experience, was compared to the same comparator group. This test eventually made its way to the US and Stanford University in 1916, which brought us the Stanford-Binet Intelligence Scales IQ test that is still widely used today.

Often left out in the history of IQ testing is that Binet himself talked about the limitations and danger of using one measure to assess intelligence. Binet argued that intelligence was far too broad a concept to quantify with a single number. He believed many factors influenced intelligence and that background and culture needed to be considered. Somewhere along the way, this was lost, since the majority of tests use a very limited comparison group to make life-altering diagnoses and decisions about a child's potential and abilities.

INTELLIGENCE REFRAMED

The intelligence model I just described is not the intellectual realm of wellness we will be exploring closely. When many of us hear the word "intelligence," we associate it with things like being smart, IQ, and education. This limited perspective of intelligence is a predominantly colonial and classist view of the world perpetuated to control and sort people. Instead, let's explore a more inclusive view of intellect. Besides, I have done many of those mentioned IQ tests, and I can share with radical candor that I did very poorly on them. As poorly as anyone else who needed and was denied an accommodation to level the playing field. ADHD and learning disabilities are not often well managed in psycho-educational assessments. It is like asking someone who needs reading glasses to read a passage without them, then claiming that since the person could not see the words, they could not read, so they simply were not as smart as their peers.

Additional theories and views of intelligence and testing have emerged to address the bias embedded within most standard IQ tests. This includes the theory of multiple intelligences by Harvard psychologist Dr. Howard Gardner, who presented a model of IQ initially with eight intelligences: visual-spatial, linguistic-verbal, interpersonal, intrapersonal, logical-mathematical, musical, bodily-kinesthetic, and naturalistic.[2] This new approach was widely accepted, especially by educational communities. When they considered more realms of intelligence, teachers developed and implemented a more inclusive approach to educating their diverse groups of students. Although the theory of multiple intelligences was a welcomed shift from the standard IQ view, it met criticism for being too broad and overly simplified. Critics said that it captured more about talent and preferences than intelligence.

However, like all advances, the theory of multiple intelligences sparked a newer idea. Gardner's work opened the door for even more inclusive ideas about intelligence, including the theory of emotional intelligence, or what is referred to more commonly now as EI (or EQ).

Emotional intelligence was first introduced by Drs. John Mayer and Peter Salovey in the 1990s. However, most people attribute and associate emotional intelligence theory with Dr. Daniel Goleman. Goleman was a scientific reporter with the *New York Times* when he came upon the work of Mayer and Salovey.[3] Goleman's book *Emotional Intelligence*, published in 1995, expanded their work to include five essential elements of EI:

- **Emotional self-awareness:** knowing what one is feeling at any given time and understanding the impact those moods have on others

- **Self-regulation:** controlling or redirecting one's emotions; anticipating consequences before acting on impulse

- **Motivation:** using emotional factors to achieve goals, enjoying the learning process, and persevering in the face of obstacles

- **Empathy:** sensing the emotions of others

- **Social skills:** managing relationships, inspiring others, and inducing desired responses from them

Emotional intelligence has remarkably changed our understanding of intelligence and was instrumental in the development of what is now called social emotional learning (SEL). This advancement of emotional intelligence was so remarkable that in 2002 UNESCO (United Nations Educational,

Scientific and Cultural Organization) developed a campaign to promote social emotional learning in classrooms world-wide. Goleman's work on emotional intelligence heavily influenced the UN's SEL principles:[4]

- Self-awareness
- Self-management
- Social awareness
- Relationship skills
- Responsible decision-making

Socrates is attributed with saying that to know thyself is the beginning of wisdom. Knowing how we socially and emotion-ally learn and function in our lives is a key to stressing wisely. Virtually all roles in our lives have a relationship component. Understanding how we interact with others, how we make decisions involving others, and how we connect with others will play into how we experience and express stress. Foster-ing this perspective on intellect seems like a great place to explore how to stress wisely.

STRESS WISELY FOR INTELLECTUAL WELLNESS

Let's dive into each of the UN's five principles for social emo-tional learning.

Self-awareness

Self-awareness is a critical aspect of how we see ourselves and how we behave. So often we feel as though our feelings and behaviours are a mystery. Yet often there may be noticeable patterns, if we pause long enough to pay attention. I see this often in my work when I am asked about certain behaviours.

The fewer the facts, the stronger the opinion.

ARNOLD H. GLASOW

"Why do I stick to my meal plan all day, religiously, then eat a whole row of Oreos at nighttime?" I am asked in an open Q & A session. My response: "Because Oreos are delicious! And perhaps you are under-feeding yourself all day. You are serving and meeting the needs of everyone else, and then you finally get a moment for you, and dammit, you want to feel good. So, you eat the Oreo. The first one is like heaven, and perhaps there is even more heaven further down the row, so you go for it. Maybe you are not self-sabotaging after all. Perhaps you are a pleasure seeker, and why not? You carry the weight of the world, and all you are asking for in return is a blasted cookie! Makes a lot of sense to me."

Have you ever watched a show in which your favourite character continually makes poor decisions? Of course you have! Stories need conflict, and personal conflict is so relatable. Try this: Imagine you are watching *you*, being *you*, doing you-type things, as if you're a character on a screen:

- What are some of the common pitfalls you would see?

- What are the themes, tendencies, or patterns?

- What would you want to tell this character they need to notice, see, or recognize?

- If you wanted the character to grow into their most "well life," what actions would they need to take?

Taking the "you" out of this exercise is key here. You need to be the observer, not the character in question. Yes, the character is you, but I want you to watch as objectively as you can. This helps us manage our unruly ego, who would prefer if our calm, clear, and steady conscious state did not notice some of the behaviours it rules when you are not paying attention.

A checked ego is a great start to building higher levels of self-awareness.

Self-management

Self-management is closely related to self-regulation, with more emphasis on aligning yourself to your future desired state. It is being your own steward to your needs, wants, and dreams as they relate to where you hope to go and what you want to achieve. Here are some self-management reflection questions:

- What is your desired state of optimal living?

- What do you have to do today to experience it as you need it to be?

- Where are you today and where do you want to be in the future?

- What has to be done today that will benefit you tomorrow?

- Are your behaviours directing you toward your future self?

- In what direction are you pointing?

- Is this behaviour getting you closer to or further away from your desired state?

Self-management is challenging for so many of us because we often rely on willpower and motivation to manage our behaviours. These two energies are fickle friends. I think and feel like I have all the willpower in the world until someone says "pizza." I have all the motivation in the world the night before an early workout, but at 6 a.m., not so much!

Self-management really comes down to pleasure and pain principles. It is quite shocking how far we will go to avoid discomfort. Our two-billion-year-old brain is not our ally here!

It has spent eons learning how to avoid discomfort for its survival. Now the threats are remarkably different, yet our need to avoid pain hits us at a primitive level. Pleasure was also so scarce once that now, when we come upon something pleasurable, like watching our favourite TV show, spending time with friends, or scrolling on social media and seeing pretty things, our brain simply prefers that. Just imagine as well how often our early brain would have contacted sugar. Very rarely. But sugar has such instant satisfying effects on our brain that, even now, millions of years later, our brain loves a sugar score!

Perhaps you are procrastinating on that assignment or report. The hard work it requires is quite uncomfortable in the moment, and the reward for finishing it is too far away, so your brain prefers to online shop. It doesn't make matters easier that when you put something in your cart and then hit buy, your brain secretes dopamine, the reward compound hormone—the very same dopamine you would experience if you finished that report, except online shopping is quicker and takes less effort. We will naturally take the path of least resistance. This is science and physics wrapped up in human behaviour. Factor in not getting enough sleep, and that lizard part of your brain takes the wheel and steers you right to Starbucks instead of the office.

There are several ways to sharpen your self-management skills. Here are a few of my favourites.

Keep your promises to yourself. Just as you protect your promises and commitments to others, show yourself the same respect and honour. Set this as a value you hold for yourself and an identity marker. *Robyne keeps her promises.* This builds self-trust and efficacy for following through. Of course, you will negotiate at times, if adapting is required. But strive to hold yourself to the highest level of personal integrity.

Know who you are and who you are not. Just because everyone else is doing the "it" thing doesn't mean you have to as well. It is hard to be accountable if the goal is not worthy of your time, energy, and gifts or not aligned with your values and your well life.

Be aware of your coveting tendencies. Coveting behaviour is when you have a deep compulsion to keep or possess something. Wanting what your neighbour has. Comparing yourself to others. Striving for an ideal or perfect life. Thinking money will solve your problems. Many of us get stuck in the outer-attainment-for-inner-attunement trap. We think something on the outside will solve all our troubles. Truth is, *you will never have enough of what you do not need.* Inner attunement holds the peace, security, and acceptance we are seeking.

Develop clarity, focus, and a realistic plan. Knowing where you are heading and why you are working in that direction matters. Your goals require a high degree of value-add in your life to make them matter enough to delay the short-term reward for the long-term gain. Keep a sharp focus on the goal in ways that are as concrete as possible. Since we have unfortunately broken so many promises to ourselves, abstract ideas won't cut it anymore. We need radical clarity. You can't run west and expect to see a sunrise. Make a sustainable, practical plan: consider the challenges and setbacks that will likely pop up, and plan accordingly. Planning matters, but having a well-developed plan that aligns with what matters most is even better!

Social awareness

Seeing things from other people's perspectives, showing empathy, appreciating diversity, and being able to read the room are practices of the intellectual realm. How often have you been in a situation or a conversation and clearly someone just did not get it? Being socially aware requires a multitude of skills put to use simultaneously. You need to be mindful of the cultural norms, the context of the situation, body language, tones, and verbal and non-verbal cues, all while being present in the moment, managing your own mental clutter, and anticipating your own scripts for responding. There is a lot going on! Yet when we get being socially aware right, the other person feels so heard, seen, and validated that the relationship is instantly strengthened.

I recall keynoting at one of my first huge conferences. Those who are familiar with my work know I always do a land acknowledgement. I have acknowledged my place and space for nearly two decades, as an educator. I thank the kind and remarkable Indigenous elders who told me it was my responsibility to do this wherever I go.

As I was about to take the stage at this event, the person with the headset holding the curtain back grabbed my arm and said, "The production crew said your first slide is something about Indigenous lands. Don't say anything about that, it's too political." Then they gently pushed me forward. I took a wobbly step. The spotlight captured me and guided me to centre stage.

Behind me on massive screens, I saw my second slide, not the land acknowledgement that is always my first slide. Without skipping a beat, I introduced myself, and I acknowledged the lands that, as a settler, I call home, and that I was a guest there that day in those lands and territories. I was on treaty land, and I had a moral and ethical obligation to do my part to recognize the original peoples of those lands. For a moment I wondered if there would be any fallout from my wee censorship rebellion.

Then, I saw her. A lone woman, sitting in the centre of this huge conference room, stood up. People turned to see what had caught my attention. I stopped talking and looked right at her. Although the house lights were dim, I saw her weary eyes filled with tears. With a strong, powerful voice, she said, "Thank you." The thank you echoed through the room. She said, "I am a survivor of the residential school atrocities, and these are the lands of my people."

We talked afterward, she and I, at great length. My being socially aware was such a small gesture on my part, but for this woman, hearing an outsider acknowledge her lands—which she had never once heard, ever—was affirming. Please never underestimate the power of being socially aware.

Relationship skills

Like communication, cooperation, and conflict resolution, the capacity to be in a relationship and in a community is a fundamental skill in the intellectual realm of wellness. We must learn how to interact with people in a "well way." For example, we must learn how to talk about difficult topics, or how to listen to really hear and understand. We will dive much deeper into the roles of relationships in the next chapter.

Responsible decision-making

Responsible decision-making includes thinking about the consequences of personal behaviour. There are five steps to making responsible decisions:

1 Identify the problem.
2 Analyze the situation.
3 Brainstorm solutions to the problem.
4 Consider ethical responsibility.
5 Implement, then evaluate and reflect.

This five-step decision-making map is just one example. There are several ways to work through major and minor decisions. But key are the pieces that consider our ethical responsibilities and our reflection. We are not just deciding for us; our decisions influence those around us, our communities, and possibly even the wider world. And if we fail to build in reflection, we miss the opportunity to learn. If we don't repair it, we often repeat it. We will repeat the same mistakes until we finally learn the lesson we need to know.

FINAL THOUGHTS ON THE MIND

The union of our mind and brain is one of the most powerful forces on earth. We cannot have a well life with an unwell mind. I have seen far too many examples of people going on vacation with their troubled mind. They can be standing in the most beautiful location, taking in the most stunning vistas in all the world, and still feel restless and angry. As the tale goes, two prisoners find one another years after being liberated. One prisoner asks the other if they have forgiven their captors. The angry prisoner replies, "Absolutely not!" The wise prisoner says, "Then they still have you captive."

My gentle invitation is to set peace of mind as your highest goal and organize your life around that. The strength of your wellness depends on the quality of your thoughts. Be sure your thoughts have a gentle place to land in your mind. Your body is always listening. And as the saying goes, if you knew the power of your thoughts, you would stand guard at the door of your mind. Only you can do this work.

"

Our sense of worthiness,
that critical piece that gives us
access to love and belonging,
lives inside our story.

DR. BRENÉ BROWN

CHAPTER 8

COMMUNITY

B EING PART OF A COMMUNITY is paramount for our survival. We are not meant to walk this world alone. Yet for many of us, finding community can be quite complex. Our first community is our biological family, which also includes the tapestry of our ancestors. This is our first relationship with others: people here and those who have gone before us. Our sense of belonging hinges on this first relationship. My research on resiliency found that belonging is the first pillar that establishes our capacity to show up in our lives. In this chapter, I revisit some of the key learning I have shared previously about the fundamentals of belonging and how to foster community.

Through my work, I have seen the effects when communities are not meeting a person's primary needs both emotionally and physically. The feeling of belonging produces a sense of safety and security that affords an abundance of privilege even in precarious life situations. Yet for many, when security and safety is not available, it becomes a life mission to find it wherever they can. This idea that people will seek out community before almost everything else speaks to the huge biological and physiological pull to belong. It is woven into our DNA to be accepted by the group.

Researcher Carl Taylor from Michigan State University has studied youth and gang-related behaviours for over forty years.[1] His work with Pamela Smith unpacks how when a person does not have their basic needs met in their home environments, they are at greater risk of seeking connection in unhealthy and dangerous ways. Their work identified that youth drawn into gang life are seeking protection, stable relationships, and access to resources that traditionally a home system would provide. Growing up in precarious and unsupportive environments does not have to be a life sentence, but for many it becomes one.

I vividly recall working with one such person. It has been over twenty years since I met him, yet his story is etched in my memory. It is the story of a boy who was willing to give up everything just to have somewhere to go. Although how he ended up where he was is not my story to tell, I can share with you the part that included me and was entrusted to me to share. It starts inside a maximum-security prison.

Kingston Pen was the oldest prison in Canada and considered its most notorious. This limestone structure, built by inmates, has a brutal history of violence and cruelty. In the early 2000s, I completed an internship there as part of my behavioural science training. Rarely do our places of employment hold such complex and tragic histories. It was not lost on me that this building not only housed some of Canada's most infamous incarcerated people, but in 1842, 10 per cent of the prison population was female, and children as young as eight years old served time there.[2] I never quite could shake the eeriness of the building, even when surrounded by prison guards casually drinking Tim Hortons coffee and talking about hockey.

As I walked through the stunning main gate house, across the cobblestoned courtyard, this magnificent structure cast grim shadows that triggered uneasiness. This place was not safe for anyone. I walked to my small student office in the Regional Treatment Centre area, knowing I was being watched. You were always being watched. As days, weeks, and months passed, I was even more convinced that this social-order, law-abiding, judicial-system–enforcing building was the least likely place for people to be "corrected," despite it being a correctional facility. Places like this breed violence, pain, and chaos. It felt void of hope. Those living inside its walls suffered. Those people on the outside, affected by those living inside, suffered profoundly, too. It was a cluster of tragedy and failed systems that seemed endless and unsolvable. One typical, nothing-out-of-the-ordinary kind of day, there was a lockdown. All regular programming was postponed. Because it was a lockdown, no one could leave, even the staff, so a psychologist and I decided to play cards with the inmates who were being held in the treatment centre.

That afternoon, I was schooled. Not only at cards, but about the realities of the lives of these inmates. I learned a raw, unabridged tale about the impacts of social injustice, violence, racism, prejudice, classism, and deviant behaviours from people who had been marked by society. These men had broken the rules and, consequently, other people's lives, and their own.

Having a new person to share their stories with (me) was a privilege many inmates with life sentences were rarely afforded. Their "tellings" were not intended to scare me but

to educate me in a way no textbook could. I felt they were
eager to change my mind or at least have their side of the
story heard. They shared candidly, casually, and with some
degree of care, not boastfully or sensationally. What became
clear to me was that they wanted me to know parts of their
stories; to know about their families, their memories of life
outside these limestone walls.

That afternoon I met a hardened yet kind-eyed man with
deep wrinkles and grey hair. He shared with me that he had
been sentenced as an adult for crimes he had committed at
around eighteen years old. He was now preparing to celebrate
his forty-fifth birthday. I did the math quickly in my mind. He
had lived longer in federal prison than he had ever lived in
society. His references for the outside world were from the
1970s. He had lived in the prison longer than I had been
alive! How does this happen? He recounted that as a child,
after years of being bounced around the system, not fitting
in anywhere and not really having a family, he had found his
people in a local gang that recruited him. The gang became
the family he had always needed and desired—he belonged to
someone; or in this case, he belonged to something. To secure
his membership within this new family and solidify his place,
as an initiation, he had to commit a heinous crime.

He knew that this crime would likely cost him his life, or
at the very least his freedom. He was well aware of the consequences for his life and also the lives of his victims. Yet the
need for a family was greater. "If I'd had somewhere to walk
to instead, I would have taken that path, but every path in
front of me eventually would lead me here, so I just checked
in sooner so I could get it over with," he said. He was still part
of that gang, or what he called family, both inside and outside
the prison walls. He said that they would help him build a new

life once he was released. He finally had someone looking out for him. He mattered to them, and they mattered to him. He'd made a family. He'd done want he needed to do.

For many of you, this extreme case of finding belonging may seem far outside your realm of experience, yet to stress wisely, we must understand as much as possible about one another to create community. And for so many, the world they have been born into is not kind.

BELONGING FOR WELLNESS

Our deepest desire is to belong—to feel that sense of security and safety that only comes when we are accepted into a community. Although we can develop solitary practices to lean into wellness, to be fully well, we need one another in some capacity. In psychology, we talk about this as empathic attunement. Empathic attunement is that moment when you connect so organically and authentically that you feel truly seen. You and your experience matter deeply to another, or someone finally gets you. You are seen, heard, and respected. You realize that you are not alone.

Recently I wrote an article for International Women's Day (IWD). I shared my frustrations with the competing systems of pressure on women both professionally and personally. I shared candidly about how when I was working in the university setting, as a scholar, I felt like I was supposed to work as though I didn't have a family. And in my personal life, I felt like I was supposed to raise my children as though I didn't work outside the home. If I needed to leave work because the daycare called and my child was sick and needed to be picked up, my boss would ask if someone else could pick them up or ask why my baby was always sick. And in my social group, the pressure to be making homemade, organic baby food and to attend every play group as critical markers for my child's success was constantly under-communicated but overtly felt. It was a losing battle. The expectations from both sides were too great. I didn't feel like I belonged at work or in my peer group. Yet, when I shared this feeling in that IWD article, women worldwide reached out to me to share similar feelings and experiences. I was not alone. Other caregivers felt the pulls, guilt, and frustration, too.

Parents are not the only ones who feel pressure or exclusion. So many women who are childless by choice share with me the constant onslaught of not fitting in with other people's norms. There is enormous pressure on women to have children, and not to carries ridiculous amounts of stigma and shaming. I think it is cruel that when a man says they don't want children, they are declared a committed and dedicated professional, but when a woman doesn't want children, she is vilified.

The idea here is that we need to find our people—the other people out there who get us and understand us. So often we feel like outsiders. Like there is something wrong with us. There is nothing wrong with you! We all want to belong. We try to fit in the best we can. When we are around the wrong people, it will never feel right. As a therapist once shared with me, "You don't have social anxiety, Robyne, you are hanging out with the wrong people!" That was a knock-you-on-your-ass truth-punch. We need that empathic attunement. That does not make us needy, it means we have needs! Also, knowing that someone has our back in difficult times, even when we may be the one who messed up, is a lifeline for true wellness.

Knowing that you do not have to walk this world alone and knowing who and where to go to for support is one way to stress wisely. To do this community-building work, you have to start with yourself and not just where you are today. You have to understand your origin story. How did you become you?

FROM CRADLE TO GRAVE

Evolutionary psychologists use the expression "cradle to grave" to summarize the need to belong and the bonding with others over the span of a lifetime. It starts from day one. Our evolutionary biology took no chances. We are pre-programmed to imprint on others. For example, when a new mother breastfeeds her baby, the distance from the crook of her arm that cradles the baby's head to her eyes is the exact distance a baby can see. Hence, when a mother is feeding her baby, all the baby can see is her face, which creates a bond. Baby smiles, Mom smiles: the baby now has a protector. And for Mom, when she sees her baby looking into her eyes, oxytocin is released in her bloodstream. She is bathed in the bonding hormone. Evolution and biology unite to pave a connection that transcends life itself. A mother is always a mother, even after her children have grown. And when mother and child are separated, the phenomenon known as *mizpah* (the Hebrew word for connection, the emotional bond between two people apart) occurs.

Belonging also introduces the feeling of trust. To understand how our earliest experiences inform our internal sense of trust in others, we turn to attachment. Psychologists John Bowlby and Mary Ainsworth studied the connection between a child and their parent and came up with "attachment theory." They concluded that the attachment style we embody in infancy carries us from our earliest days to our death.

Relationships with others are crucial for our physical, social, and moral development. Researchers have devoted their lives to explaining how our different attachment styles affect us across our lifespan.

Once we have established trust and a bond to secure our survival, we can start exploring the big world around us. As we grow, we start building wider social nets and forming connections within larger communities. With exposure to the bigger world, we start to adopt roles that inform our identity. Ideally, the roles we play serve us well, but this is not always the case. Even before toddlerhood, we start developing an internal script that tells us a story of who we are and where we fit in. As school-aged children, we decide on a label, perhaps of our own choosing, but often from someone else. This label could be "I am a good student" or "I am athletic." We test out our labels in a relatively conscious state at first. Yet over time, the more we hear labels, the quicker we internalize them without testing them first. If a sibling always tells you that they are the favourite child, you eventually believe them. Or if you are constantly told that you are too emotional, you internalize that label, and every time you experience emotion, it reinforces a negative belief about being a person who feels deeply, as if that is something bad. Regardless of whether it is a positive or negative label, eventually that label moves from the conscious to the subconscious, resulting in the embodied belief that it defines who we are. This could serve us well (as in, "I am lovable and worthy"), or it can serve us poorly ("I am unlovable and broken").

Take a moment to reflect on the labels you have used or been given to define who you are and who you are not. Please know that this is heart work. Meet your insights with compassion, grace, and patience. We have always been trying to do the best we can, in the moment, with our situations. All of us serve a purpose.

RELATIONSHIP TAX

I invite you to list all your roles and the communities you are already a part of. For me, I am a mother, a daughter, a wife, an educator, a scholar, a redhead, a descendant of Scottish immigrants, a pet parent, a teammate, a leader, an entrepreneur, a philanthropist, an author—the list could go on almost endlessly. Now, for each of your roles, think about the expectations, norms, and labour that it requires. You might need a bigger piece of paper for this!

When we take a deep look at all this, we can see clearly why we are so overwhelmed. Not only does each of our roles and communities have a set of rules and expectations, but many of them also have conflicting rules or standards. The visible and invisible pressures require our attention. Holding multiple and sweeping roles can protect us by giving us a sense of safety and connection; however, it is paramount that you are aware of the emotional cost associated with each role.

Are these roles mutually beneficial? Are they helping you become your most authentic self? What is the relationship tax for each role? The need for belonging can easily pull us away from our true self. We start changing who we truly are as an attempt to belong. Fitting in is when we shift for the purpose of being accepted by the group. Often our unconscious urges us to buy certain things, talk about particular topics, or acquire status objects that will garner respect, all in an attempt to fit in. Society also sends us messaging that, to be happy and successful, we need an army of people, a squad, a giant friend network. Although it does take a village to raise a child, the size of that village is up for discussion. Having a small, consistent, emotionally available group of people who are true allies is optimal compared to having a large gaggle of people you stress yourself to death trying to impress.

Stressing wisely here is taking an inventory of the people in your life, your roles, and your communities and ensuring that you are in equal partnerships. Several people who I have done this work alongside express that it can feel selfish at first to evaluate relationships in this way. Yet, once they start doing the "relationship tax exercise," they see that certain relationships or communities are depleting their resources so greatly that it is preventing them from truly showing up for the people who matter most to them.

We are so replaceable in almost every role in our lives. Be sure to protect, nurture, and honour the roles in which you are irreplaceable. And I am not referring only or specifically to biological family. Struggling with maladaptive family relation-ships can be the biggest stressor in many people's lives. But we can reframe by recognizing who is "family" and who are our "relatives." Family are your ride-or-die people, blood or chosen. Relatives are people with whom you share a common history, and you acknowledge them at a safe distance from which you can still feel healthy and whole. Now, I wouldn't recommend letting your relations know that you have sorted them this way! This tool is for you. Once you have those rela-tives in that boundary, your expectations for them can be set and maintained. You don't expect them to meet your emo-tional needs because those people are not your family. Doing this helps maintain and protect your peace. Navigating family systems is complex work. If this is an area that you need to nurture, I highly recommend connecting with a professional who specializes in Internal Family Systems work. It can be a game changer.

Our roles serve as avenues to belonging, yet they can also generate distress. We will never be able to know enough, love enough, or work hard enough to create belonging with people who are not available to us. To stress wisely we need to understand how to work in sync with the reality of our connections. This may unleash grief. We may need to grieve the roles we had hoped for but that are not possible at this time. The grief is evidence that these roles are important to us. And just because we may not have these roles, connections, and relationships right now, creating systems of love, support, and meaningfulness is possible as we move forward.

STRESS WISELY FOR CONNECTION AND COMMUNITY

Making new friends is relatively straightforward for many children. They are in a shared environment, like a playground. One child asks another child their name. Maybe how old they are, or if they like dogs. And then, ta-dah: they are instant friends.

As adults, making friends and connections is hard. I see the evidence of this often with sports families. I have witnessed adults who cry when their child is cut from a team. The parents are devastated for their child, yes, but mainly because the other parents are their friend circle. In parenthood, our sense of community usually comes from our children's worlds. For others, leaving a job may mean losing their work family or their social life. So, where do we go to find connection outside these social networks?

Because true belonging
only happens when we
present our authentic, imperfect
selves to the world, our sense
of belonging can never
be greater than our
level of self-acceptance.

DR. BRENÉ BROWN

Connecting and belonging in adulthood needs to start with your relationship with yourself, then your relationship with others, followed by your relationship with the broader world. Many resources, websites, and even apps for finding friends—such as Bumble BFF, Hey! VINA, and even PawDate—are simply amazing tools. Technology for good! Since these already exist, I want to offer another tool to help you seek clarity about who you are and how *you* want to be part of a community. Let me introduce one of my favourite tools: signature strengths.

SIGNATURE STRENGTHS

Signature strengths is a values-based self-discovery approach. Our values make up who we are and what we are all about. Living within our values is how we align with our truest versions of ourselves, and it allows us the clarity in our relationships to stress wisely. As I say a lot, it is making what matters most matter most.

Unfortunately, the current landscape of our many competing roles is not lending itself to values-based living. Most people struggle in this domain, which leads to overwhelm and burnout. At the heart of burnout is a deep experience of depletion. Time spent outside our values hurts us physically and psychologically and ultimately diminishes how we perform.

When we align with our values, we become accountable. We own how we show up and how we work. We practise professionalism not because we are told to; rather, because we carry ourselves with respect, emotional intelligence, and confidence. We are willing to explore new ideas and perspectives different from our own, and to accept challenges as learning opportunities. We live an inspired life and value trust, honesty, authenticity, and care. We need to ensure we build connections that do not run deficits. Enter signature strengths.

When thinking about how we cultivate values-based living, we rarely think about using our strengths. We have been conditioned to use a skill deficit approach to problem solving. Yet, here lies the key to unlocking values-based behaviours: use what you have and be who you truly are! According to Drs. Ryan Niemiec and Robert McGrath, a strengths-based approach to changing our behaviours leverages our inner capacities and character strengths that are unique to us.[3] When we are using our signature strengths, we can then be part of communities that reinforce and support our true selves.

Drs. Christopher Peterson and Martin Seligman explain that signature strengths have three key features:[4]

- **Essential:** The strength feels essential to who you are as a person.

- **Effortless:** When you enact the strength, you feel like you are tapping into something natural. There is an ease, deep familiarity, and even comfort.

- **Energizing:** Using the strength uplifts you and leaves you feeling authentic, purpose driven, and present. Your sense of balance and steadiness allows you to show up in your life more ready and able.

The table that follows shows some examples of signature strengths based on the work of Peterson and Seligman, with my prompts for understanding and application.

Signature Strength	Understanding and Application
Curiosity	**I have an inquisitive sense about the world.** You meet challenges with openness and a willingness to think about what is possible. You are eager to learn and understand.
Practicality	**I can see things in their basic form.** You can break things down in manageable and processable pieces. You have clarity for needed sequences using facts and fundamentals.
Social intelligence	**I can readily connect with others and engage and am socially aware.** You are able to read the room and you understand impacts, people, and situations with ease and accuracy.
Perspective	**I can use my lived experience to inform how I see the world.** You can hold multiple perspectives and readily zoom in and zoom out, and you can see the big picture.
Bravery	**I can move forward in uncertainty.** You can function with high degrees of discomfort and have the courage to act.
Perseverance	**I can steady myself and persist through challenges.** You can embrace the uncomfortable and manage setbacks while also recognizing when to move on, let go, or course correct.
Integrity	**I live within my values and stand for the greatest good.** You are guided by a strong moral compass, value system, and set of standards for behaviour and thoughts.
Kindness and generosity	**I readily help those in need.** You can share resources, energy, and time with ease, accompanied with a deep commitment to compassion and tender-heartedness.

Lovingness	**I readily give and receive love.** You have a remarkable ability to share affection and radical acceptance of others and self.
Loyalty	**I stand united with those who I have given my trust to.** You can hold a steadfast devotion to people, causes, and values in an adaptive and healthy manner.
Equity	**I readily treat all people equally.** You operate with a keen understanding of social justice, inclusion, diversity, and equity.
Leadership	**I can readily lead others to meet collective goals.** You can generate followership and support others as they accomplish their goals. You operate for the mission and the people.
Self-control and self-awareness	**I can self-regulate.** You have a keen understanding of your own sense of self and can operate within your personal standards.
Humility	**I practise being humble or modest.** You operate from a genuine place of reverence for your opportunities and skills while holding a recognition for your lived experience in relation to others.
Wonder	**I appreciate and savour moments of wonder and awe.** You have a remarkable ability to see and experience the extraordinary in the ordinary. You can hold space for the mysteries of life.
Hope	**I readily practise living filled with hope.** You operate from a deep knowing that all will be well, inspired by trusting yourself, others, and the world.
Spirituality and faith	**I live and practise by a divine or higher purpose.** You lean into an awareness of and reverence for forces greater than the individual and strive to align with spiritual values and teachings.

Playfulness and humour	**I readily bring merriment and joy into my days and the days of others.** You operate with an air of ease, youthfulness, and cheerfulness that enhances the mood of the community.
Passion and enthusiasm	**I live engaged, inspired, and with energy flowing.** You operate from an energy-inspired state that motivates deep engagement and zest.

These examples are just a selection of key signature strengths that you can use to understand your place, space, and natural traits as a community member. I truly believe that every person has skills and talents. Often when we embrace our gifts, we discover our signature strengths.

So, let's tie this all together. For you to create, foster, and nurture your communities and relationships, I invite you to use your signature strengths to find your people. Think of how your signature strengths can be part of community. Where are these gifts shareable? Who could benefit the most from your wisdom? What situations or environments will let your signature strengths grow? Our signature strengths are our gifts to be shared with the world. They help us know a very special ingredient of who we are; we benefit from this, then we can share it generously with others. This sharing is a springboard for being of service, which is the greatest stressing-wisely practice within the social realm.

A LIFE OF SERVICE GIVES *YOU* A BETTER LIFE

Being of service to others increases your life expectancy, your health, your well-being, and even your life satisfaction.[5] When we realize that we can be of service to others, our sense of connection to the world around us yields benefits that outweigh our own output. Physiologically we change by helping others. Researchers at University of British Columbia showed that when people were given forty dollars to spend and half were instructed to spend it on themselves and the other half to spend it on others, weeks afterward, those who spent the money on others had a significant decrease in their blood pressure that compared to starting an exercise program or healthier eating practices.[6]

Another researcher, author, and social change leader, Allan Luks, spent his lifetime studying what he called the healing power of doing good. He reported that being of service and helping others enormously benefits the person helping, such as strengthening immune system activity, decreasing intensity and awareness of physical pain, activating positive emotions that support well-being, reducing negative attitudes that deplete well-being, and enhancing the functioning of various body systems.[7] Luks wrote about the "helper's high": "Helpers experience a high similar to that of a runner following a workout. After helping someone, the helper's body releases endorphins, brain chemicals that reduce pain and increase euphoria. This creates a rush of elation followed by a period of calm." There is evidence that helpers can re-experience this high by remembering their altruistic acts long after they take place.[8]

The benefits of being of service are remarkable, and with all good things, moderation and intention are equally important. One gentle awareness note I would offer here is to know why you are doing what you are doing. Are you being of service because of your "disease to please"? There is a difference between helping others and trying to please others. Are you doing it for ulterior motives? Or perhaps you may be feeling pressured, or even resentful. Can you be of service while also managing your own needs? It is important that you feel good and be well, apart from helping others or being of service, too.

True altruism can provide a sense of meaning, direction, and purposefulness to your life. The important idea here is that you also look after yourself and understand how your origin story affects how you show up for others and yourself.

THE SAILBOAT

Being part of a community is such an important component to our well-being that Abraham Maslow categorized belonging immediately following essentials like food and safety. The Maslow hierarchy of needs is a well-known theory that helps us understand what we need to survive, and it is often represented as a pyramid. I would like to share a different take on the pyramid: the Sailboat of Needs introduced by Scott Barry Kaufman.

The Sailboat of Needs

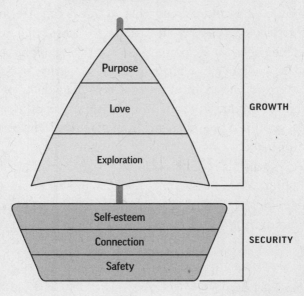

Source: Scott Barry Kaufman

The idea here is that life is not a climb to the summit, as the pyramid suggests. Life is meant to be an experience, not a competition or race. Kaufman proposes this:

> It's more like a vast ocean, full of new opportunities for meaning and discovery but also danger and uncertainty. In this choppy surf, a pyramid is of little use. What we really need is something more flexible and functional: a sailboat. With holes in your boat, you can't go anywhere. All of your energy and focus is directed toward increasing the stability of the boat. The human needs that comprise the boat are safety, connection, and self-esteem—security needs that, under good conditions, work together toward greater stability.[9]

There will be times in our lives when we need to focus on us, our own sense of security. And to experience that, we will need connections with others. When our foundation is solid, we then have the spaciousness to experience growth. Humanist psychologists refer to this as transcendence, which is when we move from our own experience to helping others, loving others, and finding our true purpose or calling. (Small side note: You can have more than one purpose or calling, and these can change over time.)

I like thinking of all of us wee sailboats doing our best to navigate the adventures of life. Now, it is true that some may be yachts, some are dinghies, and others may be floating pieces of driftwood. And some people are staying afloat because of a life ring a stranger threw to them. I also imagine some of us are on calm waters, others are in storms; some are lost at sea, and others are just coming safely into harbour after a long journey. Nevertheless, we all are somewhere on the water, doing the best we can.

FINAL THOUGHTS ON COMMUNITY

Stressing wisely requires us to build and nurture our relationships and community. Societies thrive when people connect with one another and then expand beyond personal achievements and individual successes to the greater good for the benefit of all. This unity and commitment to one another matters. And as the amazing scholar and author Dr. Margaret Wheatley explains, "Whatever the problem, community is the answer."[10]

There is a place for you here.

"

The soil is the great
connector of our lives, the source
and destination of all.

WENDELL BERRY

CHAPTER 9

OUR WORLD

T HE PLANET IS DYING faster than we thought. This scientific fact was presented in the paper titled "Underestimating the Challenges of Avoiding a Ghastly Future," published in the *Frontiers in Conservation Science*, by a collection of the world's leading scientists.[1] In our conversation about stressing wisely, this feels like a showstopper, a career-ending injury, or Armageddon, and not the Bruce Willis feel-good kind.

"What's the point?" a second-year university student asked me when we were talking about teaching eco-stewardship and climate change to children. My student was distressed by the current realities of a hurting planet. We all should be. The truth is right in front of us. We know our earth is in danger. Biologist Jonas Salk explained that humans alone are responsible for killing our planet. He noted that if all the insects were to disappear from the earth, within fifty years all life on earth would end. If all humans disappeared, within fifty years the world could heal itself.[2]

My student, who was a pre-service teacher, felt helpless and even hopeless in the face of what he called an inevitable mass extinction. Several students were noticeably uncomfortable about this doomsday forecast. From the back row, "God, just don't think about it," said one student. "Don't have kids," came from elsewhere. "Can we just get back to the curriculum?" pleaded another student who was cheered by several classmates.

ECOLOGICAL GRIEF

When thinking about the state of our planet, people exercise many different approaches to addressing it. Some are consumed with what is known as environmental or ecological grief. Ecological grief is defined by Drs. Ashlee Cunsolo and Neville Ellis as the grief felt in response to climate change–related losses of valued species, ecosystems, and meaningful landscapes.[3] This includes

- **physical ecological losses:** physical disappearance, degradation, or death of species, ecosystems, and landscapes;

- **loss of environmental knowledge:** identity, community, and cultures that are connected directly to the environment; and

- **anticipated future losses:** future loss and destruction.

These are real feelings of loss, overwhelm, fear, anxiety, and even rage about the world. People also wonder about their futures. A poll conducted in 2019 by *Business Insider* found that 38 per cent of people surveyed between the ages of eighteen and twenty-nine considered climate change when deciding to have children.[4] Several of the university students in my class that day echoed these findings. "Why on earth would anyone bring children into this world?" lamented a student in the front row.

You may wonder where the suggestion of not having children to save the planet comes from. The theory is that fewer children will produce less greenhouse gas and reduce the draw on resources. And many like my student are concerned about what the future will be like for the children of their generation. Scientists Seth Wynes and Kimberly Nicholas recommended this in a study: "We have identified four recommended actions which we believe to be especially effective in reducing an individual's greenhouse gas emissions: having one fewer child, living car-free, avoiding airplane travel, and eating a plant-based diet."[5] Dr. Nicholas later said in an interview with the *Future Perfect* podcast that if you do still want kids, go ahead; we need better solutions to addressing greenhouse gas emissions this decade.[6] Gosh, global environmental stress is real, and what we can do about it is equally stressful!

Some people find the topic of climate change so upsetting that they avoid or deny it altogether, while others recognize it but note it is not a priority for them or they cannot afford to do anything about it. We are not programmed to take future threats as seriously as immediate threats. One student shared that they cannot worry about the planet when they are so busy trying to make rent. Another student explained that it is too expensive to buy things produced ethically. I then heard the final comment: "What difference can one person make anyhow?" I know very well the answer to that question. One person can save your life. One person can also change the way you see the world.

ONE PERSON'S CARE IS CONTAGIOUS

I had the honour of working with Dr. Dan Longboat, a Turtle Clan member of the Mohawk Nation and a citizen of the Rotinonshón:ni (Haudenosaunee—People of the Longhouse), during my time at Trent University, and every encounter with him, both big and small, gifted a lesson to me. He once shared a story about an elderly man who came upon a group of teenagers sitting in the back of a pickup truck, drinking and carrying on. The elderly man noticed they were throwing their garbage on the ground. Without saying a word, he walked gingerly over to his own truck, pulled out a plastic bag, and started collecting the garbage. One teenager noticed, mocked him, and questioned if he was so poor that he needed to collect empty cans. The elderly man smiled, said nothing, and continued picking up the garbage. The teens continued to laugh and tease him, yet the man never faltered.

His actions then stirred something deep in the heart of one of the teenagers. The teen told his friends to knock it off, jumped down, and started to help the older man. The taunting now was directed at the teen helping, but he and the man ignored it. Once all the garbage was removed from the immediate area, without saying a word, the elderly man and his new helper moved to another section of the park. Time passed and another teen joined them, followed by another. Eventually, all the teens joined the community effort, and within a short time the entire park was cleared of garbage. The teens helped the man bring the bags back to his truck. Through tired eyes, he smiled at the teens and drove away without saying a word. Sometimes the most powerful lessons are not spoken.

WE ARE PART OF NATURE

Learning from my Indigenous friends who have shared generously many of their ways of knowing and caring for the land has radically improved my hope for the future. Indigenous communities have a wealth of knowledge about how to care for, respect, and work with the lands. I wish more would listen to this wisdom. Indigenous ways of knowing can support climate change mitigation and adaptation more effectively. Julian Brave NoiseCat is a writer and advocate for Indigenous people, a member of the Secwépemc First Nation, and a descendant of the Líl'wat Nation of Mount Currie of British Columbia. Brave NoiseCat explains that one of the monumental differences between Indigenous and non-Indigenous culture is that Indigenous people know they are part of the land. Western culture believes people can "exploit and extract from nature because we are seen as a separate from it."[7]

Brave NoiseCat says that in the fast-paced industrial world, people don't realize they are in a relationship with the natural world. "An attachment to place and respect of a place and where you are in the environment, in the natural world, creates an imperative to defend and protect and preserve those places," he said in an interview with CNBC.[8] He talks about the importance of respecting and honouring the land while recognizing the reciprocal relationship and season of all things. Seeing our place within nature and holding compassion for all things is the first step in protecting the lands. After hearing Julian Brave NoiseCat speak, I wondered, How can we practise compassion for nature, like trees and wildlife, when people struggle to show empathy for our own colleagues at work? Yet, it can be done. I was reminded of this by a local educator who specializes in outdoor education. If you want kids to care about nature, they have to first be in nature!

To stress wisely, we need to have conversations about eco-stewardship and our impact on the physical world around us. I recall reading once that to feel hopeless about major social issues is to be uninformed. We can take actions, big and small, to address wicked problems like climate change. Climate psychologist Dr. Renée Lertzman, who refers to herself as kind of like an existential fixer, which I just love, says that neither polarizing view about climate change will help. "The doom-and-gloom-versus-hope dichotomy or binary is false... In actuality, the path forward is a middle path. And that middle path is one of authenticity."[9] Validate the feelings of overwhelm while also doing your part by finding actions that are within your control. All actions matter.

INSIDE WORLDS

Take a moment to check out your surroundings. How does your space make you feel? I have long told my children that a clean house makes me a better parent. When things are out of place and disorganized, my stress level rises. When my space is tidy, I have a deep sense of ease, peacefulness, and for some odd reason holiness! I know, right... clearly, in my formative years I heard that cleanliness had something to do with godliness. When my space is a mess, my thinking is a mess. When I clean up my space, my moodiness is simultaneously being cleaned up, too. This trait doesn't seem to be genetic. Exhibit A: Teenagers' bedrooms. Exhibit B: Teenagers' backpacks. I haven't appeared to pass the clean-and-organized gene to the children, yet all three, even as teenagers, agree that they love it when I clean their rooms. "Yes, you are right, Mama, this feels amazing. I bet I will even sleep better tonight and not feel as rushed finding my stuff before practice," Jax proclaimed while flopping on his bed after I had spent the afternoon cleaning his room. Jax knows the power of positive reinforcement. "Mama, you are probably the best cleaner and organizer ever. I don't think other kids get to know what it feels like to have such a great room, tidied with such care." I smiled back at Jax; apparently, words of affirmation were my love language that day (yes, my love language changes daily). Grateful words from my teenage boy made my heart smile. I asked him if he planned on keeping his room this way. A pause. We both laughed out loud as he smiled and winced ever so slightly. "Not likely, Mama, but don't let that discourage you. You are always welcome to clean and organize because I know it makes you feel better and happy, and seeing you happy makes me happy."

Plenty of research supports the idea that the need for organized spaces is critical for some of us. Researcher Dr. NiCole Keith from Indiana University discovered that there was an association between a clean house and a person's health and activity levels.[10] In a study I have referenced often to my own children, Drs. Darby Saxbe and Rena Repetti found that how a woman perceives her home is correlated with her daily mood patterns and cortisol levels. Women who described their home as "cluttered" or had "unfinished housework" were more likely to experience fatigue and depression compared to women who reported their home as "restful" or "restorative." The study also found that women with cluttered homes had higher levels of cortisol.[11] And researchers have found that 73 per cent of people reported having a better sleep in a made bed with clean sheets.[12] I have spoken with several

professionals who admitted that they would work late sometimes just to avoid household responsibilities. Others have
shared that they avoid social visits because the state of their
home creates feelings of guilt (*I should be more organized*) and
shame (*My home life is embarrassing*). People have also shared
with me that the general level of untidiness is their greatest
cause of anxiety and frustration. My friend, our space matters.

SHALL WE MARIE KONDO?

The work of Marie Kondo, author of *The Life-Changing Magic
of Tidying Up*, made its way into the mainstream in 2014. It
seemed like decluttering was in contention to become an
Olympic sport, and Marie Kondo was the ultimate coach. The
main ideas behind her approach are quite simple but definitely started a cleaning and decluttering revolution. There
are six guiding principles:[13]

1   Commit yourself to tidying up.

2   Imagine your ideal lifestyle.

3   Finish discarding first (let go of things you don't need or
love).

4   Tidy by category, not by location.

5   Declutter in order: clothes, books, papers, tools and trin-
kets, and sentimental items.

6   To decide what to keep, ask yourself, "Does this spark joy?"

Although a decluttered and organized space is very important for many of us, for some, clutter does not create additional anxiety or stress. So, for those of you not affected by your environment, that's great, you can skip this part. However, it is helpful to understand that, for people you share a space with who are affected by clutter, it is a challenge. And calling us clean freaks, Type A, OCD, and any other name meant to label our need for order is not helpful or generally welcomed.

As a person with ADHD, I have had this conversation with many people—friends, co-workers, loved ones, and family. When things are out of place, it takes me twice as much energy to listen, be present, or follow along. Unfortunately, the extent of my need to be organized is just surface deep. As long as I cannot see it, it does not affect me. That makes for some pretty packed drawers, closets, and lots and lots of storage containers!

OUR PERSONAL RETREATS

Our physical environment affects our wellness both consciously and unconsciously. Dr. Esther Sternberg, a medical doctor and author of the book *Healing Spaces*, explains that physical health is impacted by spaces and places.[14] She brilliantly describes how we can use our physical environment to promote wellness and even healing. For example, when we look at a beautiful view or picture, our brain releases oxytocin. It makes us feel good, promotes a sense of peacefulness, and can encourage healing. Dr. Sternberg has used her research to promote using art, specifically pictures of nature, in hospitals, to the extraordinary benefit of patients and staff. So, what kinds of things can you incorporate in your space to create healing? Here are a few grab-and-go ideas:

- **Bring in the outside:** You might like plants, open windows, light, pictures of nature or scenery, or flowers.

- **Use colours:** Use paint or decorative pieces that evoke a positive response in you. You don't have to stick with neutrals or earth tones if sky blue excites you or dark colours soothe you.

- **Decorate for personal meaning:** Display what makes you feel connection and fondness, such as pictures of loved ones, spiritual symbols, or meaningful objects.

- **Create an area of refuge:** This can be even a tiny corner with things that bring you comfort and a sense of safety. You are never too old to have a blanket fort, or at least a cozy blanket artistically displayed away from the outside world.

- **Activate the senses:** Candles, cozy things, and even water like a little fountain can help create a sense of escape and calm.

- **Sound:** Use music or white noise to create the desired feeling in your space.

- **Lighting:** Place accent lights, dimmer switches, mood lighting, and anything that can soften or shift the feel of a room.

WORKSPACES FOR PRODUCTIVITY

Our spaces are related to how we feel, and having the right spaces is a way of stressing wisely. When I work with high performers, I am curious about not only how they do their work, but also where they work. An office setup or workspace that is well organized for you can play a significant role in your productivity. A good setup promotes feelings of control and competence, which is helpful for productivity. The right setup and processes can also defend you against distractions.

Now, before I jump into the next list, I encourage professionals to be sure that their thirty-plus-year career isn't entombed in their office spaces. I remember an extremely successful lawyer who shared that they stayed too many years in a dysfunctional law firm, even though it was creating burnout, because they couldn't imagine trying to empty their office! I have heard teachers say similar things. They passed on a transfer to a better school because they didn't have enough energy to clean their classroom. Avoiding work usually results in more work eventually. Okay, so here are some key ideas that have been shared with me:

- **Have a non-computer workspace:** Although many careers have us on computers most of the day, we need a designated workspace or surface without a machine so we can do other things. Have a computer zone and a writing/ thinking zone.

- **Keep as few supplies as possible:** Make a list of the things you need on your desk or within reach. Everything else, remove or store separately.

- **Have a large recycling bucket:** Most people start piles when there is nowhere else for things to go. Reduce when you can, and recycle it once you are done with it.

- **Have a plant:** You need a visual reminder of nature and life beyond the ninety-degree angles of your work life. (Zoom meetings, screens, papers, reports, computers, books—we have a lot of ninety-degree angles in our workdays.)

- **Keep a "what matters most" reminder:** Keeping close a picture of what or who matters most to you is a must.

- **Post a values statement:** Knowing what you stand for and who you are is essential to keep in your line of sight. I have Theodore Roosevelt's "Man in the Arena" speech as a framed picture, along with Halbert L. Dunn's opening remarks on wellness, which I shared in chapter 4. When feedback or comments come in, I know where to look, very quickly!

- **Build in anything that promotes movement:** Having moveable furniture, wobbly chairs, stand-up options, or a cordless skipping rope for in between meetings can all help. As the saying goes, sitting is the new smoking.

Thus far in this chapter we have taken a massive, zoomed-out look at our planet and then a tight, zoomed-in look at our spaces both personal and professional. Next, I am eager to share with you another aspect of stressing wisely in our environments: the role of nature and the invitation to play.

STRESS WISELY FOR ENVIRONMENTAL WELLNESS

Every season brings about its own mosaic of elements working in harmony. In North America, the fall welcomes in the cooler air, and the leaves transform into beautiful shades of red, orange, and yellow. People gather and celebrate the previous seasons' efforts with harvest festivities. Winter tucks everyone away as the cold weather blankets our lives. We bundle up. We turn inward. We are restored by the rest as we anxiously await the spring. Spring is the season of renewal.

We awaken from the long winter days and welcome the freshness of new beginnings. And then we meet summer. Gosh, I love the seasons in Canada. Mother Nature's canvas.

WE ALL NEED SOME SUMMER (EVEN IN WINTER)

After long seasons of darkness, both figuratively and relatively, we all need some summer. Summer represents more freedom and less structure. There is a marked shift when the weather loosens its grip on us. I love that first warm day in the spring when the winter heaviness and ache lifts. We may not have even realized we were still carrying those cold days, dark nights, and deep longings. Summer also promotes play, yet play is something many of us in adulthood have abandoned.

Somewhere between childhood and adulthood, many of us stop playing. As adults, with the competing demands of personal and professional commitments, our leisure time is usually spent "doing." However, just as play is critical for childhood development, adults need to play, too. The research on adult play is convincing. Play fuels creativity, imagination, and problem-solving abilities, which are extremely important for "adulting." The research also reports that adult play relieves stress, improves brain function, boosts mindfulness, improves relationships and connections with others, and keeps us youthful and energized.[15]

WHAT EVER HAPPENED TO RECESS?

Remember recess, that fifteen-minute chunk of time to do nothing? Remember how good it felt to get outside to play for play's sake? Remember counting down the minutes? Recess equalled freedom. And when you did not recess "well," you lost your freedom. I spent many recesses indoors, standing against walls, or walking with teachers. Do you remember when you were a kid and didn't feel the cold or get out of breath quickly? I bet when you were a kid, you weren't counting your steps!

When adult systems take over and consume us, they leave little room for the curiosity, wonder, and magic of childhood, which we know has a correlation with time outdoors. In these new, somewhat more enterprising systems, we become overwhelmed with the need to be productive, accountable, and efficient. We simply do not have time for childhood freedoms, even if we long for them. We understand and, perhaps reluctantly, accept this as a rite of passage into adulthood: the cost of being a grown-up. But life does not have to be that way. It is time to lighten up, be unproductive without guilt, and take back some of your freedom. Recess for adults? Why not? Just imagine what interrupting the workday for fifteen minutes of play each afternoon could do for your health, well-being, and productivity. You may be wondering, *Where do I even start? This sounds like just one more thing I need to fit into my day.* Rest assured, my approach to play is doing less with the right mindset to experience more. So, where do you start? Outside. *Nature.* It is our first playground, a consistent friend, and a wise teacher.

The brilliant, engaging, and thought-provoking scholar Richard Louv writes about nature's power to heal, bond, and build, and how we suffer without it.[16] Outdoor time is essential for physical, cognitive, and emotional well-being. It is a canvas for mindfulness, it builds self-efficacy, and it instills a sense of appreciation and awareness of interconnected systems; it teaches respect culminating in acts of gratitude and eco-stewardship. Research has shown that when we are outdoors, our imagination is activated, instilling a sense of curiosity, wonder, and creativity. Rarely do the best ideas or discoveries happen during meetings or at boardroom tables. They happen outside. Outdoor time also encourages healthy risk taking, which is critical for teaching people how to navigate life's challenges, manage the anxieties that accompany them, and become resilient.

PLAY FOR CONNECTION'S SAKE

We know that play is not just essential for kids; it can be an important source of relaxation and stimulation for adults as well. What is more, for us, play is a gateway to empathy, communication, and relationships.

Play reinforces the ties that bind us together. It also happens to be one of the fastest ways to heal minor relationship stress. When we play together, our moods improve, we feel less stressed, and we drop our grudges and get back into sync. Play is essential to maintaining happy, healthy, and productive communities. People who play together make memories together! I am often asked what can play look like, in nature, if someone is not an "outdoorsy" person. Side note: If you are outdoors, then you are automatically an outdoor person! Here are some examples that I find helpful:

- Personify nature and honour the land. There's no better way to reconnect than to name something, befriend it, and spend time making memories with it.

- Use the outdoors as a gateway to adventure and storytelling.

- Be enterprising. Grow things with a purpose. Plant trees or contribute to your community's garden. Develop your sense of community and eco-stewardship by contributing to your local abundance.

- Play with loose parts. This is a great way to stimulate the imagination and ignite creativity. Loose parts are everywhere in nature: rocks, sand, grass, leaves, sticks, flowers, weeds... the list is endless! Just find things and do something with them. (Unless they are poisonous!)

THE URBAN LIFE CONUNDRUM

There are some barriers to outdoor experiences. Some urban life does not lend itself to outdoor time or play. Blacktop and concrete are the antithesis of green space. NatureHood is Nature Canada's response to the barriers to accessing nature that exist within urban spaces, and the growing disconnection to nature that threatens all of us.[17] It is a program aimed at reconnecting people with nearby nature, and it is a place where people can connect with nature's wonders. NatureHood is in the eye of the beholder. Reframe and reimagine your urban space into your own NatureHood:

- Instead of walking by, next time you are out, notice a tree on your street. Take pleasure in watching it change with the seasons.

- Create your own nature place. Grow something on a rooftop, balcony, or windowsill.

- Reconfigure your personal workspace to include a plant ally and a window with a view of the outdoors.

The bottom line: make nature breaks as simple and routine as possible by bringing nature to you.

APPS TO BRIDGE THE GAPS

Here is an idea: instead of trying to spend less time on your screens, try spending more time outdoors. When we try to reduce anything, we resist. When we add something, we feel rewarded. Time away from our personal devices can be tough, but using the device as a bridge to the outside holds promise. Here are some apps that will help you and your family repurpose those devices as useful tools for engaging in outdoor play:

GROW with Nature Play

This app promotes early childhood development and family health and well-being through outdoor play. It provides parents of children zero to three years of age with age-appropriate activities to do in nature that stimulate curiosity, build confidence, and reinforce family bonds, and set the stage for eco-stewardship later in life.

Nature Passport

This app includes tons of activities to encourage outdoor exploration, discovery, observation, and play for kids aged seven to ten and their families. It includes recording features for videos, photographs, and notes, a journal to catalogue memories, and reward badges for activity completion.

Seek by iNaturalist

This app encourages exploration in nature for families. It works by identifying living organisms like insects, birds, plants, amphibians, and fungi, and allowing you to observe and learn about them in the process.

FINAL THOUGHTS ON OUR WORLD

I recall working with a C-suite professional who shared that they felt as though they were letting down their family because they were not "fun" enough or into playing. If you do not connect with play in the traditional sense, my invitation is to think of play as softening. Can you take off the pressure for a wee while and soften to the ideas of wonder and awe?

When was the last time something took your breath away, when time seemed to stand still, just for that moment, so your senses could take it all in? When do you feel awestruck or mesmerized by the wonder of our world? Many of us are so busy with the constant ebb and flow of our daily lives that the idea of wonder seems distant. Maybe you reserve this notion of truly looking at the world with wonder for when you are travelling or seeing something new. Think about how you can see wonder in the everyday. Sometimes we gloss over the everyday because we believe if we stopped and looked closely at the world, we would not get anything done. Find ease and softness in your schedule to leave room for joy or perhaps even fondness.

Fondness is one of the most underused feelings. Thinking fondly can bring about a complete emotion shift, such as when an old song that you danced to in high school comes on or you find a lost picture of your child when they were young. See if you can find moments that inspire fondness, which can lead to a sense of awe, too. Researcher Dr. Pamela Paresky, author of *A Year of Kindness*, explains that wonder and awe are extremely important to our wellness.[18] Wellness discovered through kindness relates directly to our stressing-wisely practices. She describes wonder as an act of intellectual humility. If we know everything, we cannot experience wonder. We need to adopt a humble outlook and be willing to learn and take care of natural resources. Perhaps this can start by calling them natural "gifts," rather than resources to collect and use for our benefit. We also need to be sure that we are leaving the natural world around us so that there will be enough for those who come after us.

Nature is an awe-inspiring phenomenon. Awe is believed to be a sense of collective engagement and oneness with the world around us. It is how we can find our common threads and links to humanity. It is the tapestry of our lives, the lives of those who have gone before us, and those still to come. When we work with this definition, we can see why these practices are so important. Choosing to view our lives from a higher plane and operating from a deeper sense of consciousness, we can choose our actions with greater care.

Even in the direst situations, with great effort, we can choose where we set our gaze. Nature is always there. As visitors on all lands we travel, and as stewards of the lands we keep, let us recognize the life-giving properties of nature. Find wonder. Be in awe. Our planet needs us. And we need her more.

66

The reward for good
work is more work.

UNKNOWN (AND TOTALLY TRUE!)

CHAPTER 10

OUR ROLES

CIRCLE TIME IN KINDERGARTEN.
  "What does your daddy do, Robyne?"
  "He shoots people."

Gasp...

"What does your mommy do?"

"She makes people better."

My father is a television producer. He has spent most of his career shooting people and places on camera.

My mother was a nurse. She spent her career helping save lives and easing pain.

So, in kindergarten, when I was asked about my parents' occupational pursuits, I wasn't wrong, but I still ended up in the principal's office. While swinging my legs in an over-sized chair, looking down at my dirty knees and grass-stained shoes, waiting for the principal to teach me about the "wages of sin and lying" (that was what my teacher told me I was in for), I decided there was not a chance in hell I would ever want to be a teacher.

I graduated from teachers' college in 2006.

WHAT DO YOU DO?

Often when we first meet people, we ask, "What do you do?" Many of us use someone's profession or livelihood to determine their status or the amount of respect they should be afforded. An often-unwritten rule in societies is that if you work in a particular field, you are somehow more valued. Certain roles are more revered. People make quick inferences about you, your personality, your motivation, your values, your ambition, and your general health and life satisfaction based on what you "do." Your work is just one of the things people rapidly judge you for, right up there with your appearance, your voice, what you eat, how you spend your time, and who you spend your time with.

We make decisions about people almost automatically. This does not make us bad people. It is not a moral issue. From a psychological perspective, it speaks to the fact that we are mental misers! We take shortcuts whenever possible to make determinations about people. Now, of course, some people take this too far. Yet, there is a place for quick mental judgements. For example, if you were walking home late at night and a stranger with dark clothing emerged from the shadows and started following you, your "Spidey senses" would be activated. Your body would react to their fast-approaching footsteps. In this scenario, you should use snap judgement. I wouldn't want you to pause and be open minded and lean into good intentions lest you misread the situation. I would want you to act. Cross the street, have your thumb ready to make that emergency call, and get to open and public places as soon as you can. There are real dangers in our world, so knowing how to quickly assess is important. This is another example of how our nervous system keeps us alive and safe. However, this part of our psychology makes us prone to judging people, even about things that don't impact our safety. We are hardwired to make quick assessments, the quicker the better.

According to Dr. Amy Cuddy, a social psychologist from Harvard, when we first meet people, our judging is really seeking two key pieces of information: Is this person trustworthy? And is this someone to be respected?[1] Dr. Cuddy believes that knowing if someone is trustworthy and respectable connects to the dimensions of warmth and competence. We ideally want to be perceived by others as having both. Interestingly, Dr. Cuddy notes that often people emphasize being perceived as smart, competent, and strong, yet this approach can backfire if someone does not believe you are trustworthy and capable of connection.

WHAT ARE YOU GOING TO BE WHEN YOU GROW UP?

In most educational systems, children are asked to pick courses or levels of study as early as elementary school. These decisions inevitably affect their future opportunities, and children are being asked to make them when they haven't even hit puberty, yet somehow, they need to know their future! As I have shared before, my educational experiences, especially in elementary school and high school, were tumultuous. I vividly remember my grade eight teachers telling me that they wished there was a level below basic or trades that I could study, saying that I would never amount to anything and I was wasting everyone's time. I was considered a "throwaway" student. And I believed them.

These memories came flooding back when one of our children came home with recommendations for lower-level entry in high school. Now, the teacher wasn't saying our child was a throwaway like my teachers had. Yet they did claim they lacked "academic potential." They also provided a series of career recommendations, based on a computer program. It was suggested that said child pursue modelling, professional sports, or being a tour guide. I don't think this is necessarily the best approach to supporting our children exploring their futures!

I appreciate that educators have a job to do, and most are doing their very best with the tools, resources, and information they have. But I think it is a very dangerous practice to tell people what they are capable of. You cannot measure potential or loss of potential. In my work, nearly every comeback story I have heard involves at least one person who counted another person out and someone else who came along to challenge that belief. Telling people what they are capable of, or trying to measure their potential, does not stop at elementary school. All through high school, trades, college, university, and even outside of education, people are asked, "What are you going to do?" I remember being asked what I was going to do with my psychology degree. Apparently to this person, a psychology degree wasn't enough to get a job; I would have to go on to graduate studies. So, when they asked me what I was going to do with my degree, I told them I was going to frame it.

I think there are better questions we could be asking children:

- What kind of problems do you want to solve when you are older?

- What gifts do you have that you want to share with the world?

- What communities do you want to be a part of?

- Who or what causes need you the most, and how can you best serve them?

These questions inspire and ignite deeper questions in someone's heart. And pursuing those deeper questions can set us on a journey of discovery. It reminds me of the very last question I asked in my book *Calm Within the Storm*. It was proposed in 1983 by brilliant scientist, artist, visionary, and inventor Buckminster Fuller. Fuller was a revolutionary. He asked the world tough questions, kindly, in the hope of making it a better place for all of us. When I came upon this key question, it was like a battle cry, challenging me to share my theory of everyday resiliency with the world. It was very much the catalyst for writing my first book and this one, too. I believe it serves as an open call to action for all of us: What is my job on the planet? What is it that needs doing that I know something about, that probably won't happen unless I take responsibility for it?

Whatever your work may be, it is likely stress-filled or at least overwhelming at times. Work, inside or outside the home, is just that: work. Work is defined as physical or mental effort or activity directed toward the production or accomplishment of something. An occupation is defined as an activity that serves as one's regular source of livelihood, a vocation. Or an activity engaged in especially as a means of passing time, an avocation. I can't say that I have spent a lot of my adult life in an "avocation"! Yes, time has passed, yet I feel as though I have been working myself to the bone all the while. To explore the realm of stressing wisely as it relates to our work, there are key concepts that can relate to all work. It doesn't matter what you do or how the world sees what you do—these concepts support the well life.

PURPOSEFULNESS

Take a moment to reflect on *all* the career advice you have come upon in your lifetime—the good, the bad, and even the ugly! Here are some I was taught: If you love your job, you will never work a day in your life. Follow your passion. Time gaps are bad for your résumé. Don't quit unless you have something else lined up. Don't career hop. Rework your weaknesses as strengths. You have to pay your dues. Never say no to your boss. Find your why... Perhaps you could add your own here, too.

Reflecting on my own career trajectory, I can tell you most of the advice was not overly helpful and even resulted in me staying too long when jobs had run their course. I recently spoke with a teacher who shared a powerful insight: "I don't need to be reminded of 'why' I went into teaching. I need to understand, 'Why' am I staying?"

Knowing why we do what we do is important, but the reasons need to be deeper than just the surface level. This introduces us to purposefulness, which is the intention behind our actions and how it aligns with our values. Contrary to the idea that we have to love our jobs to be happy, the statement should read that we need to find purpose in what we are "doing" to be content. For example, the single parent who works multiple jobs to support their children doesn't have to love their jobs—they love their kids. If what you are doing puts food your children otherwise would not have on the table, you get up and do it. The nurse comes out of retirement to support the weary health care system through a pandemic. They don't have to love nursing; it is the call to be of service and support their fellow health care professionals. The professional athlete who uses their salary to build schools in their home country doesn't have to love football; they love their people and their country. The idea here is that our work (which we must do) allows us the opportunities to live within our values.

Research shows that our view of purpose even affects the stress associated with the work. For example, your boss calls you at 3 a.m. with a demand. You must respond immediately. How would you feel? Now, let's say your newborn baby wakes you up at 3 a.m. and needs food. Sure, you may feel tired or even a little frustrated since you are desperate for sleep, but how you perceive this interruption from your child is substantially different than a call from your boss. Why? Because of your values. Your role as a parent is different than your occupational roles. Interesting to note, however, that as children age and their demands are not as immediate, the lines start to blur. Many of us start putting the needs of our jobs ahead of our families and even ourselves.

A FACE FULL OF PURPOSE

"Mama, this basketball game after school is super important. I need you there. Please be on time. This matters to me." Hunter held hard eye contact, making sure I heard him. A trait of my ADHD is hyper-focus. I can get so attached to my own thinking inside my head that I might look present, but the information you are sharing with me might not be registering, hence not remembered. Hunter knows me well. He got right in front of me. I saw him. I heard him. I got it. This was important. "Of course, Hunter, I will be there." I smiled as I drove to work that morning because my not-even-remotely-little boy still wanted his mama to be at his game. As soon as I got to the office, I told my office mates that I was heading to my son's game after work.

As my needed departure time approached, I started packing up. A student popped in unexpectedly with one quick question. Someone else needed a signature. Someone else just needed to confirm the details for tomorrow's meeting. A delivery arrived. By the time I was finally at the high school gym, the game was in the fourth quarter. A wave of relief washed over me when I saw there were still eight minutes remaining. Hunter saw me from the court. Gave me a wink. *We are good. Wow! That was a close one*, I said to myself.

As the buzzer signalled the end of the game, the athletes returned to their benches, talked briefly with their coaches, and collected their belongings. Hunter made his way to me in the stands. I was greeted with a huge smile and a hug. I love being a mom to this big guy! Hunter released our embrace, then asked me if I was okay. "Yes, just got tied up for a few minutes at work, but I made it. You played great, Hunter."

Then, with zero ill-will or malice, he asked me, "Have you ever been late for a keynote, a research meeting, to teach, or even a flight?"

"Absolutely not, Hunter. I can't be late for those things."

Hunter nodded, then with sadness in his eyes and his voice he said, "But you can be late for me?"

It is fair to say that moment felt like an emotional two-by-four hitting me in the face. Hunter was right. Although I always claimed the purpose behind my working so hard was ultimately for my children, especially since for a long time I was the sole financial provider for us all, I had lost my way and concurrently my why. In that moment, we forged a new non-negotiable: "If I give you my word that I will be at your event, Hunter, I will be there for the beginning."

I can share with you now, four years later, that I have not missed an event or arrived late when I have committed to being there. I have also ended phone calls abruptly. Left unfinished meetings. Blocked out time in my calendar that accounts for travel. The key difference is that I let people know my stop time in advance, and I honour that non-negotiable as if the relationship between Hunter and me depends on it. Because it does.

MEANING MAKERS

We humans are drawn to making meaning. We struggle in all aspects of our lives when it is devoid of meaning. Things need to make sense. People will go to extraordinary lengths to make sense of things even when there is no sense to be made! We have just talked about purpose, and although "meaning" and "purpose" are often used interchangeably, they are different. Meaning is what we ascribe to something or is conveyed by an action. Meaning is quite personal. Purpose is the reason or motivation behind doing something. Here is an example: "They argued about the meaning of Christmas," versus, "They argued about the purpose of Christmas." Similar but not synonymous. Understanding meaning and meaningfulness in our work is another key insight for stressing wisely.

A study conducted by BetterUp, an amazing company that focuses on peak performance and wellness, found results that lead to remarkable conclusions about the power of meaning and work.[2] Looking at over twenty-five different industries and factoring in a wide range of work environments, company sizes, and demographics, they uncovered several key insights:

- Employees reported their work was as half as meaningful as it could be.

- Nine out of ten employees are willing to trade money for meaning in their jobs.

- Employees who experience meaningfulness in their work stay.

- Employees whose work feels meaningful work longer, take fewer leaves, and have less absenteeism.

- Reported meaningfulness and supportive workplaces were correlated.

- Employees were more satisfied at work and with the company when the job felt meaningful.

It may seem obvious, but having meaningfulness in our work matters. Researchers Catherine Bailey and Adrian Madden from MIT found that meaningfulness was more important to employees than any other aspects of the work, including pay and rewards, promotions, and working conditions.[3] And what was truly remarkable from their research was the role leaders and managers hold in fostering meaningfulness. They made a startling discovery: "Our research showed that quality

Far and away the best prize
that life offers is the chance to
work hard at work worth doing.

THEODORE ROOSEVELT

of leadership received virtually no mention when people described meaningful moments at work... but poor management was the top destroyer of meaningfulness." Drs. Bailey and Madden explain that they anticipated finding clear links between the factors that contributed to meaningfulness and those that eroded them; however, meaningfulness appeared to be increased and decreased by different factors. Leaders did not raise it, per se, but leaders could destroy it quickly. This presents a significant challenge for leadership.

FINDING MEANING IN OUR WORK

From the outside, it seems like certain roles have a quicker jump to meaning; for example, the firefighter who saves lives, the pilot who moves people through space, the social service worker who supports adoptions, or the health care professional who treats our illnesses. During the COVID pandemic, new emphasis was rightfully placed on essential workers, including those who worked in the food supply chain, teachers, frontline health and social services workers, pharmacists, and delivery drivers. Interestingly, if having meaning ought to serve as a buffer to our stress, then these professionals should be immune to burnout! They are doing the good work, and society recognizes them. But despite this, these groups, especially first responders, run the highest risk of occupational burnout and occupational loneliness. How can this be?

According to Dr. Amy Wrzesniewski, a researcher from Yale University, meaning has more to do with how someone *thinks* about their job than the actual job.[4] She found that people equally split into three categories when describing their work: jobs, careers, and vocations. Those who believed their work to be their vocation and described their work as a calling had the highest scores of meaningfulness, regardless of the job they were doing. When people's work is fuelled by their belief, it has a deep instinctual motivation and reward.

This reminds me of the Greek myth of Sisyphus. Zeus punished Sisyphus for escaping death twice by forcing him to roll a massive boulder up a hill, only to have it roll back down every time Sisyphus was close to the top—a task he had to repeat for eternity. I am pretty sure Jax would describe loading and unloading the dishwasher as "Sisyphean"—laborious and futile! Many of the jobs we do may feel like this. Repetition and monotony can turn the tasks of even the most service-driven and meaningful career into a painful exercise. To help understand this in practice, let's take a look at what happened with our pharmacists during the COVID pandemic.

EASING THE BURDEN

Researchers Tauqeer Hussain Mallhi, Aroosa Liaqat, and their colleagues describe how pharmacists are a critical mainstay in public health. Pharmacists can directly or indirectly support patient care in a multitude of ways, including through education, counselling, guidance, medication regulation, management of minor symptoms, infection prevention, and preparation and administration of vaccines. During the pandemic, pharmacists eased the extraordinary burden on health care facilities, yet it came at the cost of their own well-being.[5]

According to a study conducted by researchers Mary Durham, Paul Bush, and Amanda Ball in 2018, over 53 per cent of pharmacists were reporting high scores of burnout using the Maslach Burnout Inventory–Human Services Survey which measures burnout in three key areas: emotional exhaustion, depersonalization, and lack of personal accomplishment. In this study, emotional exhaustion was the most reported symptom.[6] Dr. Mallhi used the same assessment with a different group of pharmacists after COVID-19 was discovered, and over 64 per cent of pharmacists were reporting high levels of burnout. The rise of burnout and compassion fatigue within this population of health care providers needed to be addressed.[7]

Alongside Dr. Calvin Poon and PharmD candidate Nicole Gwiazdowicz, I explored pharmacist burnout.[8] For months, I worked coast to coast to coast learning about the impacts of stress and burnout for these public-health champions. I heard them speak about the joys of being of service to their fellow Canadians and the challenges that came along with being on the front lines. How many times can a pharmacist be asked the same question in one day? Well over a hundred times, reportedly. Imagine trying to do complex cognitive work while being interrupted more than one hundred times to answer the same question. Time on-task is fleeting. The demands are real. And the stakes are as high as they get! From this work, and using the Maslach Burnout Inventory, we asked key questions about workload, control, reward, community, fairness, and values. You can explore these questions, too, because they are generalizable to all of us:

- **Workload:** Are the work requirements within reasonable human limits?

- **Control:** Are there enough areas of your work and how you do your work within your control?

- **Reward:** Are you acknowledged and compensated for your work?

- **Community:** Are there opportunities within the work for community and collaboration?

- **Fairness:** Are the domains of equity, inclusion, and diversity recognized and supported?

- **Values:** Are you able to work in alignment with your personal values?

I discovered that when these six areas were improved, the levels of burnout dramatically decreased. We then took these six areas and developed a recovery plan. Here is how you can reclaim how you do the work.

Workload

Identify your top three daily priorities. Schedule time on-task to complete a task with a deadline. For example, "By the halfway point in my shift, I will have completed two of the three tasks." Use your boundaries to ensure that you can meet this goal. We often overestimate what we can do in a day and underestimate what we can do in an hour when we spend time on-task. Ultimately, your workload needs to be within the scope of your human limits. A friendly reminder: If you have fifteen priorities, you have no priorities. Pick three tasks to complete per day. This adds up to fifteen completed tasks per workweek. That is a great start!

Control

Identify the locus of control. You may not be able to control every aspect of your work, but identifying key areas helps. How can you choose to start your day? What energy are you bringing into your day? Where will you focus today? How will you choose to react? As the magazine editor Walter Anderson reflected, "Although I may not be able to prevent the worst from happening, I am responsible for my attitude toward the inevitable misfortunes that darken life. Bad things do happen; how I respond to them defines my character and the quality of my life. I can choose to sit in perpetual sadness, immobilized by the gravity of my loss, or I can choose to rise from the pain and treasure the most precious gift I have—life itself." [9]

Reward

From a behavioural perspective, if we are not reinforced often enough, it is extremely challenging to continue anything! And if we receive punishment (angry boss, negative feedback, or lack of acknowledgement), it is even more likely we will not be able to continue. You do not require money or food as rewards. Your perspective matters, though. Give yourself time off task, being unproductive without guilt. Be sure to label your behaviour as a reward to deepen the benefits. "I am having this ten-minute stillness break to enjoy my coffee in peace because I am working hard, and I deserve to take time to recharge and replenish." Give yourself daily rewards and long-term rewards.

Community

Collaboration and being part of a team are critical for preventing burnout. You cannot carry the weight of your world alone. Seek connection. Build social capital within your team wherever you can. Build trust and mutual respect, foster cooperation, and acknowledge effort. When people feel connected and share a vision of what their work culture can be, work becomes more sustainable and enjoyable.

Fairness

Ensuring that equity, inclusion, and diversity are authentically practised in all areas of a workplace is crucial for fostering a sense of fairness and respect. We need to create spaces where all people are seen and heard. It is not just about having a seat at the table. It is having a voice, too.

Values

At the heart of burnout is a deep experience with depletion. Time spent outside of our values hurts us both physically and psychologically. Ensure you are building a professional practice that does not cost your relationships, including the one with yourself. Living whole-hearted in every domain of your life is the most powerful defence to combat the celebrated norm of hustling, the praise of exhaustion, and the disease to please others.

Every role in your life will have a certain degree of stress and distress. The big idea here is to recognize what is reasonable and possible. I also appreciate that a workplace that lacks psychological safety—let's say in the form of a difficult boss or colleagues—requires more intervention. You can do all the things I've listed, but if your boss, the environment, or the culture is off, it is going to be exceedingly difficult to stress wisely in your work. My invitation here, inspired by the words of the legendary Arlene Dickinson, is to "know your worth."

CARING FOR CAREGIVERS

With the concepts of work and wellness taking shape, I'd like to look closely at one more group. This group has the most challenging yet rewarding role on the planet: caregiving.

Caregiving has been described as one of the most labour-intensive roles in the world. Whether you're caring for children, parents, a sibling with a developmental disability, or even a neighbour, being responsible for someone's health and well-being requires herculean effort. The visible and invisible labour is almost immeasurable. Yet, people have tried to measure it! Interestingly, an article on Salary.com reported that, if she were paid, a stay-at-home mother's annual salary would be in the neighbourhood of US$184,820 in 2021.[10] Mothers work an estimated 106 hours a week, fifteen hours per day, on average, seven days per week. The skills required—everything from health care provider, driver, advocate, educator, cook, cleaner, and financial planner to holiday planner —are beyond the scope of any other profession. There is no salary for this role, but there are expenses. The cost of raising one child alone, excluding the salary the parent should make, is $240,000 in a lifetime. If you are raising a child with special needs, the estimated cost skyrockets past $2 million.[11] The biggest fear reported by aging people is outliving their money, which is a reality for millions of seniors.[12] As a result, many adults look after their aging parents as well as their children. Caregiving stretches our entire lifespan in some capacity.

We must acknowledge this wicked problem. Our entire economy is built on the backs of caregivers. More than ever we need to re-imagine how we do our work and how our work is valued.

STRESS WISELY FOR OCCUPATIONAL WELLNESS

The phrase most of us know well is "work-life balance," but I prefer "life with work integration" to emphasize that *living* is the priority. Life is the main course; work is one extremely important side dish. We must find healthy ways to include work as one aspect of a multifaceted and full life well lived. Integration builds wellness into our days. Our weekends and evenings are not long enough to try and repair our stressors from work. We need to look after our well-being as we work.

SEEK CLARITY AND CREATE STRUCTURE

Life with work integration rarely just happens. It usually takes concerted effort to structure our lives in a way that works for us. To do this, we need to know what our true priorities are. From here, we can create systems for our workday that ensure our priorities are being met every day.

To begin, ask yourself:

- What are my non-negotiables?

- What is most important to me in my life?

- What are my values?

- If someone were to look at my life, would they be able to tell what my true priorities are?

- What kind of changes do I need to make to put my priorities first?

Once we know what we most value, we can create systems that support more sustainable life with work habits. Here are some key habits that promote life with work integration.

Do one thing at a time

Mono-task rather than multi-task. Work without interruptions, distractions, or multiple things happening at the same time. When interruptions are constant, recognize the impact and quality of focused work. Use your calendar to block time-on-task windows (focused work versus reactive operations). When we are in a constant state of multi-tasking, we burn through our energy stores faster. We also tend to multi-task outside of work, too. This may look like watching your favourite TV show while scrolling on your phone and having a conversation. There is a place for multi-tasking, but be mindful of the effects of making this your go-to state of being in the world!

Take regular breaks

As much as possible, schedule meetings with time in between to get up from your desk, stretch, drink water, and take some deep breaths. Have blocks of time away. Be unavailable, and explore being unproductive without guilt.

Pay yourself first

Establish practices that allow you to tend to your body, head, and heart before opening yourself up to the demands of work. Morning routines and rituals are extremely helpful patterns of behaviour to maintain clarity, intention, and focus.

Simplify the expectations

Carrying the weight of the world with only two hands, while also trying to navigate all the invisible labour, is not optimal or practical. Be mindful about the expectations you are striving for or setting for yourself. When you come upon a rule, standard, or ideal, ask where the belief came from. Who is it meant to serve? How is this belief aligned with your goal of life with work integration? How can you reframe this expectation to include compassion, flexibility, and self-preservation?

Create a joy playbook

What are your go-to behaviours or environments that help you feel better? Keep a running record or log. Add items as you discover them. In a state of distress and overwhelm, remembering things that generate positive emotions is difficult. When you notice you are feeling disconnected, low, or just not sure about your next right move, revisit your playbook. Remember, research shows that remembering things fondly changes our physiology, resulting in a shift in mood and state.

Cultivate calendar wizardry

Use your calendar as a strategic tool for building boundaries, scheduling recovery time, spending time on-task, and setting up other structures that support your wellness and productivity. Remember, as you are entering something in your calendar, if it is not a "hell yeah," perhaps it needs to be a no when that is possible. Or, if you do say yes, be extremely mindful of where you schedule it. An approach I often use when I am struggling to say no is to say, "I am going to pass.

Thank you, though, for thinking of me." "Pass" is easier for the asker to hear than "no."

Match your energy and mood

Often we procrastinate because something important is lacking—understanding, clarity, time, interest, energy. It is extremely hard to motivate yourself through work that is rid- dled with lack. My invitation is to meet the task at hand with a matched mood and energy level. Sometimes, things just need to get done. Try the one-and-done method. Embrace the discomfort of lack and just get that one thing done! But beware of the trap of trying to do multiple one-and-dones in a row. You will lose the motivation because your mind will remember that one-and-done really means just more and more work! Another idea here is to use morning energy as a protected resource. Our morning energy is the most pro- ductive, yet many of us start our day with email, which is an energy and mood drain. Complete just one meaningful task on your list before entering the email vortex. Find times or patterns that increase the likelihood of an energy and mood match.

Cope ahead of time

This is one of my active favourites. If you know you have a long day or a busy night, cope ahead of time. What can you do proactively to make "later" easier and more manageable? Knowing what's for dinner in the morning is so much easier than trying to figure that out at 6 p.m. Plan accordingly! If you know you have a difficult meeting in the afternoon, schedule a walk immediately afterward.

When a situation is
within your control, take action.
When a situation is outside your
control, make preparations.

JAMES CLEAR

Live your values

We need time living within our values to feel like our most authentic and whole-hearted selves. If you value adventure but have not travelled in years, this will start to erode your sense of self. If you want to be a present parent but you have no energy for your child at the end of the day, you feel disconnected with what matters most. Every day, set the intention to do *one* thing that connects you to your values. It can be simple, like reading your child a story, supporting a local business, or even planning a future trip. Keeping top of mind what matters most to you helps maintain perspective.

Know your home team

Knowing who is on your home team is a crucial component of life with work integration. Often, the people who get the brunt of our bad days are those who need us the most. The reality is that we are replaceable in every position, role, or job, except for a few sacred relationships. Protect the relationships you are entrusted with.

FINAL THOUGHTS ON OUR ROLES

No boss, organization, or company can make you well. You need to ensure that you are your own champion and advocate for what you need so you can work in a manner that reflects your most authentic and well self as you do the work.

Most of your adult life will be spent in a working environment or state. Regardless of where it is or what you do, how you spend the majority of your time will affect your well-being. My gentle invitation for you is to notice how your work influences your wellness. Be honest with yourself. You do not have to spend your entire adult life with the Sunday Scaries, fearing going to work on Monday. Nor do you have to miss out on all the things that matter most to you, chasing the promotion or that bigger lifestyle.

Careers are like dates. You don't have to marry the first career that comes along, and being married to your job doesn't have to be a life sentence. Perhaps you can shift your thinking from being a high-achiever to a wide-achiever! Not all career trajectories need to go up—they can expand. Think of a portfolio career versus a linear one. Try new things. When I am asked to give career advice, which makes me cringy, I offer this idea: make your career decisions on knowledge and experience versus assumptions, hearsay, or what other people think. What skills, talents, and gifts do you offer *and* like using? Note the crossovers. Just because you are good at something doesn't make that your necessary vocation.

The biggest step in the right direction for any of our work is that we acknowledge that we are *all* grown-ups! Intelligence in organizations does not run top-down. Responsibilities and pressures also don't run top-down either. Most of us are managing daily lives far more complex than what we do in our professional work. Treat people as competent adults. We are fully formed, and we know how to get the work done. And for the love of all that is holy, let's stop making the reward of doing good work be more work. Let the good work's reward be a deep sense of purposefulness, meaning, and spaciousness to make what matters most matter most in our lives.

66

You will never have enough
of what you don't need.

UNKNOWN

CHAPTER 11

RESOURCES

SCOTLAND. BOTH THIRTY-TWO YEARS OLD, with four children and minimal schooling. Denied immigration for six years.

Then, finally, it happened. They boarded the ss *Montnairn* at Port Glasgow. They sold everything they had for that voyage.

Thirteen dollars. That is how much money the Hanley family, my family, had to build a new life in Canada.

WE DON'T TALK MONEY

The realm of financial wellness is complex because so many of us have been taught not to talk about money. In many families and relationships, discussing money is more taboo than talking about politics, religion, and sex. In a survey Wells Fargo conducted, 44 per cent of people said talking about money was more challenging than talking about death and their funeral wishes with their families.[1] In another survey, people were more comfortable talking with friends and family about marital problems, mental health issues, addictions, race, and differing political views![2] Money is considered too personal a topic. Wow! I would think some of those areas of discussion could also be considered quite personal, but money takes the cake, apparently.

There is absolutely no way to deny that our financial situation influences our health. Research shows that almost 50 per cent of people in developed countries live with constant fear, anxiety, and insecurity about their financial situation.[3] Let's pause there—in developed countries. We know these sobering conditions lead to major health and wellness implications that affect every facet of someone's life. Food shortages and costs, poor living conditions, low compensation for work, and not being able to make ends meet are real social problems in our communities. Despite financial implications being the leading cause of reported stress in North America and financial stress being cited as the leading cause of divorce, we still don't talk about money.

The situations people face daily in so-called developed countries is heart-wrenching and appalling.

Days before Christmas, in Peterborough, Ontario, a community housing complex went up in flames. This was directly across the street from the elementary school all three of our children attended. The fire engulfed the townhouse on the end first. The older children escaped. Their little sister, Ava, who was two years old, did not. She burned to death.

First there was sympathy. The scope of this tragedy rippled through the community. Then it came to light that the mother had not been home during the fire. The blaming ensued. The mother had been working a night shift at a local fast-food restaurant just around the corner. The older children were looking after the toddler. There was a lot of talk about what kind of mother would leave her children alone at night. The blaming, shaming, and judging were relentless. But do you think for a second any mother would want to leave her children alone at night? Instead of pointing a finger at her, could we ask why a mother ever has to make this choice? Why do we as a society allow this to happen? Let's talk about a living wage instead of vilifying those who are doing whatever it takes to feed their kids. There is far more harm in not talking about money and the implications of living in poverty. We need these conversations for our own well-being, but also for the social implications and to address the privilege that some are afforded while others are left behind.

WHY DON'T WE TALK ABOUT MONEY?

We don't talk about money for plenty of reasons. It causes stress. We feel judged. We feel bad if we have a lot of it. We feel bad if we don't have a lot of it. It is considered rude or in poor taste. In relationships, we avoid even more financial topics: opposing attitudes about money and what to do with it; financial infidelity or lying about debts, purchases, or savings; mismatched financial priorities like paying off debt versus saving. Then you can factor in major impulse buys, the inability to compromise on spending, a lack of emergency plans, and trying to maintain independence. Talking or not talking about money is a minefield. And to stress wisely, my friend, we need to start talking about money and understanding the role it plays in our wellness.

This isn't the place for specific recommendations about money, spending, saving, or investing, or any other idea about managing resources. But let's explore relationships— in this case your relationship with resources. Understanding your relationship with your financial situation and resources is how you stress wisely about money.

The reality is that we are already always talking about money, indirectly. We talk about money when we subscribe to a "traditional" life path: go to school, get good grades, attend post-secondary education, get a job, strive for a promotion, save for a down payment, find a responsible partner, get married, start a family. We are talking about money through the clothes we wear, our photos on social media, the cars we drive, and our hobbies. Even being in nature, having access to green space, or the time we have to be in nature is a conversation about money.

Money touches every single aspect of life. But, as the popular CNBC financial analyst Jim Cramer says, "You can graduate college knowing tons about philosophy, the ancient world, or the human body without knowing how to balance your checkbook." We teach children how to measure the surface area of a triangle but not how to do their taxes. We require children to take courses on history and geography but don't teach them about compound interest. Yet money and capitalism permeate everything they will ever do. Not talking about it takes our power away.

Stressing wisely about money reclaims that power. To explore this idea more, let's boldly lean into financial wellness and get real and raw about what we need to be talking about. I promise it is a lot less awkward than you may think! Gentle side note: If you are similar to me, you might already be dismissing this chapter. For a long time, I carried the labels "I am not good with money" and "I am not a money person." I have also gone through seasons of my life when I had so little money that any conversation about it seemed irrelevant. Perhaps you are thinking, "I don't have enough money to even consider financial wellness." Please stick with me. Exploring this realm of wellness could very well be the missing piece to you living your best life.

WHAT'S YOUR MONEY STORY?

Our first step begins with a check-in. What's your money story? We all have a running narrative about money that stems from our childhood, and we do not get to pick our money stories. So, there is no need for shame or judgement. It just is.

Most money stories are complex. If you had a lot of it growing up, that may also have included significant pressures. If you didn't have money growing up, potentially your basic needs were not consistently met. Our money stories are not "all-or-nothing." Take Kevin Durant as an example. Parts of his childhood money story were downright sad, yet through his talents as a basketball player, he worked himself into abundance. While accepting his NBA MVP award in 2014, the Oklahoma City Thunder star basketball player named the real MVP. Through tears, in front of the world, Durant spoke directly to his mother. He recalled the best moment of his life was when he and his brother moved into their first apartment with their single mother, Wanda Pratt. "No bed, no furniture, and we just all sat in the living room and hugged each other, 'cause that's when we all thought we made it. You made us believe we were worth something. Kept us off the street. Put clothes on our backs, food on the table. When you didn't eat, you made sure we ate. You sacrificed for us. You're the real MVP."[4]

Money stories often include parents or guardians not talking about money ever. Some people recall their families always fighting about money. Some remember the power imbalance when one person in the family had complete control of the money. Others carry unnecessary but real shame from living on social assistance or receiving charity, or not consistently having the basics like food or hydro. Sometimes money stories may not be as explicit. You may only remember a parent always working, and as a result they missed important events in your childhood. Perhaps you remember being told money doesn't grow on trees, or "We cannot afford that," or judging harshly those who had money.

There are also neutral or positive money stories. "Although we didn't really talk about money growing up, I don't ever remember going without anything," said one workshop participant. "I remember my mom working harder than most other moms, but it made me feel proud of her. I wanted to be a hard worker like her," said another. "I remember getting money, just a few dollars when my grandparents came to visit, and it was so special."

Our money stories are the foundation of how we think, feel, behave, and talk about money. These stories shape our values and beliefs about money, and we inevitably carry them into our futures. We may carry the money stories from our ancestors, too. My paternal grandfather came to Canada with only thirteen dollars. Back in Scotland, my family had been extremely poor and struggled. They were also proud and very hard-working.

Once the family made their way to Ontario, they settled in Galt, a small town west of Toronto. They did their best, but they still struggled. My grandfather had left school in grade two to support the family. Those kinds of things happened.

He worked every day of his life. Even the day he married my grandmother, he went back to work afterward.

Now, the Hanleys were poor, but my grandmother's family, well, that was a whole other level of struggle. They were trappers. When my grandmother was a young girl, she lived in Quebec. One of the only bright spots for her family was when they had saved enough money to buy a cow. This was a big deal. But sadly, as a young child, Alice, my grandmother, was walking the cow through a field in the winter and went off the path. They ended up on a frozen river, and the cow fell through the ice. She held the rope helplessly as the cow, her family's only consistent source of milk, drowned. Eventually Alice and her family made their way to Galt, too. Her father was chasing work. When my grandfather told his parents that he was going to marry Alice White, they asked why he had chosen to marry the "poorest girl in town."

Despite the challenges, together they built a life. Four children later, my grandmother continued to work outside of the home to help however she could. She was a weaver. She made one dollar a day. Neither of my grandparents finished primary school, yet they raised my father, who was the first person in his family to go to university. My father married Lesley, who was the first woman in her family to go to university. It is not lost on me that my grandmother had less than three years of formal education, yet as her granddaughter, from elementary school to my university pursuits, I spent twenty-four years in formal education, twelve of those years being in university. I have been afforded the privilege of education because of their sacrifices.

Like so many settlers, my family came here on the promises of a better life and improved prospects. Little did they know at the time the implications of settlements for the

Indigenous people. A kind elder once counselled me not to carry settler guilt since my family, too, was once indigenous to somewhere. My family came from the Highlands of Scotland but fled during the Clearances to Glasgow, then eventually to Canada. My ancestors made this life of mine possible. By the strength of their bodies, the humbleness of honest work, and the courage in their hearts, they forged a future for their children and their children's children.

So, you see, our money stories are woven into our DNA.

Knowing your money story is an important step to stressing wisely. Here are a few key reflection questions to prompt your thinking, inspired by the work of Michael Kay, a certified financial planner and president of Financial Life Focus.[5]

1   What did you learn about money from your parents or guardians during your early years?

2   What were some of the common sayings about money in your family?

3   How did those stories affect your beliefs about money?

4   What are you carrying with you today from those early lessons?

5   Do your current beliefs support your values?

6   What would you do differently if you could rewrite your money story?

7   How would a new money story support your wellness?

8   What would support you in building a new money story for you and your family?

Reviewing your reflection, ask yourself, How can I create a money story I would want my children or loved ones to hear and learn?

REAL RECONCILING

I spent a lot of time reconciling the money story I was raised in with my current situation. Every Christmas, there appears a subtle but powerful reminder of my family's humble early years: an orange. That was both my grandfather's and my father's Christmas present when they were growing up. Now our children have come to expect a sprawl of parcels under the tree. I always ensure there is the symbolic orange in the stocking, too. It is my attempt to maintain perspective for the children. My husband, Jeff, can attest to how insistent I am on including those oranges. One Christmas Eve, we were celebrating in Florida, and after leaving midnight Mass, I remembered I'd forgotten the oranges. Now if you had to forget oranges on Christmas Eve, you would think Florida was the right place. Unfortunately not! Not a single store was open. I ended up at a gas station buying a clearance fruit basket that just happened to have three oranges inside.

Reconciling our stories can be challenging. Letting go of some of the old narratives can be difficult. There are so many feelings and memories around money, and most of them are not clear cut. My family came from very humble beginnings, but my needs were met. Yet the lessons my parents followed to make my life possible were riddled with feelings of shortage and scarcity. Money never felt like an overt stressor, yet it kept both my parents working hard. My mother also happened to be the most generous and selfless giver, to her own detriment. She sacrificed everything for her family. I grappled with profound guilt and feelings of unworthiness. I never felt I deserved her outpouring of financial and emotional generosity. In my difficult teenage years, I developed lots of stories about how I was bad and irresponsible with money.

THE POWER OF REWRITING THE STORY

It is quite shocking how long we carry old narratives about ourselves, despite the enormous amounts of current evidence to the contrary. This was obvious for me when Jeff and I decided to co-create a future together. Before we were married, I leaned into my old money stories, specifically about being irresponsible and incapable—and Jeff would have none of it! When I tried to explain that I would need him to manage all of that "financial stuff" in our marriage since I was so inept, my husband reminded me that I had managed an entire household as a single parent for many years with no support. I owned my own home, and every one of the children's needs was met. I had managed it all, plus my student debt, current tuition payments, and everything in between. I did all this while working full time and attending graduate school.

Jeff helped me see that the stories I carried did not match my reality. I may have been telling myself I was not good with money, yet I had managed very well. Of course, that time of my life had not been easy. I felt scarcity, shortage, and deep frustrations that I was doing all of this on my own. I also felt guilty because at times I needed help from my parents. I accepted that I would likely always have to say a little prayer using my debit card, hoping for that "Approved" message.

Fast-forward a decade, during which part of my development was to rewrite my money story. Within a year of leaving the university where I worked and starting my own program, I had the honour, privilege, and joy of running a seven-figure company. At the time of writing, I have a brilliant team who is paid a generous living wage. We follow the principles of life with work integration, and our families always come first. I am very proud of the community we are building, and I am most proud of the philanthropic side of my work. I ventured out on my own to be an instrument of access. I want to reduce the barriers to knowledge. I want to share this work and create the largest and most inclusive classroom possible outside of the academy. And I want to be the instrument who can channel the profits from this work to those who need it most. I dreamed that one day I could work hard enough to provide my family with financial security and then share it with others. I want to be remembered for being a giver, as someone who gave so freely of all her skills, talents, and gifts to help others. At one time in my life, only in my wildest dreams would I have imagined that this would be possible for someone like me. Maybe bold and audacious dreaming is in my DNA, too!

LYNNE TWIST UNTWISTED MY WORLD

For me to come to a place where I could reconcile my relationship with money, I needed an expert who could teach me a new perspective. Now, some of our learnings come from people we have met, while other new insights come from those who have shared their expertise in books. Like many new learnings for me, it started with a quote, which led me to a book, which introduced me to my next teacher, Lynne Twist.

Founder of the Soul of Money Institute, Twist is an expert in the areas of fundraising with integrity, conscious philanthropy, strategic visioning, and creating a healthy relationship with money. Twist introduced me to a crucial concept about financial wellness: scarcity versus sufficiency mindsets. The scarcity mindset believes there is not enough money or resources to go around, so we must hold tight to whatever we have. The classic example of an extreme case of scarcity mindset would be Ebenezer Scrooge from Charles Dickens's *A Christmas Carol*. This Victorian novel tells a cautionary tale of a character trapped in a scarcity mindset. Despite Scrooge's resources, he is a cold-hearted, selfish, and miserable miser, fuelled by fear of lack and the need for self-sufficiency. There would never be enough money in the bank to make him happy and feel safe.

We feel a remarkable pull toward acquiring so that we feel like we have enough, or that deep down we are enough. People with a scarcity mindset also feel jealous of anyone who has "more." They may even believe that those who have "more" should share it with them, regardless of how they came to have it, and even though they themselves don't share with others. Our world and our capitalist ways promote this line of thinking. Marketing and advertisements feed on these feelings of scarcity. Buy this, use this, or trade up, and then you will be fulfilled. The emptiness so many people chase to fill cannot be obtained through objects, yet it seems everywhere we look, "things" are the answer!

The alternative view is a sufficiency mindset. This mindset allows people to believe there is enough money and resources to meet their needs and to go around. Sufficiency beliefs lean heavily into trusting and appreciating what we can do and what we already have. Twist explains that sufficiency is the exquisite experience of "enough." It is knowing that your needs have been met, are met, and will be met consistently and continually. Twist shares that when a person lets go of chasing, that frantic and panicked energy moves out of the way to allow room for feelings of sufficiency. When you pay attention to what you already have, when you take care of it, nourish it, and when you are truly grateful for it—and when you can then share it—it expands. *What you appreciate appreciates.*

Now, let's look at how scarcity sneaks into our lives. It can happen as soon as many of us wake up: "I didn't get enough sleep last night; there is not enough time in the day to get everything done." Or perhaps a new graduate says, "There are not enough opportunities, jobs, or housing options." A parent goes to bed thinking, "I didn't do enough today for my child." Or a leader reflects, "There are not enough human resources to get this work done." It is remarkable how many of us hold beliefs that if we somehow had more, we would be better off. More staff, more money, more time, more understanding, more of anything will help us finally feel better. At the heart of scarcity feelings lies an uncomfortable feeling of deficiency. *Something is wrong with me. I am not enough.* Scarcity thinking also believes that once you get to a particular place or status, when you have the right job or bank statement, then you will feel like you are enough or you are safe. You made it. But the chasing feeling never goes away. The more you acquire, the greater the fear of losing it becomes. More is not always better.

SCARCITY IS IN THE EYE OF THE BEHOLDER

Sufficiency may feel ever elusive, especially if you are swimming in debt, working for a below-living wage, and really don't have "enough" of anything.

In my work, I have travelled to several developing countries, where you might think that the scarcity mindset would be quite prevalent. However, based on what I have seen, I would argue that Western culture struggles more here despite the radical differences in access to resources. I recall one passing conversation that dramatically shifted my understanding of sufficiency.

We were in a remote village in Honduras, literally on the side of a mountain, visiting a one-room schoolhouse. My students and I were bringing supplies that had been donated to the community. We brought school materials, food for the families, and simple medical aid—oh, and of course soccer equipment! Once our work was done, I brought the soccer ball out and invited the children to play with us. One very eager young boy ran up to me, asked for the ball, and took my hand. As we walked out on the rocky and uneven surface, I noticed the boy was not wearing shoes. As a mission worker in Honduras once shared with me, not having shoes is the sign of the greatest possible degree of poverty there.

I noticed the boy had sores and cuts on his feet, which looked like leather. Tenderly I knelt down beside him and said that he probably couldn't play with no shoes and hurt feet. I wished desperately in that moment that I could give him shoes. I scanned the feet of my university students hoping I could replace their shoes, if only a pair could be given to this boy. None would even remotely fit. The boy's smiling eyes met my concerned face, and in Spanish he said, "I can play. I have a ball."

Smiling back at him, I said, "Yes, you have a ball, but no shoes."

The boy laughed, furrowed his brow, and shook his head, saying, "Why say that? Why look at what I don't have when I have this?" He held up the cleanest, shiniest, whitest soccer ball in his dusty little hands. The colour contrast was as striking as my misguided beliefs. This child had known hunger. He also had known pain. Yet, it seemed to me that he did not know lack, at least not in that moment. When you focus on what you have versus what you don't have, you very well may find yourself in a place of abundance. This wee boy, who was an orphan, living in a remote village with his auntie and cousins in a makeshift wooden structure on blocks, taught me about scarcity and abundance. My students and I played for hours with the children, including our littlest friend, the boy with no shoes, who ran around overflowing with joy, merriment, and glee.

Abundance is a feeling. It comes from within. Abundance also includes everyone else having enough, too. Our collective needs are met, even those of the plants and animals, forests, and seas! Abundance is not just a capitalist ideal of "me" having it all; it means everyone is well provisioned. Sufficiency is knowing you can meet your needs. There is enough to go around, and you can count on yourself to figure things out. That little boy reminded me that we are very much our decisions, not our conditions. He decided to see what was right in front of him and what was possible.

Abundance is not something we acquire. It is something we tune into.

WAYNE DYER

STRESS WISELY FOR FINANCIAL WELLNESS

Terry Turner, a senior financial writer and a member of the Association for Financial Counseling & Planning Education, explained that "financial wellness is a state of being in which you can meet current and future financial obligations, feel secure in your financial future, and make choices that let you enjoy life."[6]

Tending to your financial wellness can reduce stress and preoccupation about money while improving both mental and physical well-being. When I first started learning about the impact of our finances and resources on our well-being, I realized I was mistaking financial wellness with financial literacy and having money. Once again, I had some unlearning to do.

Financial literacy is being able to read and talk the money talk. It is knowing the key ideas and parts and understanding financial concepts. It also includes understanding how our financial systems work. I remember stickhandling a "WTF moment" with Ava when I had to explain tax. She had worked so hard to save up for a purchase, just to find out she needed an additional 13 per cent for tax in Ontario. And the look on Hunter's face when he received his first paycheque from McDonald's and saw the money withheld for tax. We had a lively conversation about how our money is taxed several times. I also remember a conversation with two recent university grads who were planning their wedding while also trying to establish a plan to pay back the over $250,000 in combined debt from their education. These conversations matter!

Professor Kathryn Sweedler, an economics educator at the University of Illinois, brilliantly explains how financial literacy and financial wellness are related. "Financial literacy is understanding the basics, it is understanding on paper what things look like, it's knowing how to talk the talk. Financial wellness is where you start to walk the walk, where you've incorporated it into your life and where your finances start to have a spot at the table when you're making a decision."[7]

Behavioural finance is a remarkable field that braids psychology into the world of finance and well-being. Jillian Carr, Canadian financial planner and founder of Steady Gait Planning, explains that understanding your finances and your behaviours around money can change your life. Her refreshing approach to financial literacy and well-being is teach, not tell.[8] In Carr's work with clients, she supports them in building capacity by identifying their starting point and desired state of financial well-being. Other financial writers like Grant Sabatier, author of *Financial Freedom*, and Melissa Leong, author of *Happy Go Money*, offer practical, no-nonsense approaches to our financial habits. The big ideas are rooted in getting real about your current situation and building clarity on where you want to go, then pairing the behaviours and mindsets that will get you there.

Financial behavioural change is the same as any behavioural change. It usually starts with an event or a person reaching a level of discomfort that compels us into action. Things might be a wee bit chaotic in our financial lives and we feel fear, guilt, and even shame. When we hold those feelings, we tend to avoid or deny. As our financial situation continues to go unaddressed, we start to feel overwhelmed and frustrated. Financially we may have random savings, loose and inconsistent debt repayment plans, but no real course of action, yet an awareness starts to build that we need a change. At this point we may be tempted to abdicate the responsibility of "fixing" our financial situations to other people, but this is where Jillian Carr's approach of "teach, not tell" is so key. What behaviours and goals are going to help you build your desired future state? Seek out information and support from knowledgeable sources. Next, we can start creating plans to stabilize where we are today while planning for tomorrow. With a well-developed action plan and a clear course set, the higher planes of financial well-being, like stability, freedom, and fulfillment, become possible.

Money Coaches Canada curated financial insights and habits into a seven-stage model for financial well-being: chaos, avoidance, awareness, stability, security, freedom, and fulfillment.[9] Each stage has three drivers: emotions, behaviours, and achieved financial status. Although this seven-stage model is presented as a hierarchy—achieve stage one, then proceed to the next stage—my invitation is to see if you can practise financial fulfillment (feeling good about your relationship with money—how it is earned, saved, spent, shared) as you are navigating your financial growth. Can you keep a servant heart while healing your relationship with money? Many people wait until they are financially secure and beyond to think about helping others, yet the giving part, I believe, helps the other parts grow and prosper.

When you give, you are improving your overall wellness. As Winston Churchill may or may not have said, "We make a living by what we get; we make a life by what we give."

FINAL THOUGHTS ON RESOURCES

Researchers from Berkeley challenged a long-held belief that people are hardwired to be selfish. The old "survival of the fittest" mentality was replaced with "survival of the kindest."[10]

In their remarkable study, they concluded, "Human beings have survived as a species because we have evolved the capacities to care for those in need and to cooperate." In another study, economist James Andreoni introduced the concept of "warm glow giving." He explained that when people give, even if they themselves do not have much, they experience a giver's high.[11] The warm glow is what a person experiences when they feel as though they are doing their part. It is a feeling of personal satisfaction. And that feeling motivates us to do better in other life areas. Our levels of efficacy rise, meaning we are confident that we can make ourselves do and feel better by our own actions.

For me, next to the bond with my family, especially between my children and me, nothing compares to the feeling of giving. Sharing my time, giving what I have, being of service, and those moments of radical kindness and connection feed my soul. I feel most alive and connected to my purpose when I am serving. But I did have to learn to be mindful of who I am serving.

When you have a generous spirit, people will take advantage of you. Guaranteed. They may even interpret your giving as weakness while taking ruthlessly from you. This happens professionally, too, not just in personal relationships. Instead of changing who you are and what you are about, set standards for how you give. For example, when you are a "giver," the sheer amount of true need in the world can be overwhelming. You want to help, and you do, yet it might be haphazard. Or perhaps you feel pressured to give your time or resources when asked. I often experience this when I am asked to volunteer my time to speak for certain groups or organizations. Some people can be quite harsh you if don't donate your time. Guilt seems to be the gasoline that fuels this exchange. My gentle invitation is to select areas or themes to which you direct your support. In choosing a few key areas to channel your resources (for example, time or money), you can fulfill your drive to give within the parameters of what matters most to you. Then, when someone asks something of you outside those parameters, you can politely share which causes or efforts you support.

To bridge the competing pressures of our world—the giving and taking, the chasing and hustling, all with the pursuit of peace and wellness—the words of the extraordinary Dr. Erich Fromm, the social behaviourist and philosopher, are like a balm:

> Giving is the highest expression of potency. In the very act of giving, I experience my strength, my wealth, my power. This experience of heightened vitality and potency fills me with joy. I experience myself as overflowing, spending, alive, hence as joyous. Giving is more joyous than receiving, not because it is a deprivation, but because in the act of giving lies the expression of my aliveness.[12]

Now, if you think talking about money was too personal, just wait. The next chapter, and the last of the Eight Realms of Wellness, is up next: spirituality.

Lord, Universe, Zeus, help us!

"

There are only two ways
to live your life. One is as
though nothing is a miracle.
The other is as though
everything is a miracle.

ATTRIBUTED TO ALBERT EINSTEIN

CHAPTER 12

THE SOUL

"DID YOU DESERVE YOUR MIRACLE?"

In a huge ballroom, having just finished a talk for a massive pharmaceutical company, I was asked that question. I stopped in my tracks. His eyes looked accusatory, his arms folded across his chest. I was barely off the stage. Moments before I had spent an hour presenting to his group. I shared my research and ended the presentation with a rather candid disclosure about my car accident. Despite presenting to a room of mostly scientists, I still shared my personal stories. Our stories are data, after all. I am used to being asked questions about my car accident. I appreciate that this sensational near-death experience and heroic rescue sparks curiosity and wonderment. I am also totally okay talking about it, most of the time. But the particular way this stranger worded his question sent anxious tremors blazing through my body.

In an instant I knew why this question had rattled me so. It had swirled around my head and heart for years. It was an old question that had been trapped in some kind of echo chamber in my mind. This question—whether I deserved my miracle that night—had haunted me. For so many years it had scared me because I knew the answer: No, hell no. I didn't deserve this miracle. My life prior to my accident was reckless. I was hurt by people, but I hurt people, too. I held regrets.

Recoveries are never linear. As I was rebuilding a life post-accident, I struggled for many years. This question of deserving a second chance at life was like a current, pulling me off course and holding me back in my recovery. I wasn't quite sure who deserved miracles, but I was very confident that I did not. Like so many of us, I subscribed to what is known as just-world theory. Just-world theory states that if you do good things and you are a good person, good things should happen to you. You deserve them. And if you are a bad person who makes poor choices, you should experience the consequences. You should be punished for what you have done. That is only fair. It sounds simple, and it rings true on some level of consciousness for many people. But the world doesn't work that way.

Yes, I was (and am) grateful I survived my accident, and I also felt I was a burden for surviving my accident. I felt beholden to an idea that my miracle was in motion that night, before I even set off on that drive; yet good people praying for miracles for their innocents never seem to receive them. No, I hadn't deserved it. Other people who were far better than me should have miracles. Interestingly, my belief in just-world theory shifted my perspective. I definitely had not deserved my miracle, but my mother did. In time, I let this belief—that my mother deserved a miracle and I was simply a by-product of mercy shown to her—take root. I could get behind that idea.

The man was staring at me now, impatiently. I felt like he was looking for a heated discussion or perhaps an argument.

The tension was only building as he waited for my response. Thankfully, by this point in my life I had learned to embrace a pause before responding. This is no easy feat for a quick-tempered red-haired Scot with impulse issues. Practice makes better, right? And I had had a lot of practice. As words and ideas swirled, I drew in a long, deep inhalation, then tilted my head and exhaled slowly, trying to look thoughtful and contemplative.

Another memory brightened in my mind. Years ago, on the other side of the world, I had sat with a kind priest in a garden. Through tears and shame, I confessed to him that I struggled to accept my miracle. With weathered eyes, the priest asked me softly, "Which one?"

Frustrated with the question, I replied quickly, "My car accident."

"Oh, that one. My dear Robyne, you have had so many miracles in your life, I didn't know which one you were referring to." He went on to say, "We all get miracles, Robyne, each and every day. Our worlds are so full of miracles, it is hard to get through a day without one. Look for them with your heart, not your eyes or your mind, and you will see. Once you do, it will be hard to get anything done because you will be so awestruck by the love, forgiveness, and beauty all around you."

It felt as though the tears streaming down my cheeks were washing away the years of struggle and failed attempts at reconciling my miracle. The priest said, "Who are we to decide who gets the miracles? That's not our job. Our job is to learn how to recognize them, receive them, and then share them. What I have learned in my lifetime is that there are three types of business: your business, other people's business, and God's business. And you only need to mind yourself with one: your business. You don't have to make sense or meaning with any of this. That's God's job. Don't mind what other people think or what they are doing. That's their business. Do what you can with the miracles you are given. You can't earn them, and perhaps no one really ever deserves them, but nevertheless we are gifted them every day. You are not the judge and jury of miracles."

A lightness washed over me. The imaginary but very real-feeling vise around my heart loosened. With a tentative smile, I asked the priest, "Wasn't it Albert Einstein who said you can see life as everything being a miracle or nothing being a miracle?"

He nodded in agreement. "I believe so, and he knew a thing or two about the mysteries of the world."

I met myself back in the present moment. I straightened my spine, adjusted my jacket, and smiled at the now very impatient man standing in front me. "Which one, sir?" I paused momentarily, then spoke again. "I have had about 918 miracles, but I only started counting a few years ago."

WHERE TO START?

In the last chapter we talked about finances as being a personal minefield of awkwardness and taboos. Writing this chapter about spirituality reminds me of that old saying about being as nervous as a cat in a room full of rocking chairs! Talking about spirituality feels scary, yet, to me, it is the most important chapter of this whole book. Spirituality is the paramount wellness domain, yet I still write this with cautious fingertips on my keyboard. I feel vulnerable. I worry that I cannot give this chapter its due justice because spirituality permeates absolutely every aspect of what is good and right in our world. Who am I to try to write a chapter on something so colossal?

There is a hilarious social media influencer and entrepreneur from Toronto named Vivian Kaye. She has built an extraordinary empire on this simple question: "What would Chad do?" Kaye uses "Chad" to represent your average white guy. When you are the top-of-the-social-hierarchy, white, straight, English-speaking man with a moderate level of fitness, you don't have limiting beliefs. You apply for that job even though you have only two out of the ten qualifications. Women, however, often don't apply if they have 9.5 out of ten! You walk into restaurants like "Of course there is a table for me," versus, "They might have a table if I eat fast!" You walk alone at night and wonder what the big fuss is all about. Kaye promotes the idea of stopping any self-limiting beliefs. Chad wouldn't wonder who should write this spirituality chapter, so I will try and have a wee bit more faith in myself.

When a task feels gigantic, whether it is going back to school as a full-fledged grown-up, trying to clean out a stuffed closet, or writing about spirituality in a few pages, trying to sum up what people have been struggling to say for centuries, my approach is the same: take one right and solid step in the direction you want to go. I also ask the question, What do I know to be true for me in this moment?

This I know about spirituality: It is complex and mysterious. It also feels precious, sacred, and intimate. It is as personal as you can possibly get. I also know that for some the meaning of spirituality gets tied up with world religions and history, and others dismiss it as woo-woo; yet in our darkest hours, even the staunchest atheists have been known to look to the heavens for help. I have seen people from opposing religious views lay down their arms and see one another's humanity. So, let's start there. Let's untether the preconceived notions of what spirituality is and isn't so we can determine what we are saying about spirituality as it relates to stressing wisely.

WHAT IS SPIRITUALITY?

The research on the role of spirituality as it relates to wellness is complicated because there is not a consistent definition of what "spiritual wellness" is. Generally speaking, spirituality is a worldview with an assortment of beliefs, values, and morals. It recognizes external forces at work. It encompasses a knowing of a force greater than and outside oneself. The natural world is more than just purposeless mechanics, and we are more than just electrical impulses in the brain. Our lives and our world are more than just what we experience on a sensorial and physical level.

Dr. Elizabeth Scott writes that spirituality "suggests that there is something greater that connects all beings to each other and to the universe itself. It also proposes that there is ongoing existence after death and strives to answer questions about the meaning of life, how people are connected to each other, truths about the universe, and other mysteries of human existence."[1] In an attempt to simplify our understanding of spirituality, the Very Reverend Alan Jones says it is the "art of making connections." And scholar David S. Ariel calls it "heart knowledge."[2]

In the book *Music of Silence*, Brother David Steindl-Rast offers a key insight on our working definition and application of spirituality: "Sometimes people get the mistaken notion that spirituality is a separate department of life, the penthouse of our existence. But rightly understood, it is a vital awareness that pervades all realms of our being."[3] I like this definition! It's not the penthouse—it's the everyday.

There also is contention between what is considered spirituality and religion. Religion and spirituality are alike in some ways yet markedly different, too. In several respects, religion and spirituality both believe in the sacred, a higher power, and meaning-making or purpose. Each holds the belief of transcendence, a next stage or next life. They subscribe to ways of living one's life with a sense of goodness. There are also spiritual practices within religions. Yet spirituality can stand apart from organized systems. Particularly helpful for our work here is research that reveals that people who report being spiritual, versus those who report being traditionally religious, showed similar patterns of improved overall well-being compared to non-spiritual or non-religious counterparts.[4] Believing in something, whatever that might be, is good for your health!

According to Bishop Arthur Serratelli, a rapidly spreading term of identification is "spiritual but not religious."[5] This phrase sums up the idea that people may be moving away from the traditional practices of organized religions or from religious dogma. This may make some traditional religious people quite nervous, yet Franciscan Father Daniel P. Horan, who is the director of the Center for Spirituality and professor of philosophy, religious studies, and theology at Saint Mary's College in Notre Dame, Indiana, has a different take: "Perhaps the expression 'I am spiritual, but not religious' is neither as threatening nor as bad as many people think it is. In fact, it may be a great sign of possibility and hope."[6]

For some, the church has become synonymous with man-made institutions, organizations, power, corruption, scandal, and exclusion. Father Horan explains that if people are exploring their spirituality instead of religious traditions, they are still "seeking," which is a good thing. I recall one priest sharing with a group of Catholic students, "You don't have to leave Peter because of Judas." Yet many people are moving away from organized religions, nevertheless.

Regardless of where you are in this discussion, the key idea is this: spirituality and religion both can help someone manage and tolerate stress by generating opportunities for cultivating peace, purpose, forgiveness, and community. I remember reading a post that said, "Spirituality is a relationship with the Divine; religion is crowd control!" Again, I am not here to tell you what to believe, I just want you to know that believing matters, and there is a place for you here to come as you are.

In my book *Calm Within the Storm*, I shared research about what is known as the Blue Zones.[7] Blue Zones is a research program that studies the healthiest groups of centenarians (people who live to one hundred years or older) by geographical regions. This research identified a person's faith as a key determinant of their health and longevity.

Faith is knowing that there is more to this world than meets the eye. I am pretty sure Optimus Prime from *Transformers* is credited with saying that, and he is not wrong!

I think of faith as believing what you believe with your whole self, not just your mind. Faith is extremely personal. Believing in and belonging to something that is greater than yourself matters. Faith communities create places of belonging by sharing a collective consciousness of trusting in something that we cannot see, count, or measure. All faiths hold the idea that you can believe in something that exists outside time, remains constant, and is unchanging. The unchangeability is something that people can connect to and depend on. Faith in religion, or spirituality, can act as a stable resting place for us when we are weary. When life is complicated, unforgiving, and relentless, as it often can be, having a rock upon which to rest and cast your worries is the universal root of belonging and being connected to something greater. Our faith can also bind us to our past, ground us in our future, and foster hope for tomorrow.

Everyone's experience is unique. I am disheartened when people feel embarrassed or ashamed to share with me that their sense of wellness or belonging comes from their faith. This is not something anyone should be ashamed of. Faith is no less valid than someone's inspiration, motivation, and drive through nature, art, music, or science.

Being a faith-filled person does not make you anti-science, either. Scientists can also practise their faith, and belief in God or a higher power doesn't make them any less valid as scientists. An amazing study conducted by Dr. Elaine Howard Ecklund, lead researcher and founding director of Rice University's Religion and Public Life Program, found that "the divide between science and religion doesn't have to be as impenetrable as it's commonly perceived to be. Not only do scientists have many ways of viewing religion or self-identifying as religious, but they can also be generally accepting of religion in a cultural context and as a personal choice." She went on to say, "Science is a global endeavor, and as long as science is global, then we need to recognize that the borders between science and religion are more permeable than most people think." [8]

I invite you to celebrate wherever you can find community, strength, purpose, and peace of mind. Faith, spirituality, religion—heck, even rock and roll—you do you. Please don't worry so much where you find your meaning-making! Being open to what is possible and embracing the mysteries of this thing called life is a gift within itself. Being able to be faith-filled is a gift many people strive to experience, yet it remains elusive to so many.

SPIRITUAL WELLNESS

The University of New Hampshire developed a spiritual health check-in tool.[9] I have adapted their model to include prompt-style reflective statements and questions. This is meant to be a priming exercise. My invitation is for you to just notice how these make you feel. What comes up for you? What are you curious about? What questions do you dislike? Again, just notice.

- I am seeking a sense of purpose in my life.

- I hold space for reflection and time alone.

- I am open to meaning-making about the events and experiences in my life.

- I have a clear-cut sense of right and wrong and I act accordingly.

- I am open to exploring my beliefs.

- I am open to living a life in alignment with my values.

- I have people I can talk to about my beliefs.

- I practise caring and acting for the welfare of others and the environment.

- I practise compassion and forgiveness with others, including myself.

- How ready am I for presence and awareness?

- What is my deepest intention in life?

- I lead a life for the greater good.

- I strive to live my life from my highest good.

The above reflection prompts are not a checklist. Spiritual practices are part of the very fabric of how we show up in our lives every day. I don't believe we achieve some pinnacle in our lifetimes. Spiritual wellness is the ever-present mission of journeying through our days toward the greater good. We work at it every day and strive to be better than we were the day before. Maybe our goal is to react or respond in a manner that is more in alignment with our highest self rather than repeating old patterns, or to practise self-compassion, or to acknowledge that our life as we are living it is not aligned with what really matters most to us. Spiritual wellness starts with clarity. *Where am I and where do I want to be?* We do not have to sell off all our possessions and move to an ashram to explore our spiritual wellness. Just noticing how we think and feel about this topic is doing this heart work.

STRESS WISELY FOR SPIRITUAL WELLNESS

People have been thinking about spiritual matters and writing about them for millennia. These next ideas for spiritual wellness are not exhaustive but are selective based on what I have discovered in my work and what others have shared with me.

When we begin a spiritual pursuit, we often use the metaphor of a path or a journey. When the spiritual realm opens for someone by their own volition, it may be referred to as an awakening. Many people are raised within a particular religion or spiritual ideology. This often is cultural. You follow what your parents practised or did not practise. I present an example of a path next. Once we have a path, then we will explore the practices we can grow into along the way.

A SPIRITUAL PATH

The six-stage path presented here is just one example. I find it the most helpful path when I work with people who are interested in exploring their spiritual growth. I was first introduced to it through the work of Shannon Kaiser, author of several books, including *Adventures for Your Soul* and *Return to You*. In her work, Kaiser maps out what she calls six life-changing stages of spiritual awakening. I have adapted each description to reflect how this framework aligns with my scholarship and practices.

Stage one: Waking up to the void

Maybe you hear a sudden scream or perhaps a slow, faint whisper. Something inside of you shifts. You might experience an urgency or perhaps restlessness; something is stirring. You have woken up to a new idea that there has to be something bigger out there. You are uncertain but curious, so you take a first step into the unknown. Often, I see people come to this stage out of necessity. They have been sucker punched by life. Whatever it may be, life knocked them to their knees. Now they are wide awake and desperately seeking meaning, purpose—anything that can ease the pain or helplessness. Perhaps, for you, it is a spontaneous prayer for a loved one in need. A prayer into the darkness. The fragility of life or the situation scares you, and you realize that you cannot do this life alone. Or maybe it is you, standing at a crossroads. You simply cannot keep living your life like this.

Stage two: Dark nights of the soul

This stage recognizes that you now know you don't know. Before, you were living your life on autopilot, and now you are present to the vastness of the unknown. You are in the deepest and scariest stage of a personal reckoning: who you are now, in the life you have built, versus who you really are and what kind of life you actually want. You humbly stand in the collateral damage of your choices. The blast radius is wide, yet you are willing to do whatever it takes to cross the divide between here and your future. The amazing Sister Joan Chittister, a Benedictine nun, calls this holy irrationality. Nothing really makes sense, but here you are despite it all, asking the questions and feeling the feelings. Sister Chittister says, "It's the time to begin to live life fuller rather than faster."[10]

Stage three: Unlearning and discovery

This is the stage of moving from thought to action. I like to think of it as shifting from philosopher to behaviourist! You have surveyed the blast radius of all your choices to this point and seek out your truths and actionables. You evaluate it all and decide where you go from here. *What is coming with me and what is no longer needed?* I have seen people explore this stage in a matter of weeks, months, and years. Unlearning and relearning is complex work, but a renewed sense of possibility fuels you. An excitement and an aliveness course through you. You feel awake for the first time in a long time, and you see with remarkable clarity what matters most.

Stage four: Soul sessions

In this stage, the newness and excitement of realigning your life becomes more settled in your day. New routines, practices, rituals, and habits take form. You are doing the work. You are growing, evolving, and expanding internally while actively building a life that is externally aligned with your purpose and values.

Stage five: Surrendering and allowing

While many of us will always have a foot in the soul-session stage of growing and exploring, concurrently we start emerging into our newness. Here, you shift from childlike curiosity to the comforting wisdom of truly knowing who you are and who you are not. This stage represents a personal healing in your relationship with yourself. You accept your past. You are present. You can hold hope that better days are ahead. Brokenness is transformed into a mosaic of a well-lived life.

Stage six: Awareness and service

This stage is not so much the final stage as a place of culmination and sharing. Through personal growth and development, you are filled with a sense of purpose, meaning, and peace. You recognize that wellness is your birthright. Your awareness has expanded to see your unique path for living a good life—or perhaps your best life. I like to call it your "life lived wisely and well"! You are now also in a place where there is a genuine excitement to share the lessons you have come upon with others. It feels too precious, sacred, and gigantic to keep this to yourself. You feel compelled to walk gently on the earth and share boldly the truths you have experienced.

MY FRIEND, WITH ABSOLUTE HONESTY, I can share with you that I have walked this path. Okay, well, "walk" might be an exaggeration. I have tripped, stumbled, and fallen on this path. I have confidently run this path only to abandon it when life knocked me down. Humbly, I have returned to this path too many times to count. And what baffles me is that, despite it all, the path always welcomes me back. It is constant, unchanging, and always there. It holds no judgement. The only way shame, guilt, or bitterness is on the path is if I bring it with me. I believe with every part of my being that this very path is love. And this love is all encompassing, pure, true, and unconditional, and there is such an abundance of this love, it can save us all.

PLEASE START NOW

Our spiritual wellness is not a standalone realm, as perhaps the financial or occupational realms could be. Even though all the realms are interconnected in some way, we can easily tease out some—except the spiritual. Our spiritual wellness permeates everything. Our values, beliefs, morals, sense of justice, character, service, and connection to our world and one another need to be nurtured, fostered, forged, and at times even defended. It makes us *us*. A life without connection, reflection, and meaningfulness is void of what makes a life worth living. After all, a life without love is no life at all.

Now when I reflect on that idea, that love is everything, it isn't just the soul-mate, "you complete me" love so often glorified in our culture. It is the love that surpasses all understanding. It is the heartbeat of our existence. The space between the breath. It is the love we share with one another. It is the love that exists long after we are apart. It is everything that is good, right, beautiful, precious, sacred, and true in this unwell world. It is every feeling that makes our heart smile and our blood sing.

I have observed that people nearing the ends of their careers seek me out to work with me for one main reason: they want to feel again. Yes, that's right. These ridiculously successful, talented, and extraordinary professionals from virtually every industry approach the end of a career looking for guidance on how to feel feelings. They reflect fondly on their early days when they had drive and a sense of purpose. "Nothing has ever felt as good as landing my first job," said one top CEO. Another shared, "Nearing the end, I see clearly now that most of it doesn't matter. I lost my family somewhere in the chasing. I thought if I could just get successful enough, then I would have the time to get it all back, but I see now it doesn't work that way." So often, what makes people wildly successful in business—let's say, their ability to be stoic, work relentlessly for extended periods of time, make tough decisions, and carry the weight and responsibility of a company—leaves little room for emotional and spiritual wellness. They detach from certain parts of their humanity. Then, having been so detached for so long, they face a seemingly impossible task of being truly whole again.

I see similar patterns, too, when people are nearing the ends of their lives. I have witnessed a longing for more time. And it is not more time so they can finally finish their to-do list or schedule another Zoom call; it is all about relationships. Love that was withheld. Love that was lost. Love that went off course. And for a precious few, it is more time only to reflect deeply and fondly on how much love they were gifted in their lifetime. It is the memories and the moments. It always comes back to love.

I recall a member of the military sharing with me the events of one tragic day. He was with his friend in his final moments of life. The words of love shared by that fallen soldier made this once-hardened atheist believe in heaven. The two of us sat next to each other on a bench. We were looking at the sprawl of the military base as he spoke. His voice was gravelly and strong. It seemed somehow out of place that this tough man was talking with me about love and heaven. With tear-rimmed eyes, he explained, "Before my mate lost consciousness, he spoke to me about everything he loved—his parents, family, sports, women, serving his country—even with all that pain and fear there, so was love. The room smelled of death. We were in hell. Then the most peaceful look came over my friend's face. His eyes changed. All the pain vanished. He smiled like he'd finally made out a familiar face in the crowd, the person he was looking for. It was like my friend was being welcomed home by someone he was dying to see. Then, he just left, like he took off running to whoever he was looking at. He left us in that moment. I felt him leave here to go there."

The soldier paused, clearly reliving that moment in his mind. Silence held the space and stillness between us. Then, abruptly, he shook his head, bringing himself back to the moment, and with a half-smile on his face, he turned to me. The look was both serious and playful. "Doc, when my number is up, I want that, too."

Love wins.

SPIRITUAL PRACTICES IN THE EVERYDAY

Now, I appreciate that you likely picked up this book to learn how to manage stress, and now I am hitting the crescendo by saying you manage it with love. I imagine you saying, "Hell, Robyne, the Beatles told me that! 'All You Need Is Love,' right?" Okay, stick with me. Yes, stressing wisely is about a lot of things, and learning to love is a powerful tactical approach within our arsenal. Love is the atmosphere we need to keep us well and whole. Just like we cannot see the atmosphere around us on earth, it is exactly what is keeping us all from flying out into outer space. To be able to love anything, we need to first be aware of it. So, these spiritual practices I will share with you as both ideas and questions are meant to do just that. Find clarity. See what matters most, and then make it matter most.

Knowing what we value most, we can create systems that support better spiritual-wellness integration. Given the vastness of what spiritual practices can look like, I want to offer a starting point. To get clarity first is important, then you need a system for integrating practices into your life. That's where mindfulness and intention come in. So, to recap, to foster your spiritual well-being, you need

- clarity about what matters most to you; and

- a time and a place for that in your life.

I know we technically can't make time, but we can be mindful and purposeful with our time. By doing so, we can create a spaciousness in our days that feels bountiful and abundant.

SPIRITUAL INTEGRATION PRACTICES

I invite you to consider integrating some or all of these practices for spiritual wellness.

Boundaries

We all need boundaries, and most of us need help learning how to establish and maintain them. This is a practice, so be gentle with yourself. Instead of making hard-and-fast rules, decide on your top three non-negotiables. For example: *One day of the week is sacred and will not have work of any kind; I will not break a promise or commitment to my family or myself here.* Boundaries are not meant to keep people out of our lives; rather they are life-enhancing systems for who and what has access to us. Daring to set boundaries is a radical act of self-love.

Bookend your day

This is one of the most important mindful and intentional practices for cultivating spiritual wellness. Protect the time when you first awaken and again a few minutes at the end of your day. These are the easiest times to create windows for routines, rituals, or reflection. Bookending our day enables us to be intentional in setting the right tone so that we can start the day feeling grounded, connected, and aware and go to bed feeling grateful, satisfied, and purpose-focused.

Movement practices

Our bodies are not meant to just carry around our brains. They are designed to be in motion. We need movement and experiences outside our intellectual selves, just as desperately as our minds need stillness. Movement allows us to connect with and savour the world around us. Even ten minutes can profoundly affect the way we experience our day. Walking meditations are powerful for focusing and refocusing. You can reset, regroup, and recalibrate as many times as you need to in a day. And if you feel like you don't have time to move, that is your distress talking. There needs to be time in your day to not think, and just do and be.

Schedule it

Our lives have been imposed upon a calendar in some form or another. Therefore, even though scheduling sacred time may feel counterintuitive, it works. Schedule spiritual time and keep it in your calendar as if you were meeting with the most important person in the world. Even fifteen-minute blocks of rest, reflection, self-compassion, and active recovery will change your life. My friend Dr. Greg Wells points out that fifteen minutes is 1 per cent of your day. Could you devote 1 per cent of your day, or fifteen minutes, to your spiritual wellness?

Protect your peace

When we feel triggered by external events, we can remember that peace is within us. It is a place we can go to ground ourselves, and it is always available. Meditation is a good way to tap into this inner peace. If meditation is new for you, start with just a few minutes a day. Do not judge your efforts; just focus on your breathing to bring you back when your mind wanders. There are great free apps that assist with guided meditation such as Insight Timer, Buddhify, and more.

Breathing

Breathing is a vital stress-release mechanism. When we deeply inhale, it signals to our brain, "I am safe." Conversely, when we take short, shallow breaths, we signal to our brain that there is danger, and this exacerbates negative feelings and frustration. Focus on lengthening the exhale following the breath out. Rest in peace and stillness at the end of the exhale. Notice how the in-breath comes naturally. At the same military base where that soldier shared with me his experience learning about love, I learned another remarkable lesson that day. A decorated veteran spoke to the troops in the drill hall: "Each one of you, including me, has a set number of breaths we will take on this earth. Do you want your breaths to be shallow and rapid, or long and deep? You pick."

Connect with nature

Nature is our first home. It is the Vitamin N so many of us are missing in our lives. Amazing research reveals how, when we build lives that are mostly indoors, our brains are over-working certain parts and under-using others. For example, we are surrounded by ninety-degree angles all day—buildings, rooms, screens, you name it. Your brain travels this visual environment repeatedly. Yet when you go outside and are exposed to more than ninety-degree angles, you tap into a whole other part of your brain resources needed to process different shapes, sounds, and smells. Being outside changes your physiology in so many ways.[11]

Write your own spiritual-care playbook

Spirituality is very personal. You get to put meaning to the events that are unfolding. You get to decide what makes you feel the most connected, alive, and capable of experiencing love. Prayer, rituals, candles, music, an early bedtime, a spicy book, walking the dogs, gardening, calling a friend, turning off your phone—heck, it could even be a car wash, or a hot coffee, or time alone sitting in your driveway before you go into the house. Spiritual care and practices are whatever makes you feel the feelings you need to rise above the moment. When you decide the "action" you are doing is sacred and set it as so, it becomes sacred, and you experience the benefits of wholeness and the miracles all around you!

Go for the "feelings"

Often with any form of self-work, we are trying to do "something." The examples I've just provided are about the "things." But the key within doing them is the feelings that they evoke! What is the feeling or state that transports you to where you want to be and how you want to show up in your life?

FINAL THOUGHTS ON THE SOUL

Over the past few years, I started seeing the effects of high performance on the people I love the most. I witnessed our teenagers picking up extra work shifts, juggling conflicting demands, pulling fourteen-hour days, training relentlessly, never having downtime, having grab-and-go snacks as meals until it became the norm. And this realization stopped me in my tracks. Exhaustion is not a marker of success. The pace society sets for us is not conducive to a high quality of life, let alone a spiritual one. This way of living also makes having any type of spiritual practice seem impossible, or not as important as the material gains. We have every moment allotted with the "doing," and we have little or no time for the "being." And so, I stopped. I acknowledged what I was seeing, and I humbly asked my children to let me show them another way. We can be growing, succeeding, and serving while also cultivating spiritual wellness. It is possible. My hope is that you, too, can choose to slow down.

Our spiritual wellness is about choosing how we connect the dots that are our lives. Our lives are not an impenetrable line. That life as you know it today could look or be any different may be unthinkable, but life can be different, I promise. Find a why, your way, to make it meaningful. Trust in the power and might of love. Let a thread of love be sewn into everything you do. Spirituality is not for the weak. Spirituality is a calling for the brave, for those who have the courage to trust in the unseen and the uncertain. It takes audacity to step into the darkness when you can't see the ground beneath you, but you step anyway. I believe that building a life full of meaning, purpose, and values, all tethered to big love, is the most radical way to live a well life. Dr. Viktor Frankl, my forever-favourite scholar, said it best: "For the first time in my life I saw the truth as it is set into song by so many poets, proclaimed as the final wisdom by so many thinkers. The truth—that love is the ultimate and highest goal to which man can aspire. Then I grasped the meaning of the greatest secret that human poetry and human thought and belief have to impart: The salvation of man is through love and in love."[12]

"

One of the hardest
things was learning that
I was worth recovery.

DEMI LOVATO

CHAPTER 13

THE FIVE FORCES OF RECOVERY

URING THE PEAK OF COVID, I was asked to develop tools to help people manage their emotional health after the pandemic. It struck me as odd that leaders wanted tools for the "after" part. What about the "during" part? This was a classic example of the when–then trap. *Once the pandemic is over, then I will be okay.* I needed to find ways to help people be well now, not later. Just as I want you to be okay right now, as you stress wisely, not when everything is "fixed."

Wanting to help people feel okay during the pandemic led to my scholarship now known as the Five Forces of Recovery. The human condition really is a marvellous and mysterious system. What I came upon in my research is that people were intuitively doing these "things" or using these forces of recovery to feel better. My research team and I clustered these recovery behaviours into five themes:

1 Solitude and connection
2 Nature
3 Music
4 Acts of expression
5 Gratitude

People intuitively were drawn to these activities. They shared with us that when they engaged any one of these areas, they felt radically different, with little effort, and the effects seemed consistent and stable over time. These findings were remarkable! Navigating the Eight Realms is ongoing work that is vital to your wellness. And using the Five Forces, my friend, is how you can feel better in the moment. They are the life jackets to keep close, especially in stormy seasons.

SOLITUDE AND CONNECTION

The first force of recovery is on a continuum. On one end is solitude and on the other end is connection. Sometimes, to feel better, just having a few moments of solitude, to catch your breath and collect your thoughts, helps. Who would have thought that people would report missing their commutes to work? But they shared that they had unknowingly used that time, mentally and emotionally, to unpack their days. The time between work and home allowed them to shift from their workday mindset to their evening roles and responsibilities. What was particularly interesting, especially for busy people and high performers, is that they didn't need hours of quiet stillness. They just needed a few minutes each day.

Taking a few minutes to regroup, reflect, or recharge allows you to get you and your day on track. In our solitude we can also be honest with ourselves. *How am I really doing? What parts of me need extra support right now?*

We also observed that connection is related to solitude. At one end, people needed time with themselves to be real and aware, while also needing communities. They needed to be seen, heard, and accepted by others who were also being honest with themselves. We compare ourselves to others as a gauge to assess if we are doing "it" right. If all we see is that we are coming up short, we feel bad, but when we see other people who are in a similar place, there is a sense of unity and an increase in self-compassion and acceptance. This is significant. When we are honest with ourselves and find community within our vulnerabilities, we have a tremendous opportunity for healing.

My most recent experience of solitude and connection was at Hunter's basketball tournament. He had two games back to back, and during the break, the players made their way over to the stands. Several of the parents and supporters proceeded to pull out coolers filled with the loveliest home-made snacks for their respective athlete. There were fruit kabobs, muffins made from scratch, and even individually wrapped energy bites. It was a feast. Hunter sat down next to me. Feeling like the worst sports mom in history, I scoured my purse for anything I could offer him. I felt like I'd won the lottery when I discovered a crushed Clif Bar! I passed it to him with an apology. "Sorry, champ, this is all I've got."

Hunter put his arm around me while taking the sad-looking bar. "Mom, I wouldn't expect anything else!" I wasn't completely sure that was a compliment.

The mother sitting next to me, who clearly had watched the whole exchange and had also seen the mounds of snacks from the "prepared parents," smiled at us. As her son approached, she pulled out her debit card and handed it to her boy. "Maybe there is a vending machine," she said. My heart smiled. This other mama was one of my people! We shared a knowing nod.

I was wildly aware that had I not witnessed this other mom and her lack of snacks, I would have left the tournament feeling like I'd failed somehow. However, knowing there was another mama out there who also didn't bring snacks allowed me to surrender my self-judgement. Right or wrong, warranted or not, feelings don't care. They just feel. I actually think the bigger question is why we are still packing snacks for eighteen-year-old athletes. I might save that one for another day.

You are one moment of solitude or real connection away from being okay in this very moment.

NATURE

We covered nature quite thoroughly in the chapter on our world. The research on nature having almost immediate effects on mood is extensive. Spending time outdoors radically shifts your sense of being okay, and when you feel like you don't have time to get outside, that is when you need it most. When you need or want to feel better in the moment, return to nature in any form. Even opening a window or tending to a plant ally on your desk helps. Nature reminds us to hold all of life, gently and with care. Looking at nature, listening to nature, and especially being in nature all support opportunities for the wonders of nature to soothe us.

You are one moment in nature away from being okay in this very moment.

MUSIC

What would be your end-of-workday anthem? What's your life's theme song right now? What song do you play when you need to borrow courage? What nursery rhyme did your grandfather sing to you? What song would you want played at your funeral? What song can transform your mood? These are all questions I have asked in group workshops and training sessions. It is remarkable to observe how even just talking about music changes the mood and energy in a room.

Music has a brilliant capacity to promote mood congruency, regulation, and emotional release. Music naturally stimulates a range of emotions and memories since it activates the brain's amygdala, what I call our feeling factory. Music allows us to tap into this deep area of the brain that interacts with memories and feelings. One of my dearest friends on the planet is the world-renowned singer, songwriter, and storyteller Peter Katz. Peter and I have collaborated in many settings to bring the power of music and my behavioural practices of wellness to audiences worldwide. Based on the principles of the music transfer effect, using music to promote deep learning and knowledge retention, we have witnessed how music builds emotional and social capital within teams. Listening to music in any form radically changes a person's emotional experience. Take note of what music delights you, comforts you, reassures you, or strengthens you. Engage with those songs that transport you to another moment in time. Let music awaken your soul, offer you a place of rest or inspiration, or set the tone for your day.

You are one song away from being okay in this very moment.

ACTS OF EXPRESSION

Are you a bottle-er, a brew-er, or a flow-er? Do you push down the negative experience? Or do you hold on to every single emotional trigger and let it fester? Or do you let triggering things flow right on by? In my work, I often see that people have a leaning to one of the three. They bottle it up. They brew it. Or they let it go. This is what we use to explain the research finding that people who swear—not at someone directly, but just more in general—live longer![1] There is hope for many of us. We might be tapping into our immortality.

We need an outlet for emotions. In chapter 3, we learned about the emotional stress bucket and that we need releases. Expressing our stressors helps maintain a sense of being okay. The big idea here is to know what feeling you are working with. Often our feelings, thoughts, and emotions are tied up in a bundle of knots. We feel multiple things concurrently, and some of the feelings can be in opposition. You feel sad it is over and happy it happened. You feel exhausted and restless. You feel excited and too tired. I sometimes think of our emotions as similar to headphones. You put the headphones in your pocket for one minute, and now they are in a massive, tangled mess. You need to gently pull the wire to loosen the snags. This is how expression works, too, gently pulling the threads of awareness to see what needs attention.

Releases can take many forms. Here is a useful tool I use in my work: the Emotional Game Plan. You can replace the underlined words with what you know works for you (and the tendencies you want to avoid):

- When I feel angry, I exercise or get outside.

  I don't send emails or talk about it too soon.

- When I feel sad, I take five minutes of stillness or talk with a trusted loved one.

  I don't revisit the past in a destructive way or hold thoughts that it will last forever.

- When I feel anxious, I slow everything down or make lists or plans.

  I don't make sudden changes or avoid things that matter.

- When I feel envious, I look deeper: What do I think I am missing? Who says?

  I don't shop, chase, change, or compare.

- When I feel just "off," I shower, nap, or walk.

  I don't lose a day to lack of motivation or pressure to feel happy all the time.

- When I feel depleted, I go back to basics: sleep, food, gentle movement, and connection.

  I don't take on more work, people-please, or start new projects.

- When I feel self-pity or regret, I find ways to help others— any act of service (big or small).

  I don't stay in that mood or withhold empathy and compassion for myself and others.

- When I lack good feelings in general, I create, engage, serve, play, or clean.

  I don't stay trapped in "when–then" or focus on problems or what's missing.

The above planning tool is just an example of how to pair a needed emotional expression with an activity that promotes a shift. It also helps identity personal pitfalls that aren't overly helpful when you are in a particular mood or state.

You are one choice away from being okay in this moment.

GRATITUDE

What you appreciate appreciates. It really is that simple. Holding gratitude, an action, and being thankful, a feeling, is a human superpower. Dr. Amy Keller explains that "experiencing gratitude activates neurotransmitters like dopamine, which we associate with pleasure, and serotonin, which regulates our mood. It also causes the brain to release oxytocin, a hormone which induces feelings like trust and generosity which promotes social bonding and feeling connected."[2] I have also seen in my work that when someone holds space for gratitude, they are more likely to do things such as helping others and following through with wellness behaviours. Gratitude is one action that activates the four "good feeling" hormone compounds in the brain. And there are only four, so you are hitting them all! Essentially, being grateful has the same neurological benefit of running (endorphins) while petting a puppy (oxytocin), all while concurrently finishing a major task (dopamine) and being outside (serotonin). That is a big win with minimal effort.

Gratitude also doesn't have to be expressed through monumental actions. It can be noticing the wee things with deep reverence. Like being aware and grateful in the moment with that hot cup of coffee. Cherishing the memories of a loved one. Recognizing and honouring how far you have come. It is not lost on me that on any given day, my life is made up of things I once prayed for. Hold that thought. How much of your life as you know it today is made up of things you once wished and worked for? Blessings hit harder when you remember what you went through to experience them.

You are one grateful thought away from being okay in this moment.

FINAL THOUGHTS ON RECOVERY

Stressing wisely is a constellation of possibilities for finding the threads of wellness that run through daily life. Once we harness our personal truths, and by embracing the discomforts, we can then see our life through our own wise lens. It requires a degree of courage to intervene and reckon with yourself, but once that reckoning has started to unfold, the recovery can emerge. Take the time and space, and act in a way that honours your highest self. The key to your wellness is inside you—you already know what part of you needs support. The Five Forces of Recovery can help. Commit to being okay in the moment, no matter what, and trust you are okay. This is the bravest way to live your life. Trust yourself and believe in yourself, as you are right now. And then, if the time comes to explore areas of self-improvement, meet that calling with deep compassion and walk gently. I truly believe self-improvement is not about getting everything right. It is more about finding the weak spots and loving those parts the hardest.

66

You cannot fail at being yourself.

WAYNE DYER

LIGHTHOUSES
AND AN ANCHOR

MY FRIEND, HERE WE ARE. As this written portion of our journey closes, I do hope the paths before you have started to reveal themselves. Your path is yours. It is uniquely and wonderfully made for you, just as you are uniquely and wonderfully made, too!

As the brilliant Wayne Dyer once said, remind yourself that you cannot fail at being yourself. You've done the absolute best you could, up to this point, with the tools, experiences, resources, energy, knowledge, and support that you had. And you are doing the same right now, in this very moment: the best you can with your current circumstances. Sure, some things might have been a wee bit maladaptive, and maybe they still are, but you are here. Attachment researcher Dr. John Bowlby offered us all hope when he wrote, "The human psyche, like human bones, is strongly inclined toward self-healing."[1] There is still time to repair your relationship with yourself and your wellness. You are still learning. Your survival rate at life is still 100 per cent.

As a final invitation, I want to share with you my take on lighthouses and anchors. Those who are familiar with my work know I always find a way to integrate a lighthouse or two! Lighthouses are my favourite structure in the whole world. Whenever I travel, my first stop is usually at the closest lighthouse. Having recently come home from Newfoundland, I can share that of its fifty-five working lighthouses, I made my way to at least half of them in two days! The symbolism of the lighthouse speaks to my very soul. As George Bernard Shaw once said, "I can think of no other edifice constructed by man as altruistic as a lighthouse. They were built only to serve." Lighthouses serve. They don't chase boats that go off course. They don't try to be anything other than what they are and what they were made to do. They offer guidance to those seeking safe passage. They offer clarity in the storms. They represent those who have travelled a similar path and made it to safety.

When you stand next to a lighthouse, you are witnessing some of the most spectacular vistas in nature. The vastness of the oceans and lakes lay open before you. The future is limitless and full of possibilities. History is alive there, too. As I was overlooking the lighthouse at Cape Race, Newfoundland, I was aware that it had received the distress call from the *Titanic* back on April 14, 1912. Jimmy Myrick, a fourteen-year-old signal station apprentice, had been left alone that night and picked up the call.

Lighthouses serve as guides. As you embark on your path to stressing wisely, I want to offer some parting take-away insights as guidance that has served those I work with, my family, and me well. Take what you need for your journey. Imagine these awareness pauses as lighthouses along your journey. They provide guidance, clarity, and assurance you are on the right path for you and your wellness.

MORAL PERFECTIONISM

Let go or at least consider letting go of moral perfectionism. There is no such thing as a blank slate or a perfect record in life. Part of living means you will make mistakes. You will drop the ball. Things won't work out. You cannot busy yourself into rest, nor can you out-think pain, stress, or grief. There is no one right way to any of this life. We don't earn our miracles and blessings—we are innately good. We are also not being punished. I believe that hell is not so much a place; rather, it is what we carry needlessly in our time on earth. All behaviours serve a purpose, even the ones you regret or feel guilty or ashamed about. You are your decisions, not your conditions. Part of learning means you will repeat mistakes until you repair them.

YOUR TRUE VOICE

We cannot unwrite our past, but we can learn from it. Win or learn. Healing doesn't mean the damage never happened; it means the damage no longer controls us. Remember that "what ifs" in your mind are intrusive thoughts, they are not you. Fear-filled thoughts are the collection of voices that have tried to control, shape, and teach you but may no longer serve you. The voice you hear that is kind, loving, and compassionate is the real you. Trust that voice—your truest voice. It originates from your highest self, the depths of your soul, and the breadth of the greatest good. Within that inner knowing, your wisest self speaks. When you meet yourself there, accepting that love, wellness flows.

ARRIVAL FALLACY

The arrival fallacy, the when–then mindset, robs you of your joy. Today is called "the present" because it really is a gift. As you develop sustainable, authentic, and kind wellness practices, let them be to feel good in the moment. You cannot hate yourself healthy. There is not enough money to feel safe. No job or boss is worth your confidence. If it is meant for you, it will find you. You cannot miss out on something that you were born to do.

KNOW YOUR WORTH

Chasing, compensating, and hustling our way to "enough" is not a personality trait. It is a conditioned response. If you are trying to earn your worth, you have forgotten your innate value. Your value does not decrease because of another's inability to see it. Morgan Richard Olivier writes, "You have power. Stop giving it to other people."[2] And remember, don't put too much thought into anything you think about yourself after 9 p.m.

GIVING AND RECEIVING

In all things is a natural ebb and flow. The website Tiny Buddha posted, "The thoughtful also needs to be thought of. The considerate also needs to be considered."[3] Having needs does not make you needy; it makes you human. In a world that is so over-worked and under-rested, take the time you need to experience both planting and the harvest.

SPIRITUAL BEINGS ON A HUMAN JOURNEY

"We are not human beings having a spiritual experience. We are spiritual beings having a human experience." When I first read these words by the French philosopher and member of the Jesuit order Pierre Teilhard de Chardin, I was awe-struck. Imagine how different our lives would look if we embraced the immortality of our souls. Would I not want to protect my soul more than my body if my soul survived earth? Big questions for a very young mind. I came upon these words again decades later, and they struck me again on a primordial level. Our souls don't need to fit into smaller jeans, drive certain cars, or achieve a certain status. Our souls are fuelled by love. The highest good that serves all. When you get caught up in all the *doing*, remember the *being* part of you. That is immortal.

TRUSTED CIRCLE

We are not meant to walk this path alone. We need one another. However, we may find ourselves in seasons when we are alone. Our personalities are made up of parts, and we can connect with those parts for guidance, strength, courage, and comfort. Imagine yourself in a boat. Who is with you there? Who do you need? What would they say to you? Can you imagine your wisest self, your bravest self, or your kindest self? Tap into different parts of you that can offer support when you feel alone. There is no shame in not having a gaggle of friends or the family you needed. Your imagination can produce the feelings you need in the moment. My invitation is to seek out community while also embracing your oneness.

SURRENDERING

This lighthouse is about learning to accept apologies never spoken. Letting go of the need to correct every detail. Learning how to love from afar when loving up close is not good for you. Letting go of the need for other people to know your side of the story. I used to associate surrendering with weakness. Now, I see that sometimes accepting and surrendering is how we protect our peace.

PURPOSEFULNESS AND MEANING

Dr. Viktor Frankl, quoting Nietzsche, wrote that those who have "a *why* to live for can bear with almost any *how*."[4] A purpose is like a fortress that protects you on your journey of life. Frankl explained the power of meaning: "In some way, suffering ceases to be suffering at the moment it finds a meaning, such as the meaning of a sacrifice."[5] By nature, we are meaning makers. Yet we often forget that we can ascribe meaning to situations. We usually try to seek answers outside ourselves.

You are your own author. You get to determine the meaning behind each event and experience. Connect meaning with your purpose and you become an unstoppable force for good.

ALL ROADS LEAD HOME

There is a physical and emotional place on this earth, or beyond it, for each and every one of us, that feels like home. It is our area of refuge. Our safe harbour. Forging this steadfast connection is essential to stressing wisely. It could be a home, a trail, a city, or even a place in your mind that you have learned about. It could be heaven or nirvana or something else. People can also be associated with this feeling of home. It is the essence of belonging, being loved, and being you. Protect and honour this place. Let the people who are a part of this place for you know how loved they are. This home also cultivates the psychological safety we need to venture into the world. Dr. John Bowlby's attachment research makes the case that life is best organized as a series of daring ventures from a secure base. Home is that secure base. And as Ram Dass said, "When it is all said and done, we are essentially just walking each other home."

The spirit of stressing wisely is to cultivate the wisdom of knowing what you need to be well. The frameworks, concepts, and tools I have shared in this book set you up to bridge these two realms: theory and practice. Now it is your turn. The knowledge has been imparted, and what you do with it can become wisdom once you apply it to your life. According to *Psychology Today*, psychologists often agree that "wisdom" suggests some form of integration of knowledge, experience, and a deep understanding of a topic.[6] Wisdom also holds space for a tolerance of the uncertainties in life and a surrendering to how things unfold in their own time. It also confers a sense of balance.

So, for us to be wise, we need to know when to act, when to wait, when to rest, when to reflect, when to regroup, and when to try again. For example, we can know absolutely everything about the breath and the importance of breathing, but if we don't breathe, game over. We need to move our knowledge and theory into application and practice, eventually. The timing and path—that is up to you. It is hard to change. It is even harder not to. Thankfully we can do hard things. I believe each and every one of us has the capacity to move what we know into how we live before it is too late. My intention in writing this book was to do just that.

HOPE IS THE ANCHOR

My final call to action for you is this: embrace the audacious hope of what is possible in every area of your life. This is the anchor that will hold you steady even in the mightiest of storms: hope.

Life is far too precious to be wasted on things that don't matter. Make what matters most matter most. I usually say that this is "not selfish, it's science," but here I am going to change that to "It is not selfish, it's spiritual!" Your most well life depends on it.

In closing, and because I am learning to not have the last word, I am sharing a favourite quote as a love note, gifted to you. I'm sending it like a wee message that mamas tuck into lunch boxes or notes grandpas leave on the back of a napkin.

This quote inspired my heart and guided me on this journey of sharing this work with you, and now I want you to carry it, too.

My friend, may the precious insights from the beloved *Anne of Green Gables* set your stressing-wisely journey on a steady course:

> My future seemed to stretch out before me like a straight road ... Now there is a bend in it. I don't know what lies around the bend, but I'm going to believe that the best does.[7]

The End.

Okay, darn it, I had to have the last word. I will keep working on that one. Practice makes better, right?

Until next time, be well and take good care of you and one another.

Love, your friend and fellow mate who is trying her best to stress wisely here, too,

—*Robyne (with an "e")*

ACKNOWLEDGEMENTS

O H, BIG WORLD! How do I even start to thank you and acknowledge all the beautiful people, experiences, feelings, thoughts, memories, and even mistakes that made their way into my life and ultimately this wee book? Well, like every other overwhelming and seemingly impossible task I have ever faced in my life, one honest step at a time! So, in true Robyne form, I am writing this far from home, in a hotel room, with a cold cup of coffee next to me, and my iPhone is playing my favourite Peter Katz album. My weary heart is so full that tears fall relentlessly down my cheeks, making it hard to see the keyboard. As my teenagers would say, "Mama is in her feels." So, dear reader, bear with me. I am really "in my feels" about writing these acknowledgements because my words can't seem to match the gargantuan amount of gratitude I feel for the people who supported this work, let alone that this is my life! But alas, here we are. I cry and do it anyway.

To the brilliant Page Two word warriors. The pen is truly mightier than the sword, especially when I have a publishing house like you in my corner! Thank you for sharing your expertise so generously with me. You all are remarkably gifted professionals, and I credit the Page Two team for getting not one but two of my books to the moment of liftoff. As this book makes its way into the world, the journey was made possible because of each of you and the outstanding leadership of Trena and Jesse. And to Kendra, my ally in arms in the form of an editor, I gave you good, and you made great. Thank you for the calls, emails, comments, contributions, and smiles. Your words of encouragement emboldened me to tackle big ideas my way. My hope is that other authors get to experience what it feels like to be truly heard, supported, and elevated. And thank you to Jenny for her remarkable copy edit skills! I love that through track changes we can engage in conversations like old friends.

To my Speakers' Spotlight MVPs! The most professional and tireless advocates, supporters, and all-around champs, thank you for providing me with the opportunity to take my work into places and spaces I never in my wildest dreams could have found. Thank you for seeing the value in my work and sharing it far and wide. Martin and Farah, thank you for seeing something in me I didn't even know was there. You single-handedly changed the trajectory of my life; I like this new path very much! And to all the groups, companies, organizations, and event planners who took a chance putting me in front of their people and on a stage, thank you for letting me share my work with your worlds. And to my speaking colleagues who are wickedly talented, remarkably skilled, and all-around gifted humans, thank you for sharing stages, meeting rooms, conference halls, and even airports with me.

To my new friends who feel compelled to hang back after events to share parts of your stories, thank you for trusting me. And to those who reach out afterward with emails or wee notes through socials and share how my messages resonated with you, please know you honour me with your kind feedback and thoughtful reflections. I'm awe-inspired by how sharing some of my setbacks and challenges with radical candor somehow feels like giving others permission to reclaim their stories, too. I hold the stories you share with me close to my heart, and I think of you very fondly. Often our lessons are so hard-learned, and sharing them together makes me not feel quite as alone anymore.

To my fellow educators, from early years all the way to post-secondary, thank you for supporting my work and for holding space for me to be part of the conversation. I have shared time with so many of you, and I am grateful for all of it. And to my own educators and schools, thank you for inviting me into the circle of learning and shaping how I understand the world around me. I hold deep gratitude for Western University, Queen's University, and Trent University for my years as a learner, and my forever-grateful thanks goes to St. Lawrence College. Few schools were willing to give me and my cobbled-together mess of high-school transcripts a chance, but SLC did. I am proud to be an SLC Alum. Thank you, President Glenn, for keeping the SLC doors open for so many who need that one chance for someone to believe in us. And to the students who I have had the privilege to teach over the past eighteen years at Trent University, you inspire me, challenge me, and leave me with a steadfast confidence that our world and our future are in very capable hands.

A special thank you to my little but mighty Robyne HD team. The original "R-Team" is a force led by Jenna who, with such grace, ease, and humour, keeps my professional world on axis and Rich, the Amazing, who shares his skills and talents so generously. Thank you for being with me on this adventure! And to all those who work passionately behind the scenes on projects, online courses, workshops, websites, socials, and publicity. Every workday ought to be filled with as much laughter, professional diligence, outstanding work ethic, and true commitment to the things that matter most in this unwell world. You all make this work feel effortless and important. Thank you for being part of the team.

And to my other team—my forever friends, Alissa, Jill, and Stephanie, I'm thankful that you are my sisters-in-arms, and I adore you. You all make life better, much more fun, and, Jill—more expensive. BFF! A special shout-out to my dear friend Peter. You morphed from being my favourite Canadian singer/songwriter to a colleague, a friend, and then my phone call when my world wobbled. Your light shines through even the darkest moments. I'm grateful your music fills in the space where no words can touch. And to my pups! Apollo and Luna, your unconditional love and warm "welcome-homes" show me the importance of how we show up for the people that matter most to us. I promise to be as excited to see my loved ones come home as you both are to see me.

Anytime I stand on an edge, overlooking some beautiful vista, it's like the world slows ever so slightly and my heart catches up. So often, I reflect on how I got here, to this moment. Sure, I may have hiked some sort of trail, or more likely got lost trying to find coffee; nevertheless, I am here. And in that moment between breaths, I see the faces of my family, near and far, and they remind me of how far we have all come. I humbly recognize my ancestors, the women and men from my family who navigated their lives to make my life possible. Ancestral mathematics says that if you are alive today it is because of nearly 4,094 ancestors spanning over 400 years. This brings me to my knees. I imagine their struggles and battles, their love stories and dreams, their joys and tears, their adventures and misfortunes, and ultimately their hopes for their families. I can only hope my life does them justice. I also thank the Hanley, Dafoe, Stewart clans of today, the Pollacks, Grattons, Stewarts, and the Bistritans, Burnetts, Youngs, Klassens, Woodys, Epps, and the next generations. Although we may be many miles apart, I hold you close in my heart. I am also deeply indebted to my aunts who rallied around me when I lost my mom. Thank you for helping me remember how she lived and how she loved me.

I want to also thank my original home team: my parents, Michael and Lesley. I am deeply proud to be your daughter. Dad: You are my constant. My lighthouse that guides me home no matter how far I travel. Your faith in me has carried me through the darkest of seasons. You have always been there, on every mountaintop and through every valley. You loved me hardest when I asked for it in all the wrong ways. Thank you for the second and third chances and all the fresh starts. I hope I can make you as proud of me as I am of you. Mom: I might always be your wee storm in a teacup, but know your lessons landed. I am fighting the good fight for what matters most in this world: my family, my faith, and the underdogs. I have a lifetime of stories to share with you once we are together again. Please know I have carried you with me in every moment.

To my husband, Jeff: You were heaven-sent. We found one another when I needed you most, and you have never left my side. It takes a remarkable man to heal hearts he did not break. The children and I are better with you in our lives. I pick you every time. Thank you for being my best friend first, then my husband. "If my last words are not 'I love you,' ye'll ken it was because I didna have time." Oh, to adventure life with a "perfect-for-you-partner" is a gift. Thank you for letting me be not easy to love but loved dearly all the same.

And to my March Madness Miracles! Hunter, Ava Lesley, and Jaxson. Hunter: Our protector, thank you for your loyalty, your heart, and for always being my corner man. Your future is so bright. I just hope the world is ready for when you hit your stride. You are unstoppable. Ava Lesley: Daughter days are the best days. Thank you for adventuring with me so bravely through every season. I admire your courage, your "stick-to-it-ness," and your level-headedness. You are such a mighty force for good. Ava really is a big deal in our family—the one and only. And to Jaxson, you completed our family! You brought the joy, light, and humour back into our lives. I celebrate you being you and your steadfast commitment to doing your best in everything you do. Jaxson, all your dreams are within reach. It is a privilege to watch you take on this big world. Being a mom to you three is my brightest blessing, and your siblinghood is what I am most proud of in this world. Take care of yourselves and one another. Always. And remember—all roads lead home.

Hunter, Ava, and Jaxson: This is my greatest truth. I can't promise to be here for the rest of your life, but I can promise to love you for the rest of mine—unconditionally, completely, and uniquely.

PS Also hold tight to the truth that I actually do love you more than every other mother in the world loves their kids.

And lastly, to you dear reader: As I shared earlier in this book, our paths have now crossed. I am glad you are here. Of all the books in this world, you picked up mine . . . and finished it! Holy goodness—thank you for that. I look forward to our paths crossing again soon. Until next time, take good care and be well.

Sláinte!

NOTES

Getting to Okay

1 Charles Figley, "Burnout as Systemic Traumatic Stress: A Model for Helping Traumatized Family Members," in *Burnout in Families: The Systemic Costs of Caring*, edited by Charles Figley (Boca Raton, FL: CRC Press, 1997), 23.

Chapter 1: It's the End of the World as We Know It

1 "Action Research," Business Research Methodology, n.d., research-methodology.net/research-methods/action-research/#_ftn1.

2 Katherine Cooper, "'Wicked' Problems: What Are They, and Why Are They of Interest to NNSI Researchers?" Network for Nonprofit and Social Impact, Northwestern University, n.d., nnsi.northwestern.edu/wicked-problems-what-are-they-and-why-are-they-of-interest-to-nnsi-researchers.

3 Ann-Louise Lockhart, "Repeating Cycles and How to Break Them," Gottman Institute, n.d., gottman.com/blog/repeating-cycles-and-how-to-break-them.

4 Vernon Howard, *The Mystic Path to Cosmic Power* (West Nyack, NY: Parker Publishing Co., 1979), 82.

5   "Thomas Jefferson to Nathaniel Macon, 12 January 1819," Founders
     Online, National Archives, founders.archives.gov/documents
     /Jefferson/03-13-02-0511.

Chapter 2: Stress as We Know It

1   "Stress," Canadian Mental Health Association, February 28, 2016,
     cmha.ca/resources/stress.

2   Pete Walker, *Complex PTSD: From Surviving to Thriving* (self-published,
     2013), 13.

3   Henry Emmons quoted in Jon Spayde, "The Science of Stress,"
     Experience Life, May 21, 2019, experiencelife.lifetime.life/article
     /the-science-of-stress.

4   Kelly McGonigal, *The Upside of Stress: Why Stress Is Good for You and How
     to Get Good at It* (New York: Penguin Random House, 2016).

5   Alia J. Crum, Peter Salovey, and Shawn Achor, "Rethinking Stress:
     The Role of Mindsets in Determining the Stress Response," *Journal
     of Personality and Social Psychology* 104, no. 4 (2013): 716–33,
     doi.org/10.1037/a0031201.

6   McGonigal, *The Upside of Stress*.

Chapter 3: Buckets Full of Stress

1   Earl E. Bakken Center for Spirituality & Healing, "What Is Mindfulness?"
     Taking Charge of Your Health & Wellbeing, University of Minnesota, n.d.,
     takingcharge.csh.umn.edu/what-mindfulness.

2   Kenneth S. Kendler, "A Prehistory of the Diathesis-Stress Model:
     Predisposing and Exciting Causes of Insanity in the 19th Century,"
     American Journal of Psychiatry 177, no. 7 (2020): 576–88,
     doi.org/10.1176/appi.ajp.2020.19111213.

3   Irving I. Gottesman and James Shields, "Contributions of Twin Studies
     to Perspectives on Schizophrenia," *Progress in Experimental Personality
     Research* 3 (1966), 1–84.

4   Joseph Zubin and Bonnie Spring, "Vulnerability: A New View of
     Schizophrenia," *Journal of Abnormal Psychology* 86, no. 2 (1977):
     103–26, doi.org/10.1037/0021-843X.86.2.103.

5   "Adverse Childhood Experiences (ACEs)," Centers for Disease Control
     and Prevention, April 2, 2021, cdc.gov/violenceprevention/aces/index
     .html.

6   "Every Kid Is ONE Caring Adult Away from Being a Success Story,"
     Safer Society Foundation, n.d., safersociety.org/every-kid-is-one
     -caring-adult-away-from-being-a-success-story.

7   DeMar DeRozan, interview by Shannon Sharpe, *Club Shay Shay*, FOX
     Sports, July 26, 2021, 15:06, youtube.com/watch?v=uz3THND3e7U.

8   Karl Halvor Teigen, "Yerkes-Dodson: A Law for All Seasons," *Theory and
     Psychology* 4, no. 4 (1994), doi.org/10.1177/0959354394044004.

9   Alison Brabban and Douglas Turkington, "The Search for Meaning:
     Detecting Congruence Between Life Events, Underlying Schema and
     Psychotic Symptoms," in *A Casebook of Cognitive Therapy for Psychosis*,
     edited by Anthony Morrison (New York: Brunner-Routledge, 2002),
     59-75.

10   Jeremy Sutton, "10 Techniques to Manage Stress & 13 Quick Tips,"
     Positive Psychology, February 23, 2018, positivepsychology.com
     /stress-management-techniques-tips-burn-out.

11   "Burn-Out an 'Occupational Phenomenon': International Classification
     of Diseases," World Health Organization, May 28, 2019, who.int/news
     /item/28-05-2019-burn-out-an-occupational-phenomenon
     -international-classification-of-diseases.

12   Kabir Sehgal and Deepak Chopra, "Stanford Professor: Working This
     Many Hours a Week Is Basically Pointless. Here's How to Get More
     Done—By Doing Less," CNBC, March 20, 2019, cnbc.com/2019/03/20/
     stanford-study-longer-hours-doesnt-make-you-more-productive-heres
     -how-to-get-more-done-by-doing-less.html.

13   Steven Kotler, interviewed in "6 Steps to Overcome Burnout," *The Art of
     Charm*, February 1, 2021, theartofcharm.com/art-of-personal-
     development/steven-kotler-the-secret-to-flow-state-6-steps-to
     -recovering-from-burnout.

14   Arianna Huffington, *Thrive: The Third Metric to Redefining Success and
     Creating a Life of Well-Being, Wisdom, and Wonder* (New York: Harmony
     Books, 2014).

15   Charles Figley and Maryann Abendroth, "Compassion Fatigue in Nursing," in *Current Issues in Nursing*, 8th ed., edited by Perle Slavik Cowen and Sue Moorhead (St. Louis: Mosby Elsevier, 2011), 757–64.

16   Charles Figley, "Compassion Fatigue: Toward a New Understanding of the Costs of Caring," in *Secondary Traumatic Stress: Self-Care Issues for Clinicians, Researchers, and Educators*, edited by B. Hudnall Stamm (Lutherville, MD: Sidran Press, 1995), 3–28.

17   Sherrie Bourg Carter, "Are You Suffering from Compassion Fatigue?" *Psychology Today*, July 28, 2014, psychologytoday.com/ca/blog/high -octane-women/201407/are-you-suffering-compassion-fatigue.

18   Robin Stern quoted in Diane Cole, "The High Cost of Caring," *Psychology Today*, November 7, 2017, psychologytoday.com/ca /articles/201711/the-high-cost-caring.

19   Oprah Winfrey, "The Powerful Lesson Maya Angelou Taught Oprah," OWN, October 19, 2011, oprah.com/oprahs-lifeclass/ the-powerful-lesson-maya-angelou-taught-oprah-video.

Chapter 4: Stress Meets Her Ally

1   Ajai R. Singh, "Modern Medicine: Towards Prevention, Cure, Well-Being and Longevity," *Mens Sana Monographs* 8, no. 1 (2010): 17–29, ncbi.nlm.nih.gov/pmc/articles/PMC3031942/.

2   Halbert L. Dunn, "What High-Level Wellness Means," *Canadian Journal of Public Health* 50, no. 11 (1959): 447–57, jstor.org/stable/41981469. Emphasis in original.

3   A. H. Maslow, "A Theory of Human Motivation," *Psychological Review* 50 (1943): 370–96, doi.org/10.1037/h0054346.

4   Dunn, "What High-Level Wellness Means."

Chapter 5: The Body

1   Christoph Klebl et al., "Beauty Goes Down to the Core: Attractiveness Biases Moral Character Attributions," *Journal of Nonverbal Behavior* 46 (2022): 83–97, doi.org/10.1007/s10919-021-00388-w.

2   Alan Slater et al., "Newborn Infants Prefer Attractive Faces," *Infant Behavior and Development* 21, no. 2 (1998): 345–54, doi.org/10.1016 /s0163-6383(98)90011-x.

3 "Perceptions of Perfection Across Borders," Superdrug Online Doctor,
   n.d., onlinedoctor.superdrug.com/perceptions-of-perfection.

4 Christy Harrison, *Anti-Diet: Reclaim Your Time, Money, Well-Being, and
   Happiness Through Intuitive Eating* (New York: Little, Brown Spark, 2019).

5 William Banting, "Letter on Corpulence, Addressed to the Public,"
   Obesity Research 1, no. 2 (1993; originally published 1863): 153–63,
   doi.org/10.1002/j.1550-8528.1993.tb00605.x.

6 "Banting," *Merriam-Webster Dictionary*, medical definition, merriam
   -webster.com/dictionary/Banting.

7 Sylvia R. Karasu, "Adolphe Quetelet and the Evolution of Body Mass
   Index (BMI)," *Psychology Today*, March 18, 2016, psychologytoday.com
   /us/blog/the-gravity-weight/201603/adolphe-quetelet-and-the
   -evolution-body-mass-index-bmi.

8 "BMI: The Insurance Companies' Death Knell to Adequate Treatment
   for Eating Disorders," Kantor & Kantor LLP, December 5, 2012,
   kantorlaw.net/blog/2012/december/bmi-the-insurance-companies
   -death-knell-to-adequ.

9 Michigan State University, "BMI Not Accurate Indicator of Body Fat,
   New Research Suggests," *ScienceDaily*, March 7, 2007, sciencedaily.com
   /releases/2007/03/070305202535.htm.

10 Harrison, *Anti-Diet*, 33.

11 Samira Kawash, *Candy: A Century of Panic and Pleasure* (New York: Faber
   & Faber, 2013), 183–85. Lulu Hunt Peters's bestseller was called *Diet and
   Health: With the Key to Calories*.

12 Lulu Hunt Peters quoted in Erin Brodwin, "Restaurant Chains Now Put
   Calorie Counts on Their Menus—and It's Part of a 100-Year-Old
   American Obsession That Started with a California Doctor," *Business
   Insider*, May 8, 2018, businessinsider.com.au/calories-not-perfect
   -nutritionists-say-2017-5.

13 Evelyn Tribole and Elyse Resch, *Intuitive Eating: A Revolutionary Anti-
   Diet Approach*, 4th ed. (New York: St. Martin's Essentials, 2020).

14 Allison Lau, "The Rise of Fad Diets," CNBC, January 11, 2021, cnbc.com
   /video/2021/01/11/how-dieting-became-a-71-billion-industry-from
   -atkins-and-paleo-to-noom.html.

15   Canadian Medical Association, CMA *Code of Ethics and Professionalism*, 2018, 4, point #6, policybase.cma.ca/viewer?file=%2Fmedia% 2FPolicyPDF%2FPD19-03.pdf.

16   Greg Wells, *The Ripple Effect: Sleep Better, Eat Better, Move Better, Think Better* (Toronto: HarperCollins Canada, 2017).

17   "The Effects of Sleep Deprivation," Johns Hopkins Medicine, n.d., hopkinsmedicine.org/health/wellness-and-prevention/the-effects -of-sleep-deprivation.

18   Stephanie Watson and Kristeen Cherney, "The Effects of Sleep Deprivation on Your Body," Healthline, December 15, 2021, healthline .com/health/sleep-deprivation/effects-on-body.

19   Matt Walker quoted in Fiona Macdonald-Smith, "Can Sleep Deprivation Be the Cause of Mental Illness?" *Telegraph*, March 2, 2009, telegraph .co.uk/news/health/4862280/Can-sleep-deprivation-be-the-cause-of -mental-illness.html.

20   "Sleep, Performance, and Public Safety," Healthy Sleep, Harvard Medical School, December 18, 2007, healthysleep.med.harvard.edu /healthy/matters/consequences/sleep-performance-and-public-safety; Eric Suni, "Excessive Sleepiness and Workplace Accidents," Sleep Foundation, May 13, 2022, sleepfoundation.org/excessive-sleepiness /workplace-accidents.

21   Laura Smith, "53 Sleep Statistics: What Percentage of the Population Is Sleep Deprived?" The Good Body, July 27, 2022, thegoodbody.com /sleep-statistics.

22   Bettina F. Piko, Annabella Obál, and David Mellor, "Body Appreciation in Light of Psychological, Health- and Weight-Related Variables Among Female Adolescents," *Europe's Journal of Psychology* 16, no. 4 (2020): 676–87, doi.org/10.5964%2Fejop.v16i4.2183.

23   Tracy L. Tylka and Nichole L. Wood-Barcalow, "The Body Appreciation Scale-2: Item Refinement and Psychometric Evaluation," *Body Image* 12 (2015): 53–67, doi.org/10.1016/j.bodyim.2014.09.006.

Chapter 6: The Heart

1   Francine Shapiro, *Eye Movement Desensitization and Reprocessing: Basic Principles, Protocols and Procedures*, 1st ed. (New York: Guilford Press, 1995).

2   Simo Knuuttila, "Medieval Theories of the Emotions," *Stanford Encyclopedia of Philosophy*, Fall 2022 ed., edited by Edward N. Zalta and Uri Nodelman, plato.stanford.edu/entries/medieval-emotions.

3   Oscar Wilde, "The Soul of Man Under Socialism," *Oscar Wilde Online*, n.d., originally published 1891, wilde-online.info/the-soul-of-man -under-socialism.html.

4   Joe Humphreys, "Unthinkable: How Many Emotions Can One Person Feel?" *Irish Times*, January 26, 2016, irishtimes.com/culture /unthinkable-how-many-emotions-can-one-person-feel-1.2505786.

5   "About Marc Brackett, Ph.D.," Marc Brackett, Ph.D. (website), n.d., marcbrackett.com/about/about-marc-brackett-ph-d.

6   Marc Brackett, *Permission to Feel: The Power of Emotional Intelligence to Achieve Well-Being and Success* (New York: Celadon Books, 2019), 55.

Chapter 7: The Mind

1   Charlotte Ruhl, "Intelligence: Definition, Theories and Testing," Simply Psychology, July 16, 2020, simplypsychology.org/intelligence.html.

2   Kendra Cherry, "Gardner's Theory of Multiple Intelligences," *Verywell Mind*, October 19, 2022, verywellmind.com/gardners-theory-of -multiple-intelligences-2795161.

3   "Daniel Goleman's Emotional Intelligence Theory Explained," Resilient Educator, updated November 29, 2022, resilienteducator.com /classroom-resources/daniel-golemans-emotional-intelligence-theory -explained. See also Daniel Goleman, *Emotional Intelligence: Why It Can Matter More Than IQ* (New York: Bantam Books, 1995).

4   "Social and Emotional Learning (SEL)," International Bureau of Education, UNESCO, n.d., ibe.unesco.org/en/glossary-curriculum -terminology/s/social-and-emotional-learning-sel.

Chapter 8: Community

1   Nancy Ritter, Thomas R. Simon, and Reshma R. Mahendra, "Changing Course: Keeping Kids Out of Gangs," *NIJ Journal* 273 (2014): 16–27, ojp.gov/pdffiles1/nij/244146.pdf.

2   R. Jacques, "The Warden and the Doctor: Kingston Penitentiary in the 1840s," *Clinical and Investigative Medicine* 30, no. 4 (2007), doi.org /10.25011/cim.v30i4.2782.

3   Ryan M. Niemiec and Robert E. McGrath, *The Power of Character Strengths: Appreciate and Ignite Your Positive Personality* (Cincinnati: VIA Institute on Character, 2019).

4   Christopher Peterson and Martin E. P. Seligman, *Character Strengths and Virtues: A Handbook and Classification* (New York: Oxford University Press, 2004).

5   Frank Martela, "Helping Others Is Good for Your Health," *Psychology Today*, September 4, 2020, psychologytoday.com/us/blog/insights -more-meaningful-existence/202009/helping-others-is-good -your-health.

6   Ashley V. Whillans et al., "Is Spending Money on Others Good for Your Heart?" *Health Psychology* 35, no. 6 (2016): 574–83, doi.org/10.1037 /hea0000332.

7   "How Helping Others Benefits You," New Jersey City University, n.d., njcu.edu/student-life/campus-services-resources/counseling-center /additional-resources/articles/how-helping-others-benefits-you.

8   "Allan Luks' Helper's High: The Healing Power of Helping Others," Allan Luks (website), n.d., allanluks.com/helpers_high.

9   Scott Barry Kaufman, "Sailboat Metaphor," Scott Barry Kaufman (website), n.d., scottbarrykaufman.com/sailboat-metaphor.

10   Margaret Wheatley, "Margaret Wheatley: Whatever the Problem, Community Is the Answer," CLD Standards Council for Scotland, June 20, 2012, Glasgow, youtube.com/watch?v=fPvEKP1cUZA.

Chapter 9: Our World

1   Corey J. A. Bradshaw et al., "Underestimating the Challenges of Avoiding a Ghastly Future," *Frontiers in Conservation Science* (January 2021), doi.org/10.3389/fcosc.2020.615419.

2   David Shearman, "Human Survival Cannot Be Left to Politicians. We're Losing Our Life Support Systems," ABC News, September 13, 2018, abc.net.au/news/2018-09-14/climate-change-insects-life-support -species-extinct-shearman/10230188.

3   Ashlee Cunsolo and Neville R. Ellis, "Ecological Grief as a Mental Health Response to Climate Change–Related Loss," *Nature Climate Change* 8 (2018): 275–81, doi.org/10.1038/s41558-018-0092-2.

4   Eliza Relman and Walt Hickey, "More Than a Third of Millennials Share Rep. Alexandria Ocasio-Cortez's Worry About Having Kids While the Threat of Climate Change Looms," *Business Insider*, March 4, 2019, businessinsider.com/millennials-americans-worry-about-kids -children-climate-change-poll-2019-3.

5   Seth Wynes and Kimberly A. Nicholas, "The Climate Mitigation Gap: Education and Government Recommendations Miss the Most Effective Individual Actions," *Environmental Research Letters* 12 (2017), doi.org/10.1088/1748-9326/aa7541.

6   Sigal Samuel, "A Climate Scientist Explains Why It's Still Okay to Have Kids," *Vox*, April 29, 2021, vox.com/future-perfect/22399882 /climate-change-kids-children-overpopulation.

7   Julian Brave NoiseCat, interview by Catherine Clifford, "What Indigenous People Can Teach Us About Fighting Climate Change," CNBC, January 29, 2022, cnbc.com/2022/01/29/what-indigenous -people-can-teach-us-about-fighting-climate-change.html.

8   Brave NoiseCat, "What Indigenous People Can Teach Us."

9   Renée Lertzman, interview by Catherine Clifford, "Climate Psychologist Says Neither Gloom-and-Doom nor Extreme Solution-Obsessed Optimism Is the Best Way to Discuss Climate Change Productively," CNBC, September 26, 2021, cnbc.com/2021/09/26/how-to-discuss -climate-change-productively.html.

10 IU News Room, "Tidier Homes, Fitter Bodies?" Indiana University, n.d., newsinfo.iu.edu/web/page/normal/14627.html.

11   Darby E. Saxbe and Rena Repetti, "No Place Like Home: Home Tours
     Correlate with Daily Patterns of Mood and Cortisol," *Personality and
     Social Psychology Bulletin* 36, no. 1 (2010): 71–81, doi.org/10.1177
     /0146167209352864.

12   Danielle Vayenas, "How Clean Sheets Can Help You Sleep Better,"
     PRweb, July 9, 2021, https://www.prweb.com/releases/2012/7
     /prweb9672953.htm.

13   Marie Kondo, *The Life-Changing Magic of Tidying Up: The Japanese Art of
     Decluttering and Organizing,* translated by Cathy Hirano (New York: Ten
     Speed Press, 2014).

14   Esther M. Sternberg, *Healing Spaces: The Science of Place and Well-Being*
     (Cambridge, MA: Belknap Press, 2010).

15   Catherine O'Brien, *Education for Sustainable Happiness and Well-Being*
     (New York: Routledge, 2016).

16   Richard Louv, "Ten Reasons Why Children and Adults Need Vitamin N,"
     Richard Louv (website), June 24, 2011, richardlouv.com/blog/Ten
     -Reasons-Why-Children-and-Adults-Need-Vitamin-N.

17   "What Is NatureHood?" Nature Canada, n.d., naturecanada.ca/enjoy
     -nature/your-naturehood/what-is-naturehood.

18   Pamela Paresky, *A Year of Kindness: Discover How Journaling About
     Kindness Leads to a Happier, More Meaningful Life* (self-published, 2010).

Chapter 10: Our Roles

1   Craig Lambert, "The Psyche on Automatic: Amy Cuddy Probes Snap
     Judgments, and How to Become an 'Alpha Dog,'" *Harvard Magazine*,
     November–December 2010, harvardmagazine.com/2010/11/the
     -psyche-on-automatic.

2   "Meaning and Purpose at Work," BetterUp, 2018,
     f.hubspotusercontent40.net/hubfs/9253440/Asset%20PDFs
     /Promotions_Assets_Whitepapers/BetterUp-MeaninG&Purpose.pdf.

3   Catherine Bailey and Adrian Madden, "What Makes Work Meaningful—
     or Meaningless," *MIT Sloan Management Review*, June 1, 2016,
     sloanreview.mit.edu/article/what-makes-work-meaningful
     -or-meaningless.

4   Shankar Vedantam et al., "Finding Meaning at Work: How We Shape and Think About Our Jobs," *Hidden Brain* (podcast), NPR, September 12, 2019, npr.org/2019/09/12/760255265/finding-meaning-at-work-how-we-shape-and-think-about-our-jobs.

5   Tauqeer Hussain Mallhi et al., "Multilevel Engagements of Pharmacists During the COVID-19 Pandemic: The Way Forward," *Frontiers in Public Health* 8, no. 8 (2020), doi.org/10.3389/fpubh.2020.561924.

6   Mary E. Durham, Paul W. Bush, and Amanda M. Ball, "Evidence of Burnout in Health-System Pharmacists," *American Journal of Health-System Pharmacy* 75, no. 23, Supplement 4 (2018): S93–S100, doi.org/10.2146/ajhp170818.

7   Mallhi et al., "Multilevel Engagements of Pharmacists During the COVID-19 Pandemic."

8   Robyne Hanley-Dafoe, Calvin Poon, and Nicole Gwiazdowicz, *Easing the Burden: How Pharmacists Are Supporting a Depleted Healthcare System at the Cost of Their Own Wellness*, robynehd.ca, August 2021, robynehd.ca/wp-content/uploads/2021/08/RHD_EasingtheBurden_August2021.pdf.

9   Walter Anderson, *The Confidence Course: Seven Steps to Self-Fulfillment* (New York: HarperCollins, 1997), 18.

10   "How Much Is a Mom Really Worth? The Amount May Surprise You," Salary.com, n.d., salary.com/articles/how-much-is-a-mom-really-worth-the-amount-may-surprise-you.

11   Logan Wilkes, "The Surprising Costs of Raising a Special Needs Child," Digital Storytelling, October 26, 2016, digitalstorytelling.uga.edu/2016/10/26/the-surprising-costs-of-raising-a-special-needs-child.

12   "Outliving Money Is Top Retirement Concern According to New AICPA Survey of CPA Financial Planners," AICPA, April 8, 2015, aicpa.org/news/article/outliving-money-is-top-retirement-concern-according-to-new-aicpa-survey.

Chapter 11: Resources

1   Ingrid M. Paulin and Wendy De La Rosa, "Why Is It So Hard to Talk About Money?" *Scientific American*, March 22, 2018, blogs.scientificamerican.com/observations/why-is-it-so-hard-to-talk-about-money.

2   *Confronting the Money Taboo*, Wisdom of Experience Investor survey series, Capital Group, December 2018, capitalgroup.com/content/dam/cgc/shared-content/documents/reports/MFGEWP-062-12180.pdf.

3   "New Research: Money Is the Leading Source of Happiness—and Stress," Northwestern Mutual, June 12, 2018, news.northwesternmutual.com/2018-06-12-New-Research-Money-Is-The-Leading-Source-Of-Happiness-And-Stress.

4   "Kevin Durant to His Mother: 'You're the Real MVP,'" CBS News, May 7, 2014, cbsnews.com/news/kevin-durant-to-his-mother-youre-the-real-mvp.

5   Michael Kay, "Overcoming Your Money Story," Financial Life Focus, December 6, 2016, financial-lifefocus.com/overcoming-money-story.

6   Terry Turner, "Financial Wellness," RetireGuide, August 12, 2021, retireguide.com/retirement-planning/financial-wellness.

7   Kathryn Sweedler quoted in Samantha Rose, "What Is Financial Wellness?" OppU, April 29, 2022, opploans.com/oppu/articles/what-is-financial-wellness.

8   Kira Vermond, "Learning About Finance," *Forum*, November–December 2018, 11, steadygaitplanning.com/wp-content/uploads/2019/07/p10-14-Financial-Literacy_NOV-DEC2018-1.pdf.

9   "7 Stages of Financial Well-Being," Money Coaches Canada, n.d., moneycoachescanada.ca/7-stages-financial-well-being.

10 Yasmin Anwar, "Social Scientists Build Case for 'Survival of the Kindest,'" UCBerkeleyNews press release, December 8, 2009, newsarchive.berkeley.edu/news/media/releases/2009/12/08_survival_of_kindest.shtml.

11 "Warm Glow Giving," Decision Lab, n.d., thedecisionlab.com/reference-guide/psychology/warm-glow-giving.

12 Erich Fromm, *The Art of Loving* (New York: Harper Perennial, 2006; originally published 1956), 21.

Chapter 12: The Soul

1   Elizabeth Scott, "What Is Spirituality? How Spirituality Can Benefit Your Health and Well-Being," *Verywell Mind*, November 14, 2022, verywellmind.com/how-spirituality-can-benefit-mental-and-physical -health-3144807.

2   David S. Ariel quoted in Frederic Brussat and Mary Ann Brussat, "What Is Spirituality?" Spirituality and Practice, n.d., spiritualityandpractice .com/about/what-is-spirituality.

3   David Steindl-Rast and Sharon Lebell, *Music of Silence: A Sacred Journey Through the Hours of the Day* (Berkeley, CA: Ulysses Press, 2002).

4   Mark Travers, "A New Study Explores the Upsides of Being Spiritual but Not Religious," *Forbes*, November 26, 2021, forbes.com/sites /traversmark/2021/11/26/a-new-study-explores-the-upsides-of -being-spiritual-but-not-religious/?sh=2eaa5215e29e.

5   Arthur Serratelli, "What Does 'Spiritual, but Not Religious' Really Mean?" Catholic News Agency, January 30, 2014, catholicnewsagency .com/column/52793/what-does-spiritual-but-not-religious-really-mean.

6   Daniel P. Horan, "Perhaps Being 'Spiritual but Not Religious' Isn't Such a Bad Thing," National Catholic Reporter, May 4, 2022, ncronline.org /news/opinion/perhaps-being-spiritual-not-religious-isnt-such -bad-thing.

7   Blue Zones, bluezones.com.

8   Elaine Howard Eklund quoted in Kelly Tatera, "Contrary to Popular Belief, Many Scientists Are Religious," *Science Explorer*, December 7, 2015, thescienceexplorer.com/humanity/contrary-popular-belief-many -scientists-are-religious.

9   "Spiritual Wellness," University of New Hampshire, n.d., unh.edu /health/spiritual-wellness.

10   Joan Chittister, *The Sacred In-Between: Spiritual Wisdom for Life's Every Moment* (New London, CT: Twenty-Third Publications, 2013).

11   Jill Suttie, "How Nature Can Make You Kinder, Happier, and More Creative," *Greater Good Magazine*, March 2, 2016, greatergood.berkeley .edu/article/item/how_nature_makes_you_kinder_happier_more_creative.

12   Viktor E. Frankl, *Man's Search for Meaning* (Boston: Beacon Press, 2006), 65.

Chapter 13: The Five Forces of Recovery

1   Brian Crans, "Don't Watch Your Mouth. Swearing Can Actually Be Good for Your Health," Healthline, February 3, 2021, healthline.com/health-news/dont-watch-your-mouth-swearing-can-actually-be-good-for-your-health.

2   Amy Keller quoted in Barbara Field, "How Gratitude Makes You Happier," *Verywell Mind*, May 17, 2021, verywellmind.com/how-gratitude-makes-you-happier-5114446.

Lighthouses and an Anchor

1   John Bowlby quoted in "Why Psychotherapy?" Bowlby Centre, n.d., thebowlbycentre.org.uk/psychotherapy.

2   Morgan Richard Olivier, *The Tears That Taught Me* (self-published, 2022).

3   @tivrax, "The Healer Also Needs Healing," Tiny Buddha, n.d., tinybuddha.com/fun-and-inspiring/the-healer-also-needs-healing.

4   Friedrich Nietzsche quoted in Frankl, *Man's Search for Meaning*, 108.

5   Frankl, *Man's Search for Meaning*, 147.

6   "Wisdom," *Psychology Today*, n.d., psychologytoday.com/us/basics/wisdom.

7   Lucy Maud Montgomery, *Anne of Green Gables* (Duke Classics, 2012), 483.

INDEX

ABOUT THE AUTHOR

DESCRIBED AS ONE of the most sought-after, engaging, thought-provoking, and truly transformative international speakers and scholars in her field, Dr. Robyne Hanley-Dafoe is a multi-award-winning education and psychology instructor, author, resiliency expert, and philanthropist. She specializes in resiliency, navigating stress and change, personal wellness in the workplace, and optimal performance—both personal and organizational. In her speaking and teaching, Dr. Robyne offers us accessible and practical strategies grounded in global research that fosters and cultivates resiliency within ourselves and others.

Dr. Robyne Hanley-Dafoe joins a group of highly esteemed authors from around the globe as a Nautilus Award recipient with her debut book *Calm Within the Storm: A Pathway to Everyday Resiliency*, which won the 2022 Silver Nautilus Award in the Psychology/Mental & Emotional Well-Being category.

Robyne lives in Central Ontario with her husband, Jeff, and three amazing teenagers, Hunter, Ava Lesley, and Jaxson, who remind her each day that she still has a lot to learn about mostly everything! On most days, Robyne runs on her love of family above all else, historical fiction, coffee, and puppies—oh, and the ever-elusive clean kitchen in the morning.

WORK WITH
DR. ROBYNE HANLEY-DAFOE

THE DR. ROBYNE HD TEAM is committed to helping people find their own path for carrying the weight of the hard parts of their lives. We embolden and empower people through our sharing of practical, research-informed strategies and community. We strive to break down barriers so people can live their well life. We believe that each and every person can do hard things and great things.

Be sure to follow us on social media and sign up for our newsletter!

⊚ 𝕐 ▶ @dr_robynehd
in f drrobynehd

Together, we will explore the challenges that humanize us all. There is a place for you here.

Dr. Robyne is available for keynotes, consultation, training, and professional development opportunities ranging from one-on-one to company-wide initiatives.

Learn more about Dr. Robyne's innovative programs, including cutting-edge open educational resources, engaging online courses, and supplementary book tools, including a free book club guide, at robynehd.ca.